Eighteenth-Century Watercolors

With the assistance of R.J.A. te Rijdt

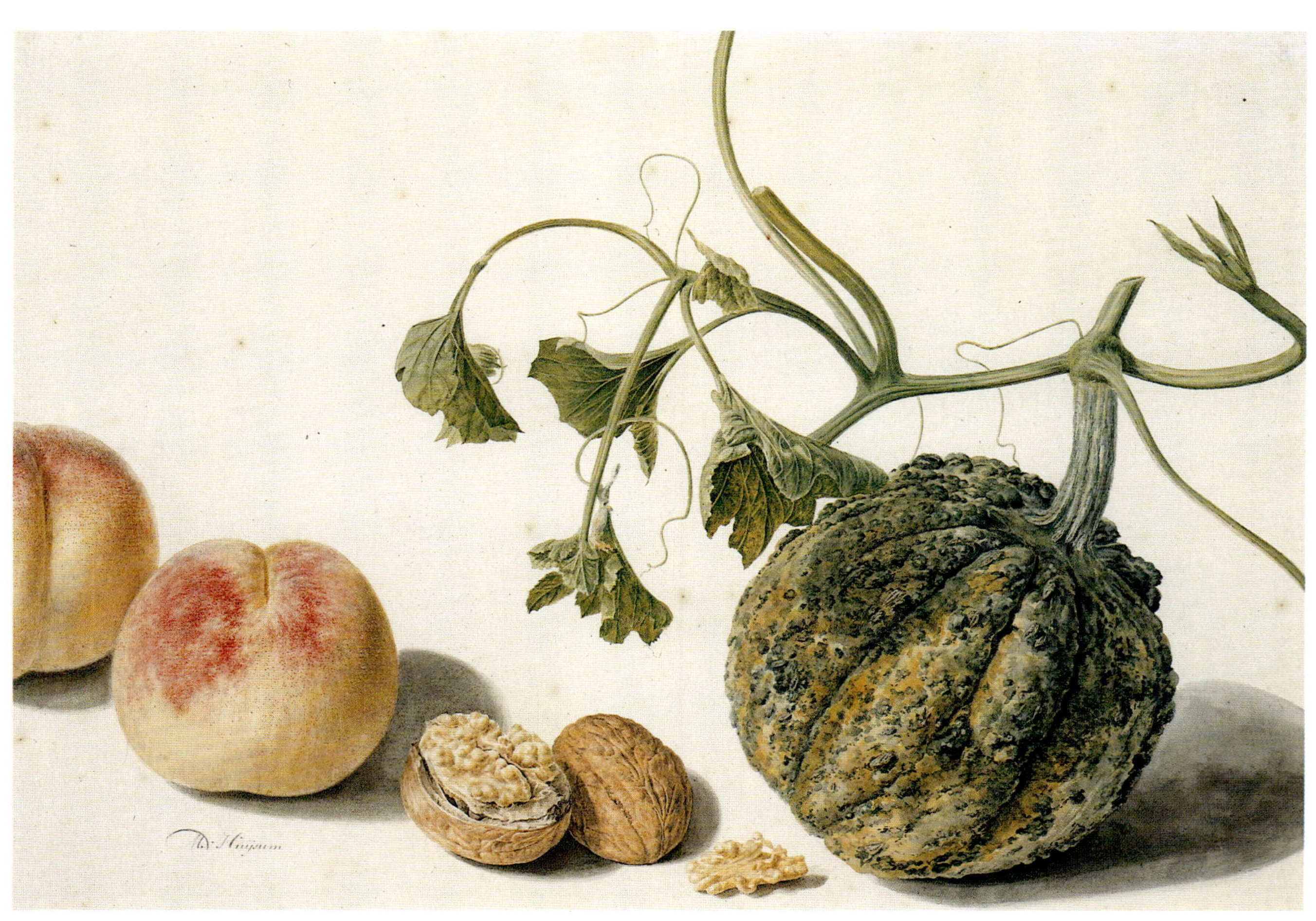

Eighteenth-Century Watercolors

from the Rijksmuseum Printroom, Amsterdam

J.W. Niemeijer

Art Services International
Alexandria, Virginia
1993

Participating museums

The Frick Collection
New York, New York

Center for the Fine Arts
Miami, Florida

Flint Institute of Arts
Flint, Michigan

This exhibition is organized and circulated by Art Services International, Alexandria, Virginia.

Cover: Hendrik Kobell, *Strollers and Skaters on a Frozen River with Ships* (cat. no. 33)

Frontispiece: Michiel van Huysum, *A Calabash, Two Peaches, and a Walnut* (cat. no. 31)

Colophon

Translator: Michael Hoyle
Editor: Nancy Eickel
Designer: Roelof Koebrugge bNO
Printer: Waanders Printers, Zwolle

Library of Congress Cataloging-in-Publication Data

Niemeijer, J.W.
[Hollandse aquarellen uit de 18de eeuw in het Rijksprenten-kabinet, Rijksmuseum Amsterdam, English]
Eighteenth-century watercolors from the Rijksmuseum printroom, Amsterdam / J.W. Niemeijer : with the assistance of R.J.A. te Rijdt : [translator, Michael Hoyle].

The present work is from the French translation: Aquarelles hollandaises du XVIIIe siècle du Cabinet des dessins du Rijksmuseum d'Amsterdam: the original Dutch is published under title: Hollandse aquarellen uit de 18de eeuw in het Rijksprentenkabinet, Rijksmuseum, Amsterdam.
Includes bibliographical references and index.
ISBN 0-88397-107-0
1. Watercolor painting, Dutch - Catalogs. 2. Watercolor painting - 18th century - Netherlands - Catalogs. 3. Watercolor painting - Netherlands - Amsterdam - Catalogs. 4. Rijksmuseum (Netherlands). Rijksprentenkabinet - Catalogus. I. Rijdt, R.J.A. te. II. Rijksmuseum (Netherlands). Rijksprentenkabinet. III. Title.
ND 1967.N5413 1993
759.9492`074`74-dc20 93-492
CIP

Contents

Acknowledgments

Watercolor stands out as one of the most visually arresting, though one of the most fragile, of the varied media available to the artist. Despite its inherent delicateness and susceptibility to light, artists for centuries have been entranced by the rich colors, subtle washes, and minute details that can be created with watercolor. The finesse that Dutch artists in the eighteenth century achieved with this challenging medium is well represented by the works seen here, all drawn from the world-renowned collection of the Rijksmuseum Printroom in Amsterdam. Opportunities to tour such esteemed European collections in the United States are indeed rare, and it is with great pleasure that Art Services International has accepted this responsibility and honor.

Guiding us in this effort has been Dr. J.W. Niemeijer, Director Emeritus of the Rijksprentenkabinet in Amsterdam. As Guest Curator of this exhibition, he has selected over seventy of the Rijksmuseum's most beautiful and important watercolors for tour. His years of scholarship and genuine affection for these works is evident in this catalogue, in which he describes the careers of many of the Netherlands' most talented artists. It has been a wonderful experience to collaborate with Dr. Niemeijer on this international project, and we thank him for allowing us to do so.

Also deserving special recognition at the Rijksprentenkabinet are Peter Schatborn, Keeper of Prints and Drawings, who encouraged the realization of this project, and Ger Luijten, Keeper of Prints. They have been particularly attentive in providing assistance at every stage, and we are grateful for their cooperation.

We are extremely pleased that Ambassador Hans Meesman of the Netherlands has agreed to serve as Honorary Patron of this exhibition. His interest, along with the valuable assistance of Andreas te Boekhorst and Frans L.E. Hulsman, Counselors for Press and Cultural Affairs at the Embassy of the Netherlands, proved significant as this project developed.

The support provided by the National Endowment for the Arts has been invaluable in bringing these treasures to the United States. Once again we extend our heartfelt thanks to Dr. Anne-Imelda Radice, Acting Chairman, and Alice Whelihan, Indemnity Administrator. We are deeply indebted to the Robert Lehman Foundation and Paul Guth for recognizing the importance of this project. In addition, we send our special thanks to KLM Dutch Royal Airlines and Odette M. Foder-Gernaert for providing valuable assistance as the exhibition progressed.

Additional encouragement in the initial phases of this noteworthy exhibition of Dutch watercolors came from three experts in their respective departments of Old Masters Drawings: Edward Lewine of Christie's in New York; Johan C. Bosch van Rosenthal, a specialist at Christie's in Amsterdam; and Gregory Rubinstein of Sotheby's in London. Their practical advice and concern for our endeavor contributed to its ultimate success.

Similarly, our colleagues at the American museums that are hosting this international presentation have provided the enthusiasm so crucial in the organizing of this tour. We offer our heartfelt thanks to Charles A. Ryskamp, Director, and Edgar Munhall, Curator, of The Frick Collection; Mark Ormond, Director of the Center for the Fine Arts; and John Mahey, Director, and Christopher Young, Curator, of the Flint Institute of Arts. To them we send our sincere thanks.

Documenting the exhibition is this catalogue, another product of international cooperation. Dutch translator Michael Hoyle and American editor Nancy Eickel pooled their professional skills in determining the final form of this manuscript. Contributing to their joint effort was the printing firm of Waanders in Amsterdam, which melded text and image with beautiful results.

Without the continued support and dedication of the staff of Art Services International, this stunning collection of Dutch watercolors might never have left the Netherlands. Once again, Grace Eleazer, Ana Maria Lim, Douglas Shawn, and Kirsten Simmons have proven themselves to be true professionals, and we acknowledge them with respect and gratitude.

Lynn Kahler Berg
Director

Joseph W. Saunders
Chief Executive Officer

Author's Notes

During the preparation of this catalogue, I received vital information from various quarters. Joke van Pelt and Ben Albach offered their views on the stage play depicted by an anonymous artist (cat. no. 73). Charles Dumas provided assistance with the watercolor by La Fargue (cat. no. 36), and Renske Jellema shared her findings on Cats's series of the months (cat. no. 15). J. van Tatenhove was consulted for the entries on Jacob de Wit, while S.A.C. Dudok van Heel identified the house occupied by De Moucheron (cat. no. 71). Els Verhaak pointed out the connection between Lauwers and Senave (cat. no. 41), and Bert Sliggers lent his expertise on the Haarlem artists. M.D. Haga was once again a wealth of knowledge and advice. I am grateful to all these persons for their interest and their readiness to assist me in this task.
I was particularly fortunate in having R.J.A. te Rijdt as a collaborator. His valuable contributions to many a discussion warrant his separate mention at the very front of this book.
The presentation of this selection of Dutch watercolors to the American public was suggested by Mrs. John Pope of Washington, D.C., and was made possible by Lynn Kahler Berg and Joseph W. Saunders of Art Services International. The translation into English was reliably handled by Michael Hoyle.

J.W. Niemeijer

Introduction

Like the colored print, the colored drawing reached its heyday in the eighteenth century. In the extensive oeuvre of Cornelis Troost, the greatest Dutch painter of the period, are found very few black-and-white drawings, and even those that do exist are often on tinted paper. Color was also an essential component when making copies on paper of seventeenth-century paintings. The lively demand for such reproductions among collectors assured many artists of a solid source of additional income. In fact, the intense desire to have color in drawings drove artists to add color to original seventeenth-century landscape drawings. Artists such as Isaac de Moucheron, Dirk Dalens, and Jacob de Wit in the first half of the eighteenth century, and Simon Fokke and Abraham de Haen in the second half, made a specialty of this, and they were so proud of their skill that they added their signatures to these "finished" products. Undoubtedly, others indulged in this practice, but they retained their anonymity in their attempts to embellish Old Master drawings. Their motives, after all, were not always of the noblest sort. Commercial considerations aside, this need for "finish" stemmed from the same eighteenth-century predilection for the completed accomplishment, fully crafted in all its parts, which also accounted for the popularity of the type of drawing presented here under the name "watercolor."

The vast majority of these sheets are equally worked-up, autonomous creations with a *bildmäszig* nature, for lack of a better term. Included here are few true sketches or studies, and in the category of design drawings (of which no more than eight or nine are featured) most again have a high degree of finish. Thus, more than just the tastes and wishes of countless collectors prompted artists to lavish such care on their drawings, for those types of design were never intended to leave the artist's possession. It is conceivable that in many cases the draftsmen were prepared to show their designs for wall and ceiling paintings to potential clients, if requested to do so. That, though, does not apply to the collaborative design by Jacob de Wit and his friend Isaac de Moucheron for a ceiling decoration in De Moucheron's own house (cat. no. 71). Yet that drawing, too, was painstakingly executed. This leads to a distinctively Dutch offshoot of the visual arts in the eighteenth century: painted wall-hangings. It is no coincidence that more than half of the thirty-nine artist in this catalogue trained as painters of decorative canvases or were closely associated with that industry. Until the third quarter of the century, this flourishing craft not only paid well but also offered its practitioners the opportunity of genuine artistic development. Many of these works – no, by far the majority – have since been lost through wear, tear, and neglect. Others fell victim to changing fashions or were destroyed by fire and acts of war. Many were shortened or radically cropped when the owner sold them or moved to a new residence. It is not widely known that this process began as early as it did. Back in 1805, whole series of works for individual room, ceiling, and overmantel paintings were sold at a public auction in Amsterdam on July 10. Fortunately, a number of superb and imposing ensembles continue to survive *in situ*. In Amsterdam, a room by Isaac de Moucheron and Jacob de Wit is found in the Theater Institute, the Andriessen Room is with the Stichting Van den Santheuvel-Sobbe, and the Dalens Room can be seen in the Van Brienenhuis, all on Herengracht. In The Hague is the Schweickhardt Room at No. 32, Lange Voorhout; in Leiden remains a suite by Dirk Kuipers and Dirk van der Aa at No. 67, Rapenburg; and in Breda are found the wall-hangings by Dionys van Nijmegen in the Academie van St. Joost.

While more examples of a similarly high standard could be cited, and those of a slightly lesser caliber are even more numerous, all told there remains only a tiny fraction of the decorations that once must have graced Dutch homes. This thriving branch of art stimulated both painting and drawing enormously. It is true that "fine art" painters looked down their noses at these wall-hangings, and not entirely without reason. Admittedly, huge paintings that covered an entire wall left little room for cabinet pictures, but weighed against this the wall-decoration workshops did provide countless young artists with employment and training. Of course, monotony and lax standards were a danger inherent in the repetitive, routine production of Arcadian landscapes replete with nymphs and shepherds disporting themselves beneath stately trees. Certainly countless idyllic rural scenes of meadows stretching to a waterway, where a ship sails by while a diminutive figure fishes on the bank, were produced, but lack of creativity plagues other genres of art as well. In many cases, the large surfaces that required painting gave the artists – both designers and executors – a breadth of vision and facture, and saved them from the persnicketiness to which some of their less-gifted brethren were prone. In many ways, wall-decorations served as the truly Dutch equivalent of the incentive sparked by the commissions for murals in churches, monasteries, and palaces that were granted in more southerly countries. In addition, the insatiable demand for painted rooms and halls spawned a new genre of drawing: colorful designs for wall surfaces, overmantels, overdoors, and ceilings. The watercolor, in its broadest sense, was the ideal medium for these preparatory drawings.

Despite the importance that is attached to the distinctive nature of the Dutch watercolor, it should be remembered that many, and indeed some of the finest, works produced were by artists who were not born in the Dutch Republic. Some came from border regions, such as Westphalia and Flanders, while others claimed distant parts of Germany, or even Switzerland, as their birthplace. Just among the artists represented here, De Beijer was born in Aarau (Switzerland); Cats in Altona, near Hamburg; Haag in Kassel (central Germany); and Lauwers in Bruges. Pieter Barbiers's father came from Flemish Brabant, Grandjean's parents were French, the Kobells hailed from Germany, and De Moucheron was of Norman stock.

It seems fitting, in this presentation of Dutch art to an American audience, to consider the implications of this international component. For a long time the tendency was to regard eighteenth-century Holland as a nation isolated and complacent. Like a wall that is not easily demolished, that preconceived notion has obscured recent views of the art of the period. A large hole was knocked in the idea by the exhibition *Herinneringen aan Italië*, which was shown at three venues in the Netherlands in 1984. Suddenly, the public became aware that along with – and sometimes even before – the English noblemen, French savants, and Russian, German, and Scandinavian aristocrats, the Dutch had embarked on the Grand Tour, visiting Florence, Venice, Rome, Naples, and places even further south.

Viewers came to realize as well that in the eighteenth century, Holland had been an integral part of the cosmopolitan network that extended throughout Italy and into the other European countries as well. What a good idea it would be to mount an exhibition illustrating the cultural and, above all, artistic contacts between the Dutch Republic and the *dix-huitième* in France, or Georgian England, to say nothing of Switzerland. In all these cases the interest and esteem was mutual, but it was most intense with the French. Any attempt to convey a sense of this intellectual intercourse would go far beyond the scope of this introduction, so suffice it to recall the visits of men such as François Boitard, the comte de Caylus, and Hubert Gravelot in the first half of the 1700s, and of Aved "le Batave," J.B. le Prince, the engravers Boily and Duboulois, Noël Challe, Quentin de la Tour, Charles Eschard, and Etienne Falconet in the second half. J.B. Perronneau journeyed to Holland no fewer than six times between 1754 and his death there in 1783. Voltaire made seven visits between 1713 and 1750, and Diderot two, in 1773-74. At the same time, Dutch painters and draftsmen were traveling to Paris. Several who made the pilgrimage to the French capital around 1700 include Hermanus Numan, Reinier Vinkeles, Tethart Haag, Hendrik Kobell, and, for a protracted stay, Willem van Leen. They were, by no means, the only ones to do so, though. It seems to have been in the second half of the century that Dutch artists felt a particularly strong call to go to Paris, and even to push on to Bordeaux and, *en route* to Rome, to the south of France. Some went in search of further training in the studios of Le Bas, Wille, or Delaunay; others hoped to develop their painting techniques and style in the circles around Greuze, Noël Hallé, and the Van Loos. The vast majority of them returned home with their horizons broadened and their style enriched. A few, such as the flower painters Van Spaendonck and Van Pol, were seduced by success and put down permanent roots in foreign lands.

England, too, must have attracted far more artists than is realized. Apart from four artists represented here – Hendrik Kobell, Hendrik Meyer, Wijbrand Hendriks, and Aart Schouman – the Channel crossing was made by Jan van Gool, Gerard Wigmana, Simon Hardimé, Jacob Campo Weyerman, the Van der Mijns, F.A. van Bloemen, Arnold Houbraken, Theodoor Netscher, Theodoor van Pee, Michiel Carrée, and Hendrik Schweickhardt, among others. A number of them worked there for years before returning to Holland, matured and brimming with visual impressions. Very little information exists, however, on English artists visiting Holland. Thomas Sandby traveled in Flanders in 1743, 1745, and 1746, but it is not clear whether he ventured north into the Dutch Republic. Thomas Rowlandson visited Holland in the 1790s, and James Adam, brother of the famous architect Robert Adam, was here in 1754-55. Robert Adam himself, incidentally, was a friend of the immensely rich Dutch collector Jan (or John) Hope. The most important event seems to have been Sir Joshua Reynolds's tour of Dordrecht, Rotterdam, Delft, The Hague, and Amsterdam in 1781 – important because here was a great painter who also published a travel diary. Reynolds's notes, for they amount to little more than that, actually say little about contemporary art. He evidently felt that only Jan van Huysum and Jacob de Wit were worthy of record (and they had been dead for thirty years by then), and he did not mention a single living artist. The same is true of Diderot, who, as a critic of the Salons in France, was accustomed to viewing works of art by his contemporaries and delivering an opinion on them. He, too, devoted barely a word to Dutch art of the period. Did these foreign visitors, who considered themselves intellectual enough to record and publish their observations and reminiscences about their journeys, not look at the modern works of art, from portraits and still lifes to landscapes, townscapes, marines, and domestic interiors, that were hanging on the walls all around them? Did their hosts never display their albums and portfolios of watercolors, drawings, and prints? And, strangest of all, did they not notice the wall-hangings that enlivened the halls they entered and the rooms in which they were invited to partake of Dutch hospitality?

An investigation of more than fifty published memoirs of foreign travelers in the Netherlands in the period from 1700 to 1800 yielded little information. Although replete with details on myriad aspects of Dutch life – on hotels and inns, the sights and street life of the towns and cities, the character of the people, customs and dress in the countryside and elsewhere, transportation and shipping, gardens, the stage, and occasionally, music – these primary sources proved to be far less of a source on the arts of painting and drawing than was hoped. One or two admitted this openly. Writing in 1787 (his book was published the following year), Thomas Bowdler stated, "I employ no part of my time in looking at pictures or at churches." Most of these authors were not that explicit, but they nevertheless displayed little more interest.

To start with wall-decoration, which was of cardinal importance to Dutch painters and draftsmen, the Englishman Sir James Thornhill, father-in-law of William Hogarth and himself a painter of decorative ensembles, is almost the only visitor to have noticed them or to have discussed their significance. In Rotterdam he mentioned the ceiling decorations, many of them with painted clouds and birds, in the houses of notabilities. Like the wall-hangings, they kept out the cold and damp. The collector Jacques Meyers had one by "Nimegen" – probably the Elias van Nijmegen who executed the design for a similar decoration (see cat. no. 49). Other foreigners, though, passed them by in silence. Mrs. Calderwood, who journeyed to Rotterdam thirty years later and commented on the interiors at length, noticed the decorated gilt leather, silk wall-coverings, and tapestries, but said not a word about wall-hangings. And in 1732, when houses throughout Amsterdam boasted ceilings and walls by Jacob de Wit, the German Baron von Pöllnitz claimed that the interiors of the city's mansions made for a sorry show. An occasional Flemish tapestry could be found, but there were no marble busts or statues, no pieces of furniture upholstered with velvet and embroidered with gold thread, and not a single crystal chandelier in sight.

Fortunately, more attention was paid to framed paintings. Pilati de Tassulo admitted in 1780 that he knew of no other country where the passion for collecting, where "amateurism," as it was then called, was as keen as in Holland. Even though artists, including landscapists, were living there, "the nature which these Dutch painters have chosen is so loathsome that the more perfect the imitation the more disagreeable it is." An earlier French visitor had already inveighed against Dutch painters' choice of subjects. In his view, few had attained the "grandeur and nobility" of the Italians, and several had not progressed beyond "smoking dens populated by dissolute students, or scenes of sottish peasants." Others had confined themselves to depictions of insects, fruit, and fish. Some had specialized in nocturnes modeled on Bassano or in battle scenes, but their efforts are generally too polished and detailed. Of course, equal weight does not always have to be attached to the opinions of foreign visitors. The English novelist Thomas Holcroft, who journeyed through Holland around 1799, solemnly assured his readers that Jacob de Wit, whose painted grisailles he had seen in the Amsterdam Town Hall, was a pupil of Rembrandt. A similarly shallow knowledge of art was displayed by Madame de Bocage (or Boccage), who had ventured to Holland in the summer of 1750 (reminiscences published in 1762), and had seen a superb "Wanuzzen" (Van Huysum, see cat. no. 29) belonging to the collector "Grankam" (Braamcamp). Van Huysum's virtuoso flower pieces do appear to have appealed more to an international taste. Reynolds paused to admire them, and the fine paintings owned by Gerrit Braamcamp also caught the eye of Thomas Pennant in 1765. It is an exception when a foreign visitor made a point of visiting a painter's studio. One who did was Sir Matthew Decker, who called on the Hague portraitist Philips van Dijk in 1748, but then Sir Matthew had the advantage of being of Dutch descent.

Beyond such passing comments, it is mainly in the writings of three foreign travelers that more substantial information on contemporary Dutch art and its creators is found. All three were professionals: the German connoisseur and print-room director Karl Heinrich von Heinecken; his compatriot, the painter Wilhelm Tischbein; and the English print dealer Samuel Ireland. Their visits took place in 1768, 1772, and 1789, respectively. (Heinecken had traveled to Holland earlier, but he left no report of that trip.) Once again, most of what these insiders relate is no longer news, but it is still worth considering their observations. Heinecken, for example, after calling on Jan de Beijer in Amsterdam (see cat. nos. 8-10), reported that this draftsman of town and village views also painted small cabinet pieces in the same manner, as well as large landscapes. A few of De Beijer's small pictures are still known today, but they are not true landscapes, so on this point Heinecken's journal is a very early, and reliable, source. Heinecken also provided interesting information on Jan Punt, who was born in 1711 and whose chief claim to fame was as an actor. At the age of fifty-five, Punt took up painting, producing ceilings and history pictures in the manner of Mattheus Terwesten. He also made "relief paintings in stucco: a form of painting which is still in fashion in Holland" (meaning grisailles produced in the manner of Jacob de Wit). Needless to say, Heinecken also inspected the large private collections. He referred to the famous Johann Goll van Franckensteyn as Baron van

Gool, confusing him with the Hague animal painter Jan van Gool, as Tischbein did. The German traveler also concluded that the Dutch love of art had declined sharply since 1754. Dealing in prints had moved to Paris, and the book trade seemed to be following suit.

When Wilhelm Tischbein arrived in Holland – in Amsterdam to be precise – he learned of the recent death (on November 11, 1772) of the elderly portrait painter Johan Maurits Quinkhard, who had not worked for many years. Tischbein was mainly interested in the masters of the Golden Age, but, of course, he also met fellow artists. His description of Hendrik Kobell furnishes an idea of that artist's irascible and unconventional character (see cat. no. 33). Wilhelm was not the first Tischbein to venture to Holland, nor was he the last. Since 1750, his uncle Johann Valentin had painted portraits while on visits to the country, including those of members of the House of Orange, which his nephew, to his surprise, found hanging in the parlor of the Blau-Jan Inn in Amsterdam. In 1791, Valentin's son Johann Friedrich August, who happened to be born in the southern Dutch city of Maastricht, moved from Germany to settle for four years in Amsterdam, where he enjoyed a great reputation as a portrait painter.

Samuel Ireland divulges the most about late eighteenth-century painters and draftsmen. His two-volume reminiscences of his travels – the first devoted to the Northern Netherlands, the second to parts of what is now Belgium – were so popular that a second edition was published only six years later, in 1796. Another indication of the work's success is that as early as 1792, a German book by J. Grabner appeared. Entire passages were copied verbatim from Ireland, even down to idiosyncratic spellings of the names of Dutch artists. Ireland must have been a fervent supporter of the neoclassicist ideal, and he made no secret of his views on Dutch architectural monuments. Leiden's magnificent sixteenth-century town hall is dismissed as "an uncouth style of architecture," and the charming country houses and gardens displayed "no simplicity or grandeur, with monstrously distorted trees and thick-legged goddesses." Wassenaer-Obdam House in The Hague, designed by Daniël Marot, was deemed inferior to the modern Nassau-Weilburg Palace (the building of which never progressed further than the wing that still stands today). In general, most of the living artists and draftsmen came off well in Ireland's account, although they are too often described as imitators of seventeenth-century artists: Jacob Cats worked in the manner of Adriaan van de Velde, Jan Ekels in the style of Metsu, Egbert van Drielst followed Ruisdael, Barend Thier imitated Potter, and Prins echoed the style of Jan van der Heyden, Michiel Versteegh of Schalcken, and Gerard van Nijmegen of Pynacker. There is certainly some truth in all this, but it does betray a certain lack of understanding and a blindness to the individual, contemporary features of the work of these artists. Sometimes, too, the associations are a little far-fetched. That the drawings of Jean Grandjean (see cat. no. 22) are "somewhat in the style of Both" is not what would come to mind first. Hendrik Meyer (see cat. no. 44), "a painter of landscapes, whose designs and drawings would credit any artist," was living in London at the time of Ireland's visit in 1789. "Mr Biiys" (meaning Jacobus Buys, see cat. no. 11) is "excellent in history painting," not a genre with which he is immediately associated nowadays.

At the time of Ireland's tour, the production of wall decorations was on the decline. In 1754 there were three hundred journeymen who, with their families, depended on the Amsterdam workshops for their livelihood, but by 1816 this number had fallen to eleven. Printed cotton and paper had ousted the far more expensive painted canvas, with the result that walls could again be hung with easel paintings and framed watercolors. For although only one or two of the sheets in this catalogue are known to have been used to adorn walls, there is abundant evidence that this was a perfectly common practice. An examination of several hundred auction catalogues from the period of 1730 to 1810 shows that works by almost half the artists featured here were offered with frames, and that almost all were watercolor drawings, apart from the pastels by Cornelis Troost and the cherubs in colored chalk by Jacob de Wit. Still lifes by Michiel van Huysum and Henstenburgh, townscapes by De Beijer, Van Liender, and Schouten, genre scenes with allegories of the months or seasons by Jacobus Buys, country retreats by Schouman, an interior or a fruit piece by Hendriks, summer and winter landscapes by Cats, marines by Kobell – all graced eighteenth-century interiors from behind glass in "modern frames" or in "brown or black frames with gilt edging."

One interior that must have been particularly well appointed in this respect was that of Burgomaster Pieter Cornelis Hasselaer (died 1795) on Keizersgracht in Amsterdam. Hanging there were large watercolors by De Beijer, Pronk, Van Liender, Kobell, Buys (who was represented by no fewer than twenty-three works), and Jacob Cats. The latter were the four famous views in the Gooi region between Amsterdam and Utrecht that Cats had drawn, at Hasselaer's behest, with the "pen and colors." They have been in the Van Eeghen Collection for the past sixty years.

These are just the masters who are discussed on the following pages, but naturally the work of others was found sufficiently attractive for framing and hanging. Among seventeenth-century works that were particularly popular were the delicate watercolors of birds by Johannes Bronkhorst and Pieter Holsteyn and, from a later period, the miniaturistic gouaches by Gerrit van Battem, Abraham Rademaker, and Louis Chalon. Topographical views, too, were often hung in frames, as were the numerous watercolor copies of seventeenth-century paintings. Fortunately, only a fraction of the total output of eighteenth-century watercolorists were put on extended display in this way. The vast majority of these delicate sheets remained safely in the dark between the pages of art albums, where they retained their pristine freshness.

All the works in this exhibition and catalogue are from the collections of the Rijksprentenkabinet in the Rijksmuseum in Amsterdam. This by no means implies that the cities of Haarlem, Leiden, and Rotterdam, for instance, lack important collections. The Low Countries are still blessed with an abundance of eighteenth-century watercolors, for until recently, foreign buyers were not active in this area. The selection was made with an eye to variety in subject, date, and size. All were acquired by the Rijksprentenkabinet in the past one hundred years: twenty-two at the end of the nineteenth century, when a start was made on building up a collection of drawings alongside the museum's fabled print holdings; more than twenty from 1900 to 1945; and twenty-nine from the post-war period. They come from a wide range of sources, with some being bought at auction or from dealers, donated by private individuals, transferred from other institutions, and acquired as single works or as part of a group. In the latter category, mention should be made of the bequest of Joannes Gerardus de Groot Jamin. This Amsterdam collector, who was born in 1842 and lived at No. 224, Amstel, bequeathed 465 drawings and watercolors to the Rijksprentenkabinet in 1921. Eight of them are included here: one by De Beijer (cat. no. 10), two by Dupré (cat. nos. 19 and 20), and images by Grandjean (cat. no. 22), Laquy (cat. no. 40), Van Noorde (cat. no. 46), Schouten (cat. no. 61), and A. van Strij (cat. no. 62). The remainder are more or less random acquisitions, with the most recent ones entering the Printroom in 1987 (Cats, cat. no. 13), 1988 (Lauwers, cat. no. 41), and 1990 (Cats, cat. no. 15).

A few of these watercolors are perhaps known to a wider public, since they have been loaned to other exhibitions or reproduced in books and periodicals. Most, however, will be unfamiliar. Significantly, this is the first time that a separate publication has been devoted to this part of the Rijksprentenkabinet collection. These watercolors may not be the most prestigious of the Rijksmuseum's possessions, but they certainly are attracting the growing attention that they deserve, both at home and abroad.

Jurriaan Andriessen (Amsterdam 1742-1819 Amsterdam)

An important and prolific designer and painter of interior decorations in both a neoclassicist and Dutch naturalistic style, and creator of occasional history pieces. Jurriaan Andriessen studied first with Antonie Elliger (1701-1781), a specialist in history paintings, and then spent a year with the elderly portraitist Johan Maurits Quinkhard (1688-1772). In 1760, Andriessen enrolled as a member of the Amsterdam Drawing Academy (of which he became a director in 1794). After spending some time as the assistant of Joannes van Dregt (1737-1807), he went into partnership with Izaak Schmidt (1740-1818) in a wall-decoration workshop. Schmidt resigned in 1772, the same year that the City Playhouse burned down. Andriessen executed a number of important decors for its replacement, assisted by Hermanus Numan (see cat. nos. 47, 48).

The previous year, 1771, Andriessen had painted the splendid room at No. 524, Herengracht. (The paintings now belong to the Rijksmuseum.) When the fashion for interior decorations on canvas waned, robbing him of his main source of income, Andriessen turned to teaching. He instructed more than forty pupils, many of whom went on to become prominent artists in their own right, among them Jean Grandjean (see cat. no. 22), Jacques Kuyper (1761-1808), Hendrik Voogd (1768-1839), and Wouter van Troostwijk (1782-1810). In later years Andriessen was plagued by poverty and ill health. He was predeceased by his younger brother Antonie (1746-1813), who assisted him in the wall-hangings shop. His son Christiaan Andriessen (1775-1846) is today known chiefly as a draftsman of everyday scenes, which are contained in a visual diary that covers the years 1805 to 1808. Andriessen was the leading wall-hangings artist from the period before the genre went into its terminal decline. His inventiveness, broad vision, and lyrical style can be seen in a number of extant rooms that he decorated, and above all in the two large ensembles of design drawings in the Rijksprentenkabinet and in the Amsterdam City Archives.

1 Design for a Wall with a Fireplace

Pencil, pen, and watercolor; gray border
320 x 511 mm
Below painted compartments: *Schipvaart* (Shipping) and *Visscherij* (Fishing); above overmantel: *Godsdienst* (Religion)
No inv. no.

On numerous occasions Andriessen received commissions to decorate one or more rooms in a house. His clients sometimes asked for a preliminary design for an entire interior or for isolated elements, such as a pair of wall-hangings, an overmantel, or an overdoor painting. In this particular case, the marble Louis Quinze fireplace, and possibly the mirror as well, may already have been installed in the room. They certainly display a very different and earlier style from the strict rectilinearity of the rest of the ensemble.

For the two wall compartments, Andriessen designed charming rural scenes illustrating some of the daily activities of people who work outdoors. Here, ferrymen cross a river and fishermen haul in a net. The dotted line on the right probably marks the position of a door. The depiction of Religion above the mirror takes the form of a classical scene of sacrifice.

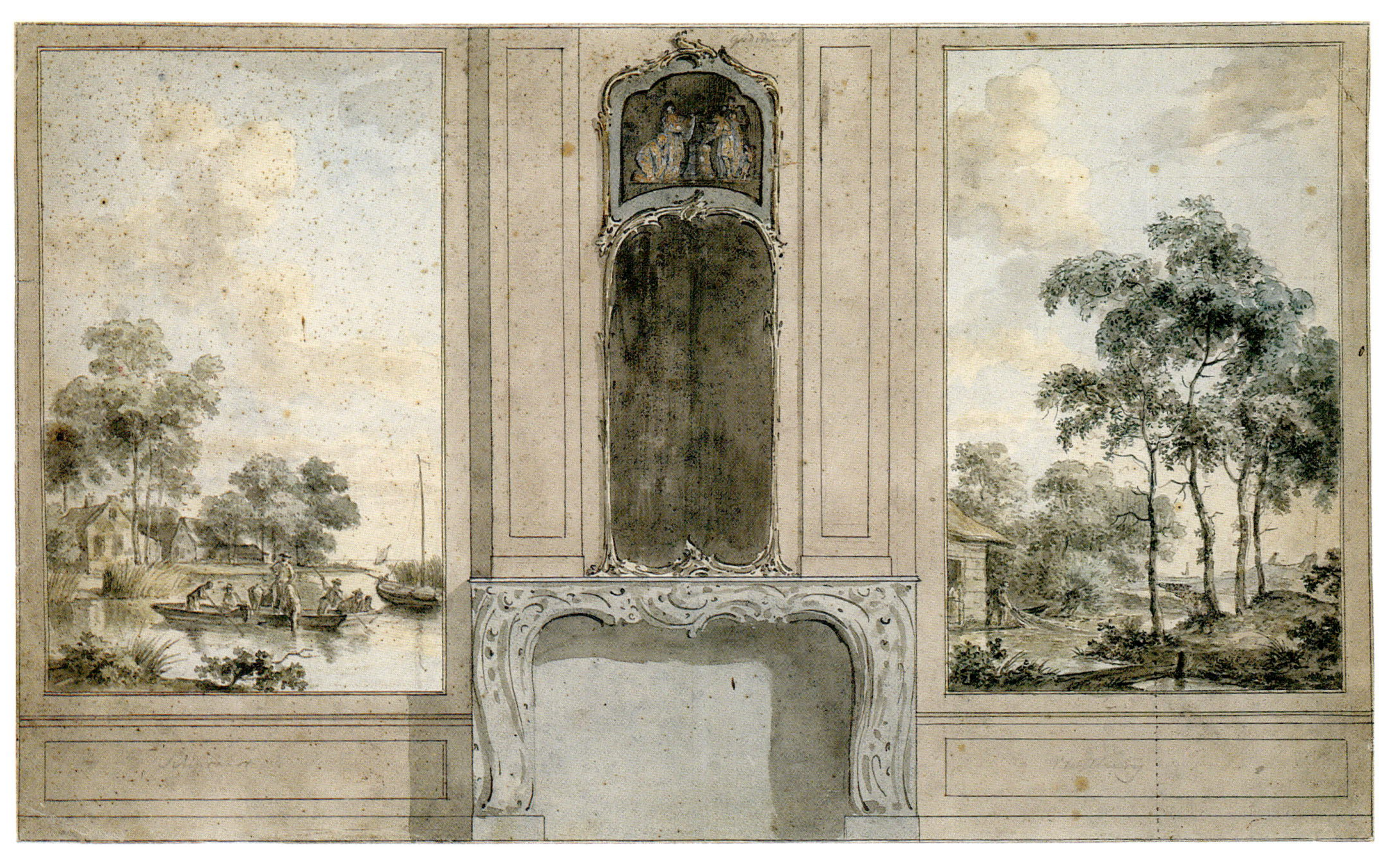

2 Mediterranean Coast with Pyramid

Pencil, pen, and watercolor; gray border; traces of squaring
187 x 405 mm
On verso, in Andriessen's hand, in pencil:
Zykam G La Borde
Inv. no. 1898 A 3570

In addition to characteristically Dutch scenes, such as the preceding one (cat. no. 1), Andriessen's wall-decoration shop also supplied classical, idyllic landscapes. That this design was actually executed is suggested by the grid drawn over the scene, which would have been used to scale the drawing to the requisite size, and also by the annotation on the back, which states that the painting was installed in a side room in the house of G. la Borde.

The name of La Borde (which was not common in Amsterdam at the time) is found on several other drawings by Andriessen, including one that reads *by den Hr La Borde aan de Vuurst* (in Mr La Borde's house at De Vuursche). This has enabled Andriessen's client to be identified as Gerrit la Borde (born 1740), a councillor of De Vuursche, a village near Utrecht, around 1790. La Borde, an Amsterdamer of humble origins, was raised in the city orphanage. In 1777 he married Adriana Josèphe in Amsterdam, which gained him entry into a family that had earned a fortune in the colonies. Two years later his nephew by marriage, Coert Simon Sander, became the owner of Drakensteyn Castle (now in the possession of the Dutch royal family), which stands in De Vuursche, and this may have given Gerrit la Borde the idea of settling in the same neighborhood. His relatives could also have been instrumental in putting him in touch with Jurriaan Andriessen, for Coert Simon Sander ordered from the artist room paintings that depicted Mediterranean harbors (originally in Drakensteyn, now in the Museum van Loon, Amsterdam), as well as a design drawing that was, until recently, in the collection of L. Houthakker, Amsterdam. Other harbor scenes that bear the name Sander are now in the Amsterdam City Archives, and decorative designs *voor de slaapkamer op Drakesteyn* (for the bedroom at Drakènsteyn) are in the Rijksprentenkabinet. Andriessen also produced designs for a room decoration (Haarlem City Archives) for A. Josèphe, possibly Andries Josèphe, who was born in Batavia (modern Jakarta) in 1756 and was an honorary member of the Amsterdam Drawing Academy from 1780 to 1809.

It is difficult to pinpoint the house that contained the side room for which this drawing was made. De Vuursche had other fine houses apart from Drakensteyn Castle, such as Klein Drakensteyn and Pijnenburg, and the country mansion known as De Hooge Vuursche. Little more is known of the latter than the five colored drawings made of the house and park in 1786-87 by Johannes van der Wal, who died while working on wall-hangings in a country house at De Hooge Vuursche in the summer of 1788. It is not known, however, whether Gerrit la Borde owned this house at the time, and it is even debatable whether this drawing has any connection with La Borde's house in De Vuursche, for this place-name appears after La Borde's name on *another* drawing.

In other words, the "side room" may have been in La Borde's Amsterdam home. In 1806, he and his wife were living on Prinsengracht near Berenstraat (now No. 469, which bears a wall tablet dating from 1713), but this was a rented house. No earlier Amsterdam address for La Borde is known.

The commissions from Sander and La Borde naturally brought Andriessen to De Vuursche from time to time. A view of the main street of the village, drawn in the fall of 1800, is part of the substantial Andriessen collection in the Rijksprentenkabinet (inv. no. A 3942). That same year he also made a drawing of the large lake at Drakensteyn. Other artists of his time found the village attractive as well, for views of De Vuursche by Jacob Cats and Egbert van Drielst are known.

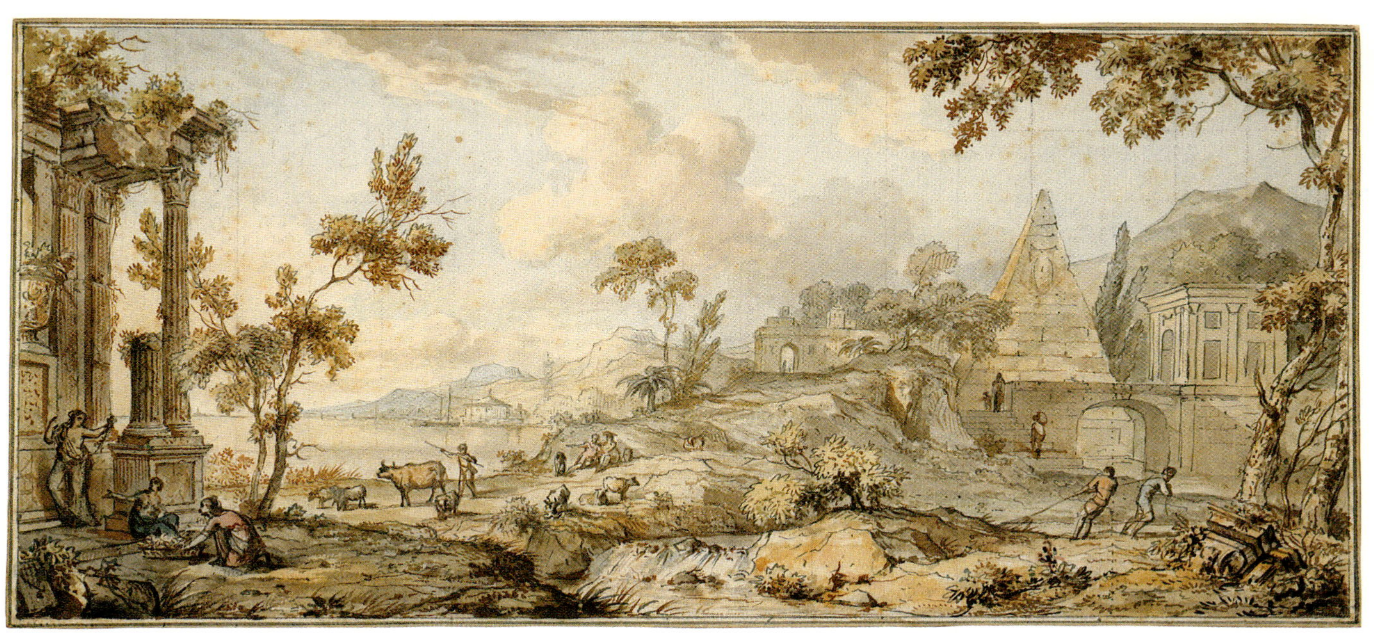

3 Idyllic Landscape with Classical Monuments

Pencil, pen in gray, and watercolor
234 x 307 mm
In left border, a dotted line with abbreviation:
hor[izon] On verso, in Andriessen's hand, in pencil:
Van Lennep
Inv. no. 1898 A 3580 (as Isaac de Moucheron)

This broadly brushed scene evokes the Arcadian life of a long-lost *aetas aurea*, a golden age, in which mankind could carefreely revel in play and dance. This nostalgic vision is seen through a stone aperture, at the edges of which are entwined vine tendrils.

It is difficult to identify the "Van Lennep" mentioned on the back of this design for a wall-hanging. There were many Van Lenneps, and several of them could have afforded such a commission. In 1767, Aernout van Lennep, owner of Manpad House near Heemstede (see cat. no. 5), gave Andriessen his first major commission for a painted room, which is still preserved there. The present design, however, does not match that decoration. Among the numerous drawings by Andriessen in the Rijksprenten-kabinet is an uncolored, outline sketch of a similar composition, which even has the location of a door marked in the same position. The sketch bears Andriessen's annotation *op Assumburg* – the name of a castle near Alkmaar that still stands today – but that castle did not belong to a Van Lennep, and it no longer has any painted rooms. The connection between the two drawings and the painted versions remains unclear.

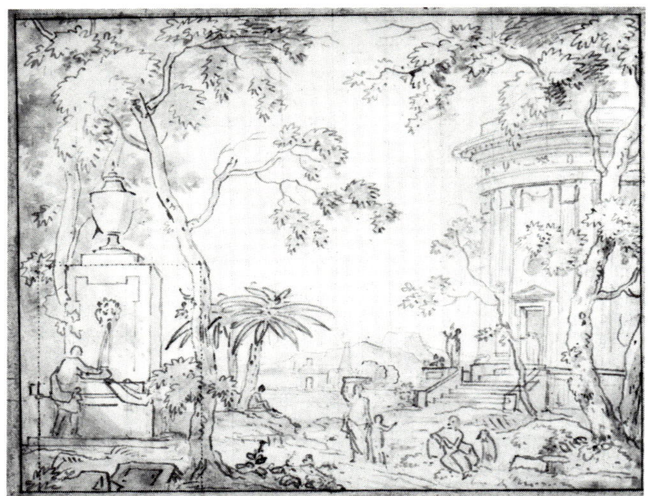

Jurriaan Andriessen, design for a wall decoration in Assumburg Castle. Amsterdam, Rijksprentenkabinet.

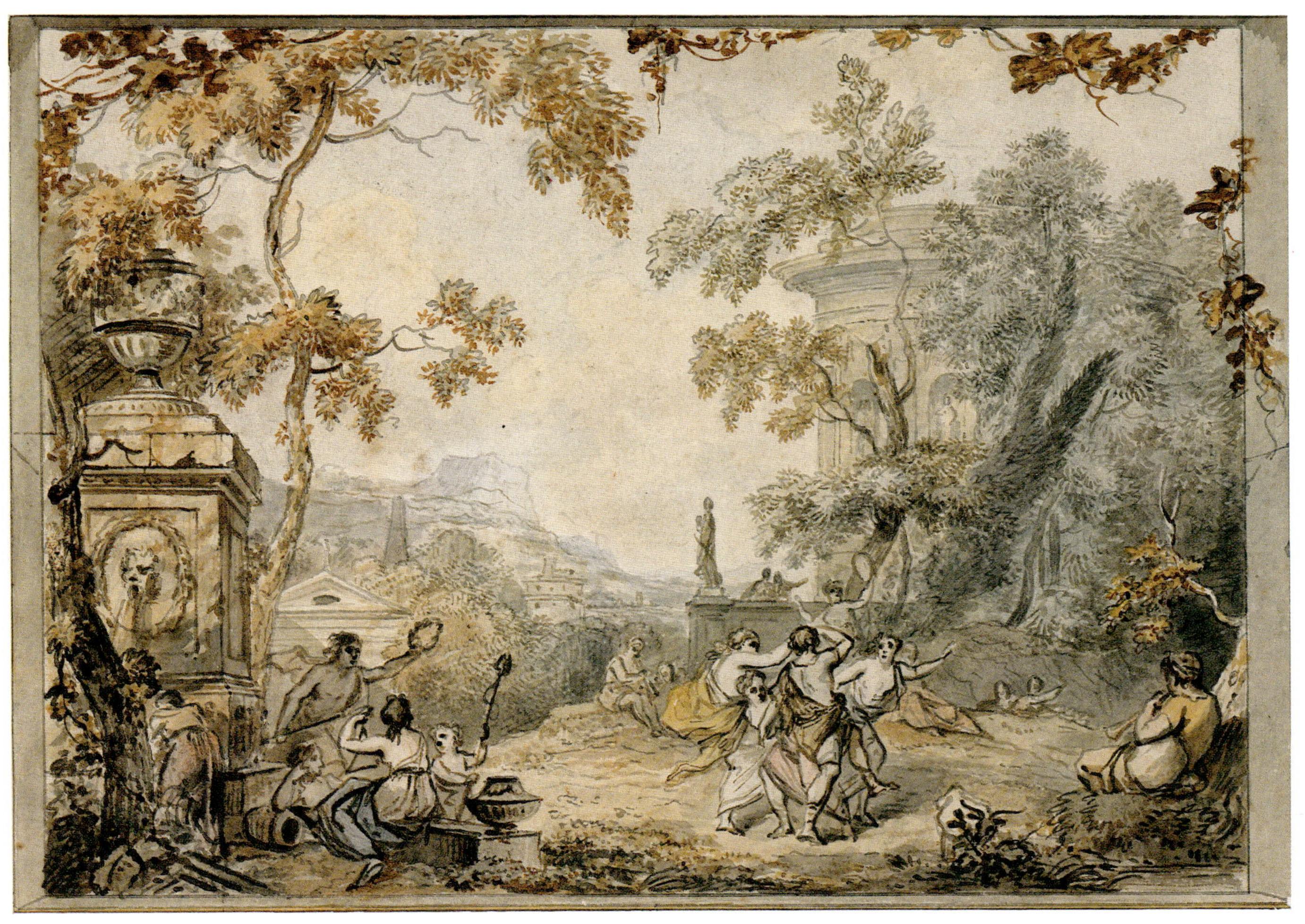

4 **View of a Dike outside Amsterdam**

Pencil, pen in gray, and watercolor; pencil border
145 x 185 mm
Above buildings: *Muyderberg, Slot, Muyden, Naarden, Vislust, Weesp, Diemen*
On verso, a fisherman at a bend in a waterway. Identical technique, with inscription: *den opgang na de hogendyk 1785* (the road to the high dike, 1785)
No inv. no.

It seems a remarkable paradox that the groundwork for the innovations that began appearing in Dutch landscape painting around 1800 was laid by artists working in the very traditional, and even regressive, manner of the wall-decoration shops. This is illustrated in a surprising way by this watercolor by Andriessen of a simple dike separating land from water to the north of Amsterdam. Assuming that the date on the verso also applies to the scene on the front of the sheet, it must be concluded that Andriessen drew this spare, unpretentious view of a polder at a time when he was also designing landscapes of a classical dream world, complete with temples and scenes of sacrifice, for the homes of wealthy patricians. Although initially little more than an undercurrent, this new, refreshing view of nature ultimately led to *plein-air* painting and thence to Impressionism.

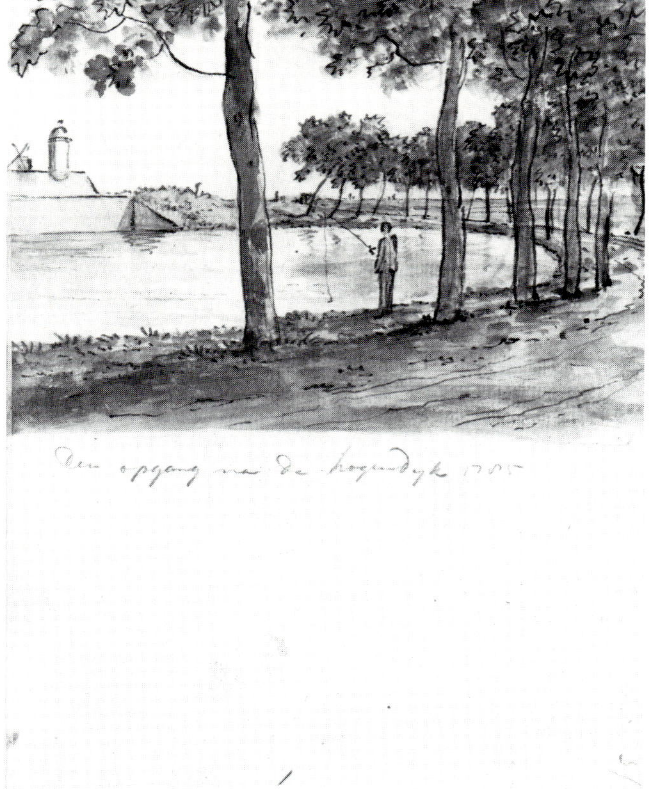

Jurriaan Andriessen, verso of View of a Dike outside Amsterdam.

The artist labeled the buildings on the distant skyline, but there was no need to identify the large, square house in the middle, for it was, and still is, recognizable as the Gemeenlandshuis (polder authority house) of Diemermeer. Some of the foreground details indicate that Andriessen made this watercolor from the vantage of Zeeburg Inn. A contemporary print shows that the enclosure at lower left surrounded a ground where the old game of *kolf* was played. The signboard by the fence may have listed the bill of fare at the inn, or it may have been used for public announcements. The inn was quite a popular site for artists from Amsterdam. On a drawing in the Rijksprentenkabinet (inv. no. A 4224), Andriessen's colleague Jacob Cats used it as a setting for a group of two men and four women who have imbibed a little too freely of the landlord's wine.

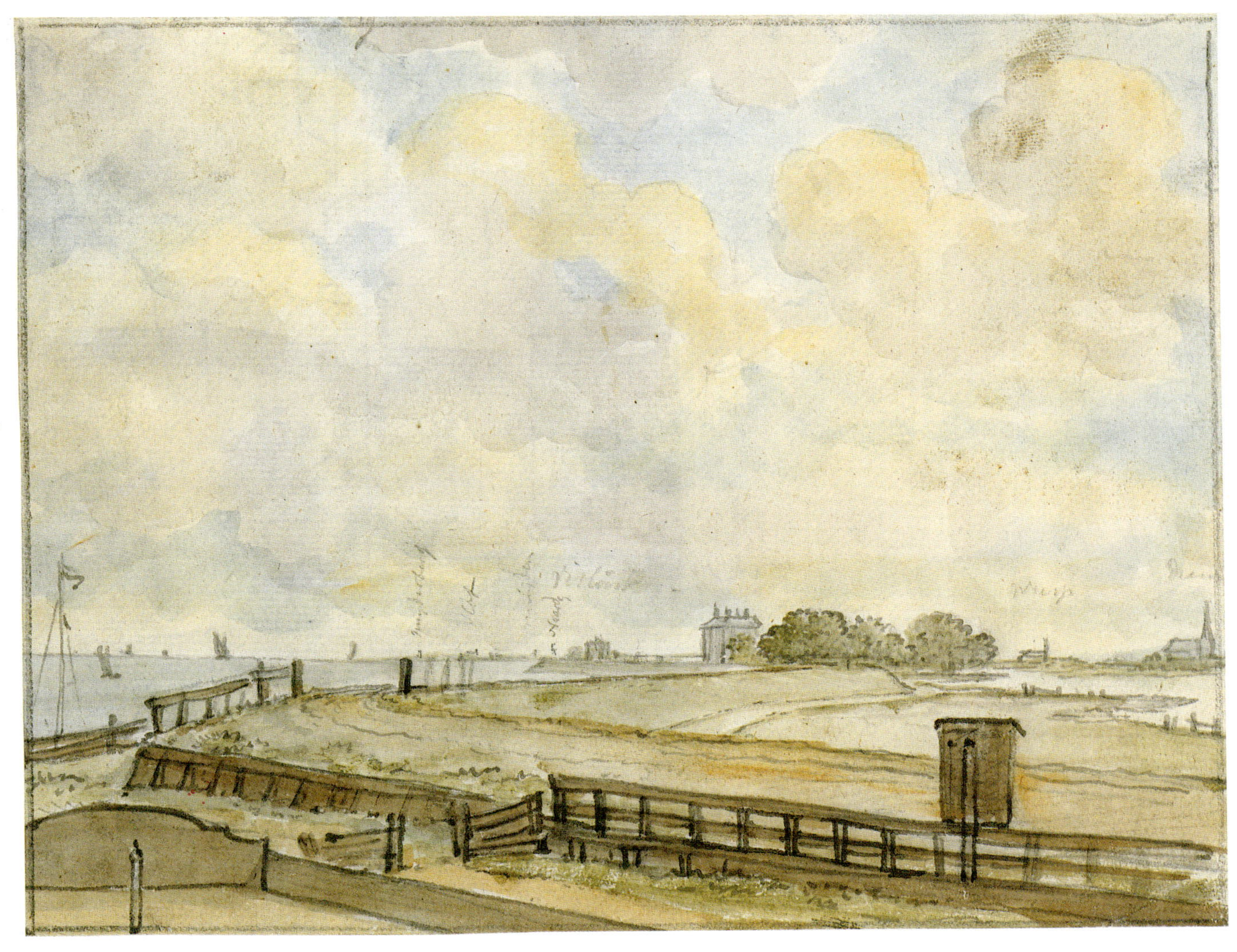

5 **Strollers on a Woodland Path near Heemstede**
Black chalk and/or pencil, and watercolor; brownish black border
220 x 180 mm
On verso, in Andriessen's hand, in pencil: *op de weg van / heemstede na de buytenplaats / 't huys te Manpad* (on the path from Heemstede to Manpad House, the country estate) [misspelling corrected].
In a later hand, in pen: *J. Andriessen*
Inv. no. 1943:70

The inscription places this woodland view in the beautiful stretch of countryside found behind the dunes south of Haarlem, an area which, in the eighteenth century and later, had numerous country estates and mansions, including Manpad. In 1767, Andriessen decorated one of the large rooms in Manpad with painted wall decorations that can still be seen there today.

This watercolor dates from much later – some time after 1800, judging by the dress of the couple out for a stroll. By then, the wall-decoration industry had collapsed, yet this woodland scene, seemingly so directly observed and freely rendered, is composed entirely in accordance with the principles of that decorative tradition. The two foreground trees flanking the path leave an open space in the sky to feature the fan-shaped foliage of the three birches, which the artist carefully placed in the very center of his composition. Less conventional is the way in which he used chalk to sketch in the main motifs before he completed them in watercolor.

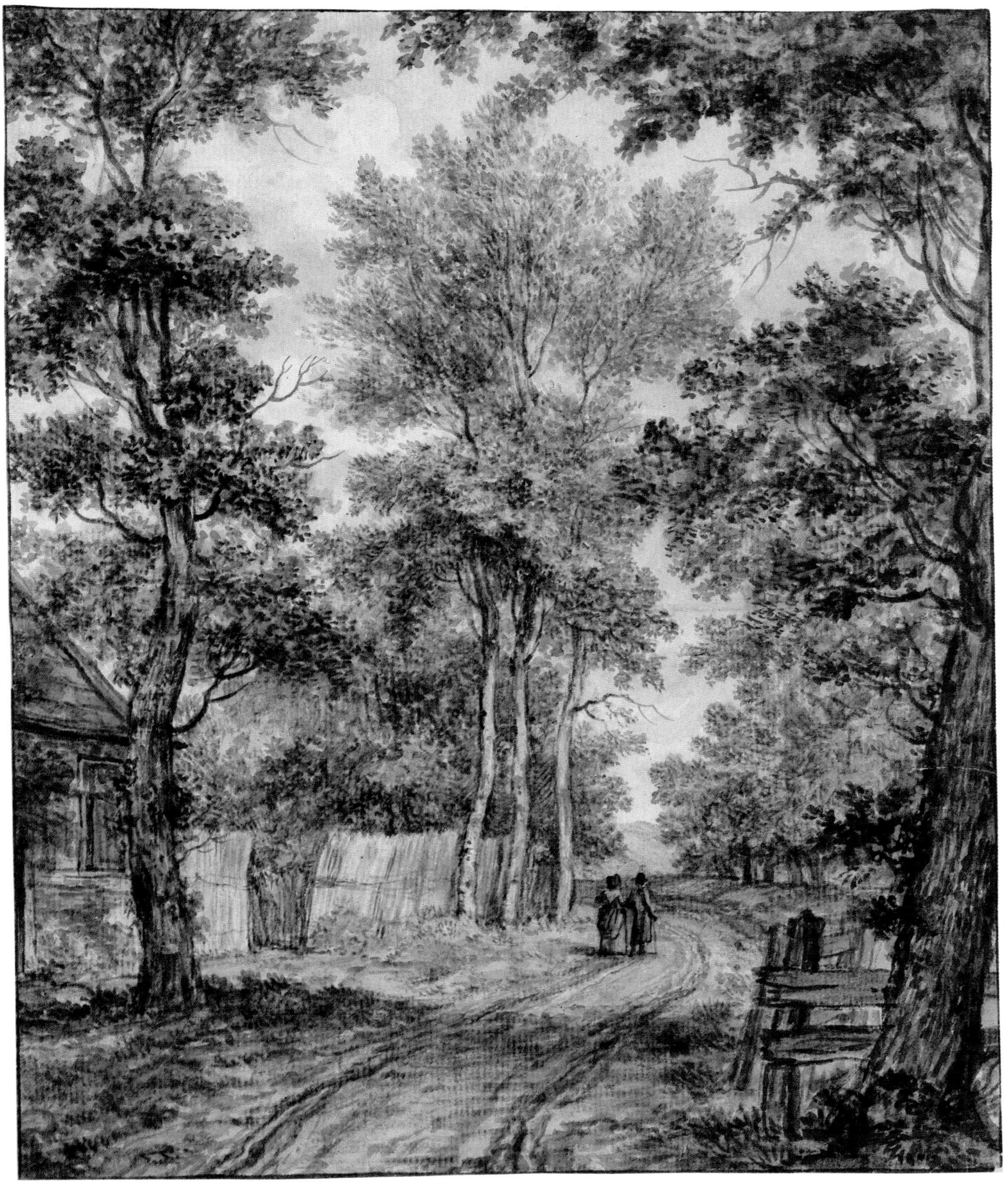

Pieter Barbiers Pzn (Amsterdam 1749-1842 Amsterdam)

Painter of wall-hangings and landscapes, draftsman, and occasional etcher from a family of Flemish artists. His father, Pieter Barbiers Azn (1717-1780), originally had a fan workshop in Amsterdam, but he later turned to wall decoration and scenery painting. Two of his many children became painters: Bartholomeus (1740-1808) and Pieter. Bartholomeus had an artist son called Pieter (1772-1837), who passed the same name on to his son (1798-1848), who also became an artist. In turn, Pieter Barbiers had a son called Bartholomeus, who was a landscape draftsman. Separating one from the other is no easy task.

For Cornelis Henricus à Roy, court physician to King Louis Napoleon – Roy died in 1833 in Amsterdam – Barbiers painted a series of wall-hangings in which the human figures were added by Jacobus Johannes Lauwers (see cat. no. 41). This is probably a suite of six works that was formerly in the Thurkow Collection and is dated 1792.

6 Hilly Landscape with Stately Trees and Human Figures

Gouache; black border with gold edging
405 x 486 mm
Signed on verso, at lower left, in pen: *P. Barbiers*
Inv. no. 1893 A 2795

Pieter Barbiers rarely dated his drawings, so it is difficult to arrange them in chronological order. Since he lived to the great age of ninety-three, he was one of the few artists who witnessed the evolution in style from the heyday of the wall-decoration industry to the Romantic landscapes of Andreas Schelfhout and Barend Cornelis Koekkoek, although he did make his own contributions to the innovations associated with the latter artists. One is inclined to date this large landscape gouache well before 1800, given its wealth of narrative detail and the decorative linearity of the spreading branches of the trees. Compositionally, it combines the type of dune landscape found near Haarlem with the hazy vista of mountain ranges, which was a popular motif in the Mediterranean scenes that were often depicted in wall-hangings. The human figures in this and other landscapes by Barbiers are reminiscent of the kind used by many of his contemporaries. Some, such as Abraham Johannes Ruytenschildt (1778-1841), Pieter Gerardus van Os (1776-1839), and Albertus Brondgeest (1786-1849), are known to have taken them from their stock of life studies.

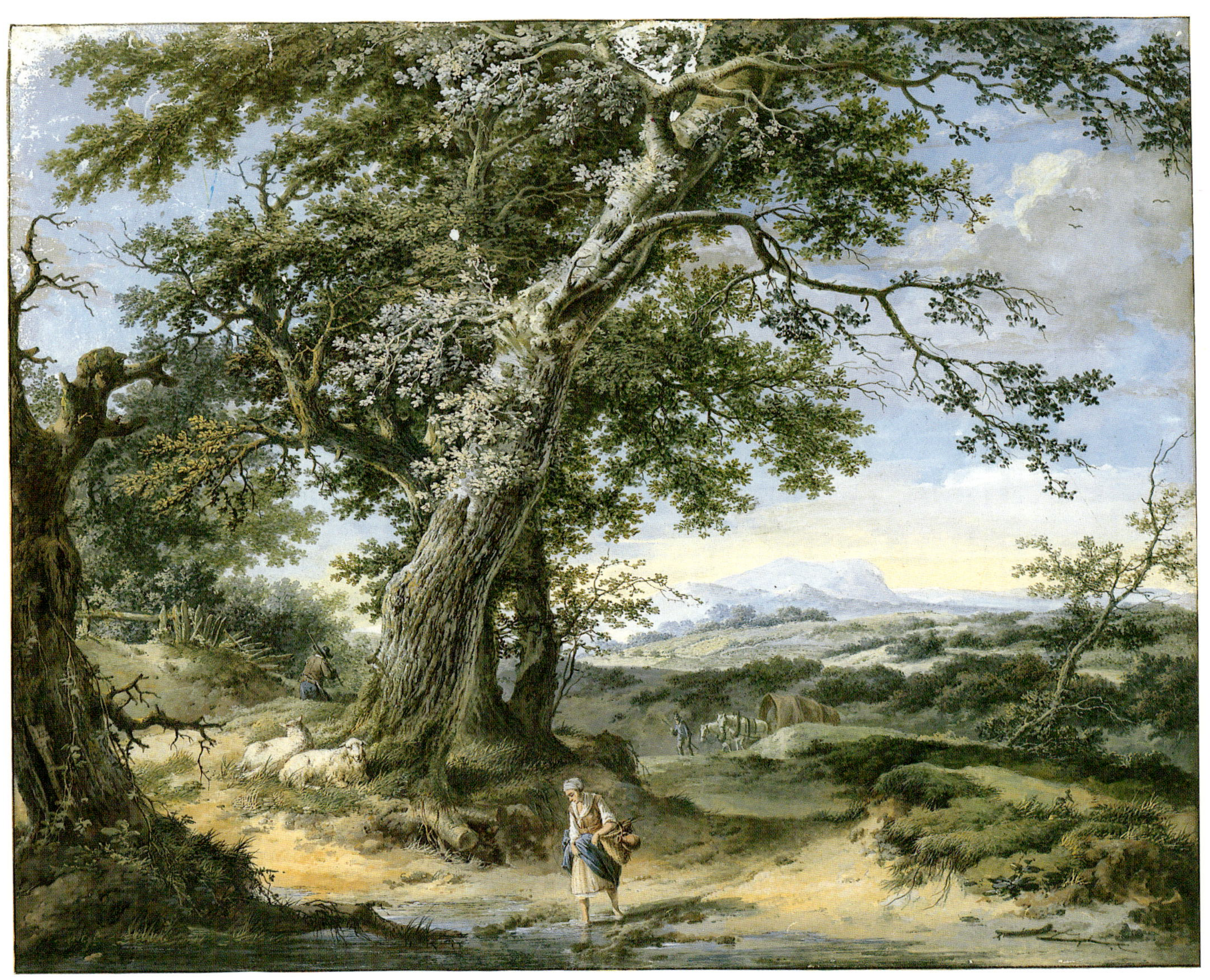

7 Argus Pheasant

Pencil and watercolor; gray border
338 x 512 mm
Signed on verso, in pen: *Pr-Barbiers*
Inv. no. 1905:254

This pheasant (*Phasianus argus*) derives its name from its tail markings. According to legend, the goddess Hera gave it the hundred eyes of her faithful servant Argus after the giant had been slain by Hermes. The bird, which could attain a length of two meters from its beak to the tip of its tail, lived in the forests of Thailand, Malacca, and Sumatra. Barbiers probably used a stuffed specimen as a model.

As it happens, a superb specimen of an Argus pheasant was on display in Haarlem, where Barbiers worked a great deal, in the natural history collection of Dr. Martinus van Marum (1750-1837). It stood in the middle of the room beneath a bell jar. This information comes from a visit to the cabinet made by members of the Caledonian Horticultural Society, who published an account of their travels. "The Argus pheasant," the reporter wrote, "is particularly fine. The specimens of this splendid bird are generally mutilated, or deprived of their feet, before they leave China; this one, however, is quite perfect."

The drawing is from a set of six sheets of pheasants and peacocks. They were bequeathed to the Rijksprentenkabinet in 1905 by Miss Elisabeth van den Brink, a descendant of the seventeenth-century marine artist Ludolf Bakhuysen, together with some drawings by that artist and various documents relating to him.

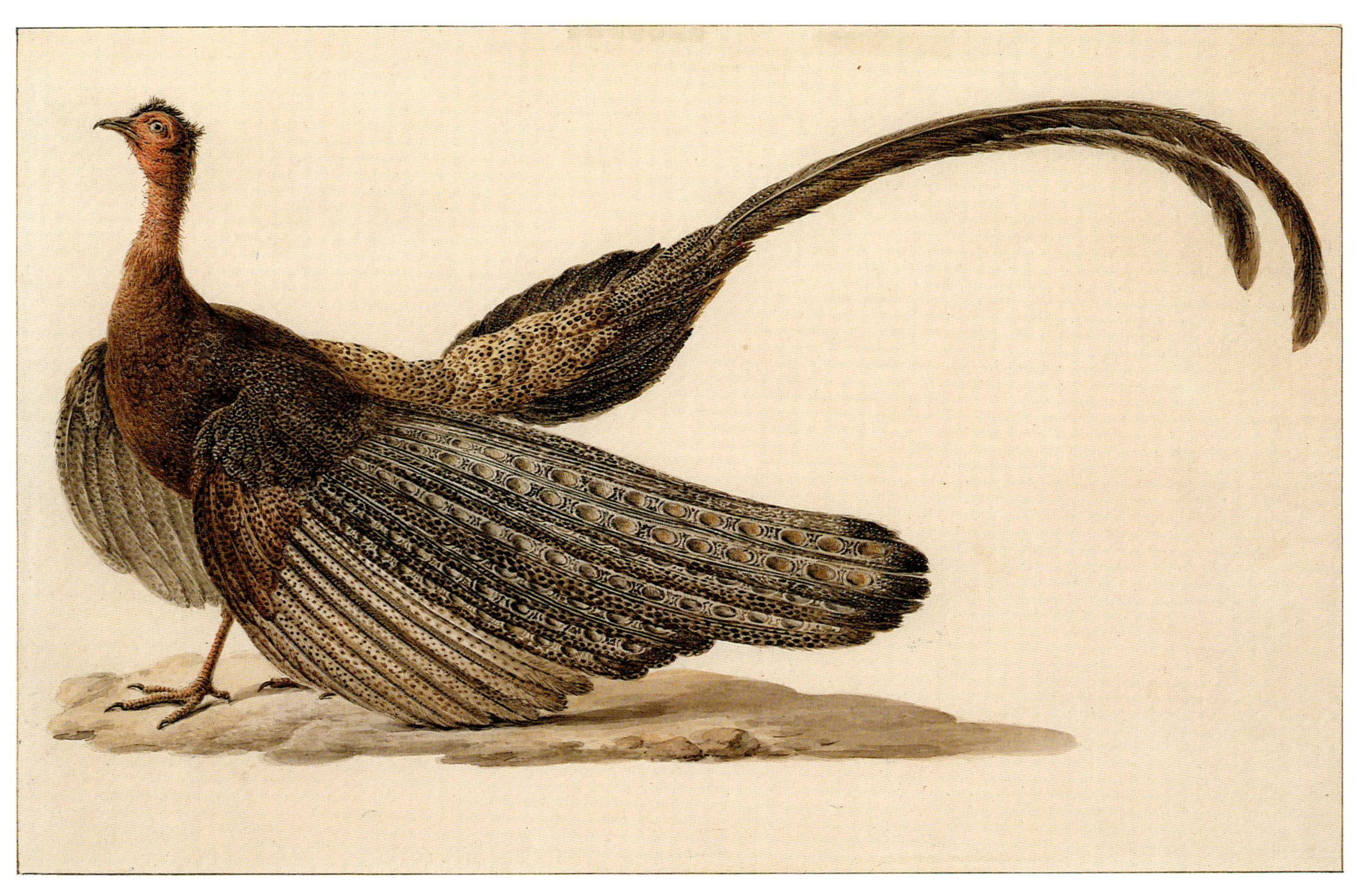

Jan de Beijer (Aarau [Switzerland] 1703-1780 in or near Emmerich [Germany])

Draftsman of hundreds of meticulously detailed views of towns, villages, castles, monasteries, and similar subjects. Jan de Beijer reached adulthood in Emmerich, just over the border in Germany, in the 1730s, before he spent some years in Amsterdam as the pupil of Cornelis Pronk (see cat. nos. 52-54). As his teacher had done before him, De Beijer then began specializing in topographical scenes and became the main supplier of drawings for the ten-part illustrated work titled Het verheerlijkt Nederland (The Netherlands Glorified), which was published by Isaac Tirion between 1745 and 1774. In 1751 or 1752, De Beijer decided to settle in Amsterdam, where, apart from a break of a few years, he remained until 1769. He took up painting under the guidance of his compatriot, Johan Maurits Quinkhard, who was born in Rees, not far from Emmerich, but had been living in Amsterdam for years. De Beijer calmly continued to draw views of towns and villages, and today only a handful of his oil paintings are known.

De Beijer, who never married, was known as an equable and good-humored man. In Amsterdam, he and his colleagues founded a drawing society, but in 1770 he returned to Emmerich, where he died ten years later. Although trained by Pronk, De Beijer developed a more linear style of drawing, which served as a model for the brothers Pieter Jan and Paulus van Liender (born 1727 and 1731, respectively). His influence on them was such that they even imitated De Beijer's inscriptions. Their drawings, dating from mid-century, are often very difficult to distinguish from those produced by De Beijer.

8 Leiden Town Hall

Pen, watercolor, and gouache; gray border; various corrections
251 x 327 mm
Signed at lower left, in pen: *J:De Beyer ad viv. delin.1751*
Inv. no. 1959:72

In De Beijer's case, the inscription *ad viv.delin.1751,* which he added to this large, accomplished cityscape, does indeed mean that it was executed in 1751, but not necessarily that it was done *ad vivum* (before the subject). His life sketches were often made years before, although, as it happens, this particular one does date from 1751, from June 29, to be precise. It is now preserved in Leiden University Library. De Beijer made at least two detailed watercolors from that first drawing, which is uncolored and almost devoid of staffage. In addition to the sheet seen here is a much larger version, also inscribed *ad viv.delin.1751,* in the Printroom at Weimar. The two completed watercolors differ only in details, the most obvious being the addition of awnings on the fourth house from the left in the Weimar sheet. They are missing in both the sketch and the Amsterdam version, which suggests that the one in Weimar is the last produced in the series.

In 1763, Abraham Delfos (1731-1820) reproduced this view, in a print of the same size, as an illustration in *Beschrijving der stad Leyden* (Description of the City of Leiden), by Frans van Mieris the Younger and Daniël van Alphen (vol. 2 [Leiden, 1770], facing p. 365). An inscription on the print states that De Beijer's original was then "in the collection of Mr Johan van der Marck Aeg.Z., chief official of the City of Leiden." The print is virtually identical with the watercolor, with the absence of one or two signboards in the print possibly being due to physical changes in the appearance of the street in the interim. This, though, does not explain why the soldiers (or militiamen) in both the Amsterdam and Weimar watercolors have been replaced with more "neutral" figures in the print. It is not inconceivable that De Beijer placed the parade conspicuously in front of the town hall in an effort to please Johan van der Marck, for in 1751 the latter was not only Burgomaster of Leiden, but also, in that capacity,

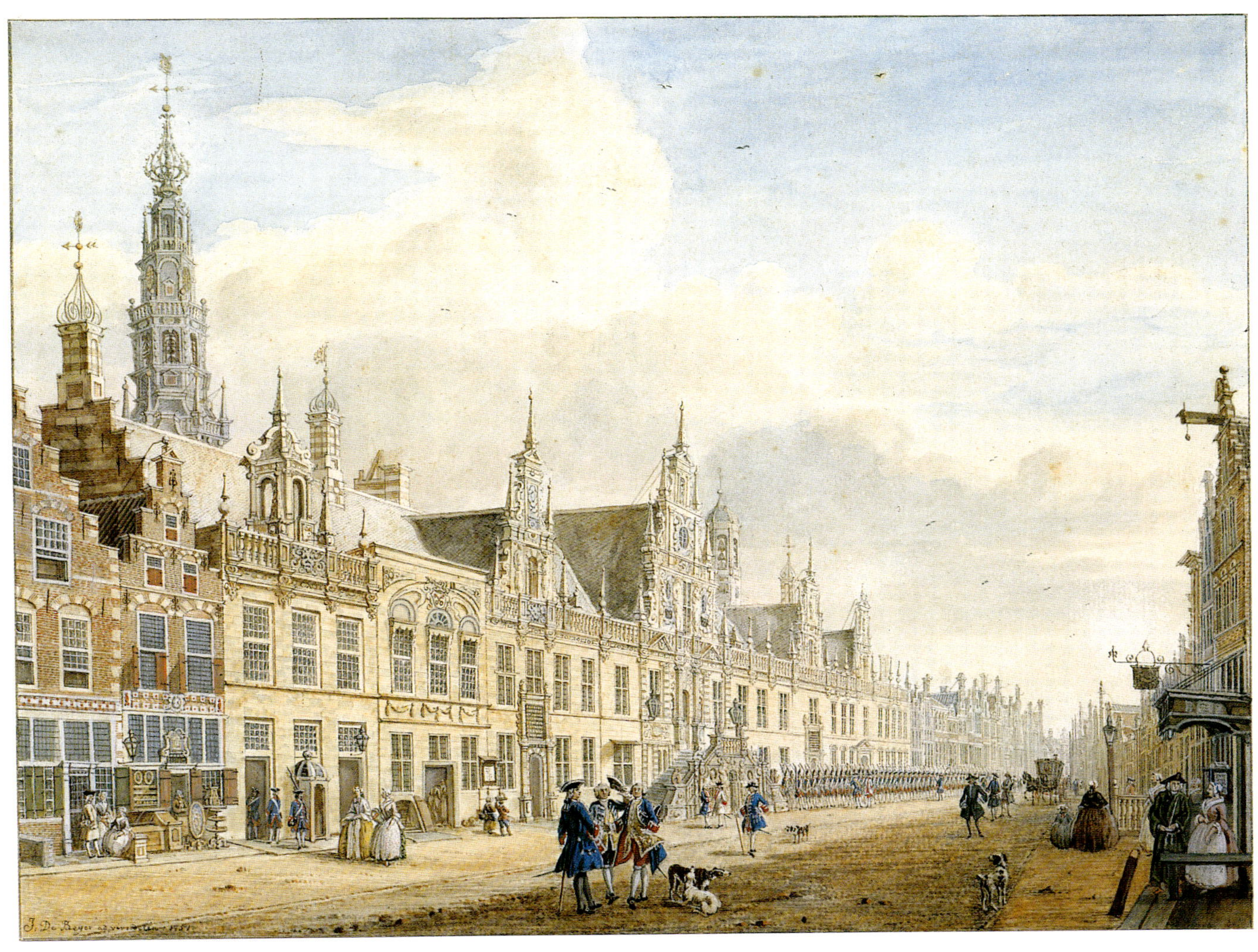

Warden of the War Council. This art-loving dignitary owned three other views that De Beijer had made in and around Leiden. They, too, were turned into prints by Delfos and published in Van Mieris's description of the town. Van der Marck also had a portrait of De Beijer drawn by the man who must have been the artist's inspiration as a topographer: his teacher Cornelis Pronk.

9 Merry Company in the Village of Houten

Pencil, pen in brownish gray, and watercolor; fragmentary brownish gray border
163 x 198 mm
Inv. no. 1888 A 1567

A group of countryfolk enjoy themselves outside a tavern beside a highway. Parked beneath the trees is the cart in which they arrived, and a second one is just drawing up with another party of revelers, who are being hailed by a man jauntily raising his glass to them. De Beijer, who was first and foremost a topographical artist, has situated this scene of rural junketing in the village of Houten, near Utrecht. This location is recognizable from its massive Gothic church tower and its large inn, which was called "De Roskam" (The Currycomb) because of its role as a staging post. Taverns of this kind were one of the centers of village life in the eighteenth century, and they often doubled as courthouses, as De Roskam did.
This watercolor, which lacks inscription, signature, and date, would have been made from a sketch done on the spot, which does not seem to have survived. A second drawing in the Musées Royaux des Beaux-Arts in Brussels, however, shows the church and inn from a slightly different angle. On the verso it bears an annotation in De
It was De Beijer's practice to go on annual sketching trips in search of subjects, and in 1741 he set out to explore the region between Emmerich and Venlo, along the Ditch border with Germany. On this tour he must have made the sketch that served as the basis for this watercolor and for an uncolored drawing of the same scene that is now in the Municipal Museum in Roermond. This view of the small town of Venlo, which stands on the River Maas in the province of Limburg, is the most elaborate of the two.

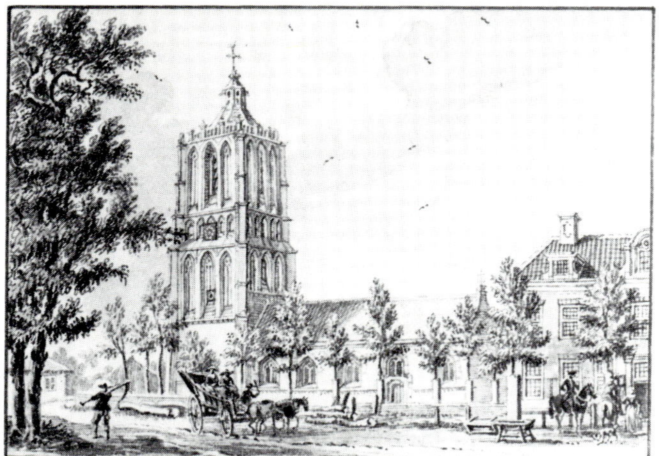

Jan de Beijer, The Village of Houten. Brussels, Musées Royaux des Beaux-Arts.

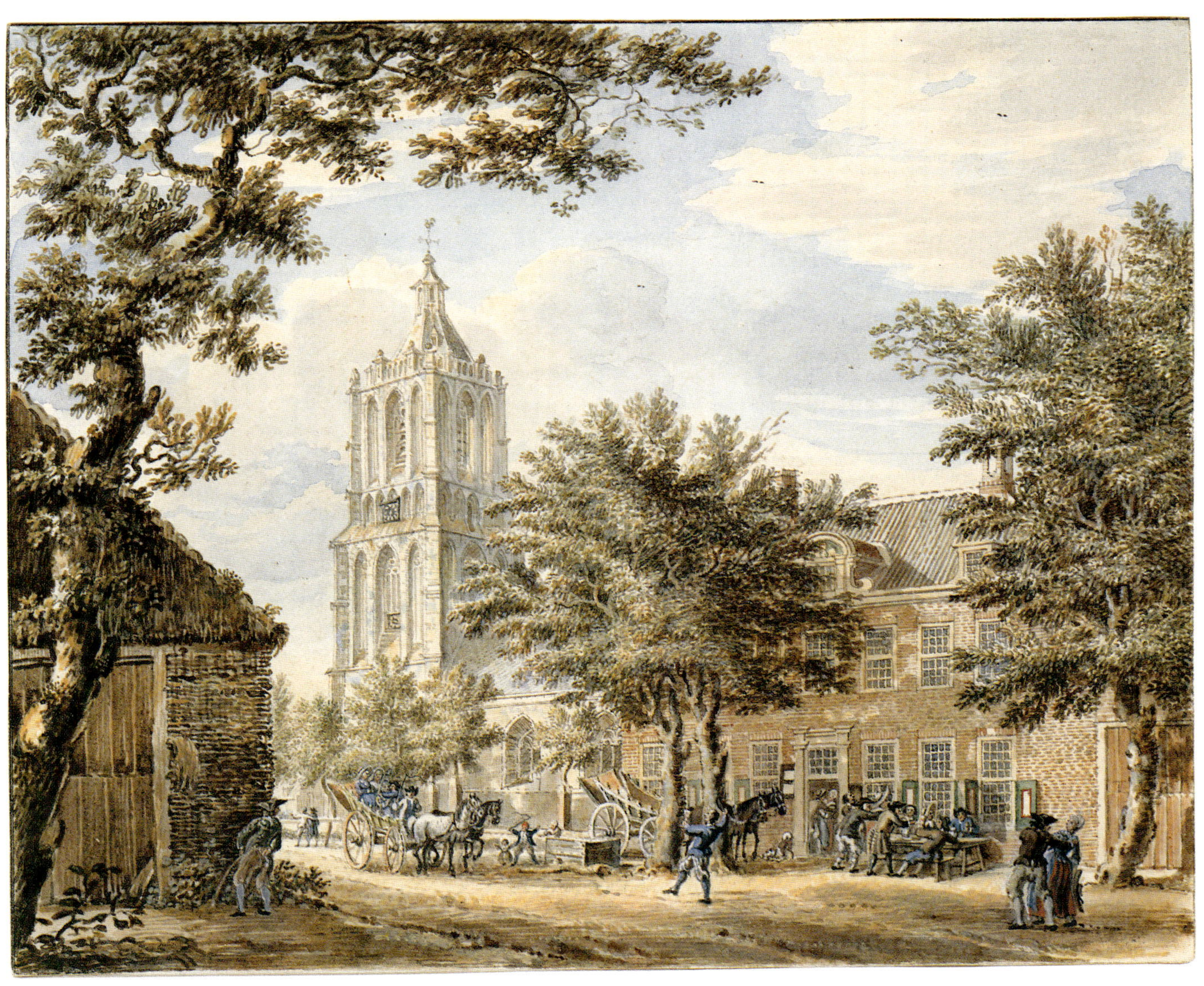

10 The Town Hall at Venlo

Pencil, pen in gray, watercolor, and gouache; gray border
210 x 254 mm
Signed on left, in pen: *JDB* [interlaced] *ad viv / delin 1741*
On verso, at bottom, an autograph inscription, half trimmed off: *JDB* [interlaced] *Raedthuys te Venlo 1741* (Venlo Town Hall, 1741); repeated slightly higher up in a later hand: *Raedthuys te Venlo 1741*
Inv. no. 1921:48

In front of the town hall, which is the main subject, a crowd of people have been brought together in a colorful composition in miniature. They have gathered to watch a court sentence be carried out. Just right of center a woman is being paraded with an instrument of punishment fastened around her neck. On the left, three men pay for their misdeeds astride an oversize wooden horse. The periwigged gentlemen surveying the scene from the town hall windows may be the judges who imposed the sentences, although the rod of justice that was usually extended from the window on such occasions is not evident. Also missing is a scaffold.Beijer's hand: *t'Dorp Houten.* That sheet was the model for a small etching by Hendrick Spilman in the large topographical publication *Het verheerlijkt Nederland* (The Netherlands Glorified), and it, too, bears the title *Het Dorp Houten.* In the drawing and print, though, the staffage is far simpler and more in keeping with the generalized nature of topographical views of this kind. The scene in this particular watercolor is unusually boisterous.

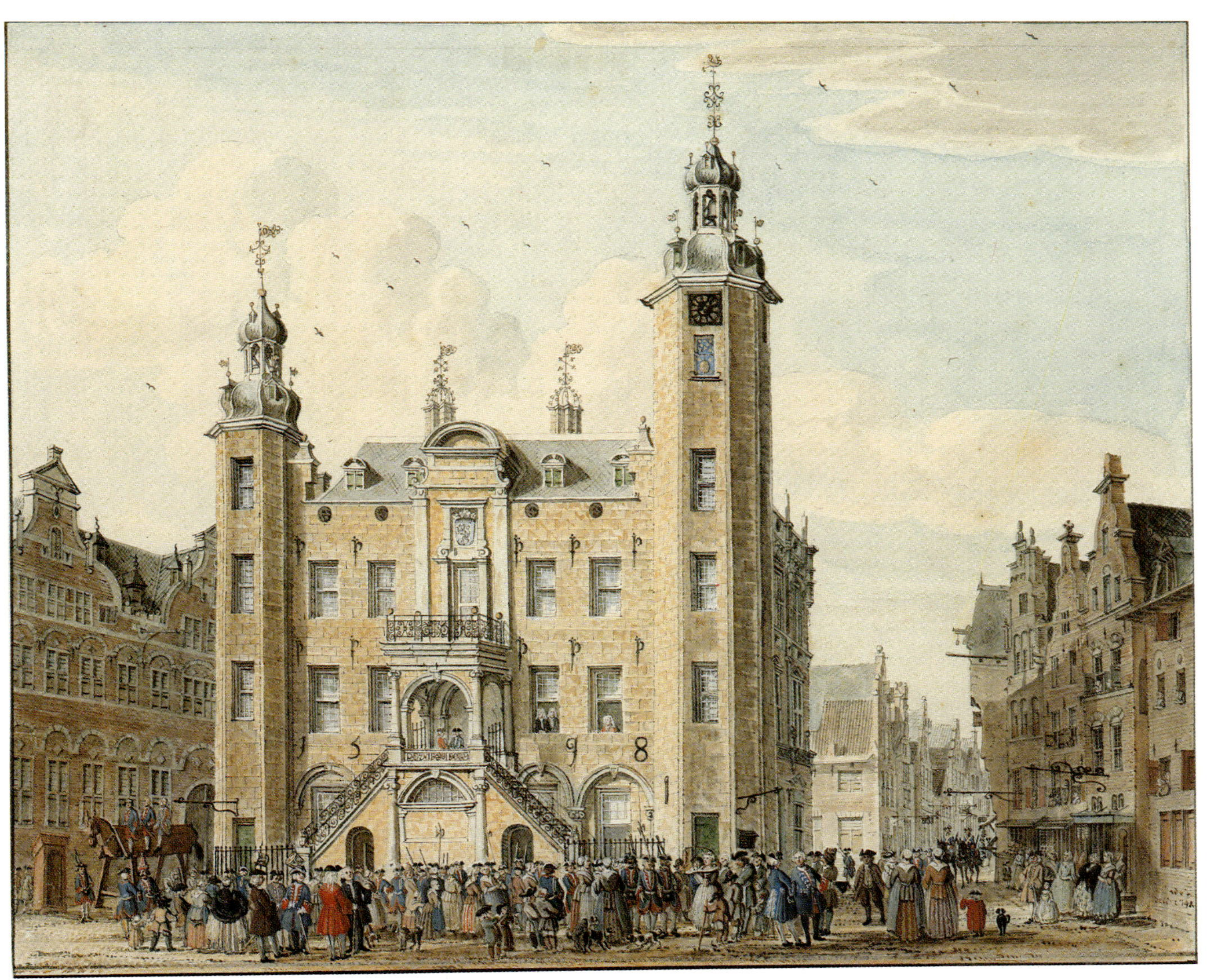

Jacobus Buys (Amsterdam 1724-1801 Amsterdam)

Portrait, genre, and occasional history painter, and a prolific illustrator. After a short apprenticeship to Cornelis Pronk (see cat. nos. 52-54), Jacobus Buys entered the studio of Cornelis Troost (see cat. nos. 65-68) and enrolled in the Amsterdam Drawing Academy (1743). Troost's influence is less evident in Buys's style and execution than in his choice of subject matter, which he derived from the popular theater of the day. Buys's work, however, is smoother and more stylish than that of his teacher, and his figures often have a rather stereotype appearance, with expressions, stances, and poses seemingly taken from a manual on gesticulation.

After Troost's death in 1750, Buys gradually developed into an independent master, and from 1770, through his work as a book illustrator, he championed a cool, modern classicism. His drawings and watercolors, though, do not belie his early years with Troost, to whose circle he belonged in Amsterdam. In 1770, Buys bought No. 1091, Prinsengracht, next door to the house in which Troost had died (No. 1093). He was also on close terms with Cornelis Ploos van Amstel (1724-1798), who later married one of Troost's daughters. Buys's directorship of the Amsterdam Drawing Academy, which he assumed in 1768, is evidence of the high regard in which he was held in the city's artistic community.

11 The Unexpected Twins, a Scene from the Farce 't Koffyhuis (The Coffeehouse) by Willem van der Hoeven

Pen and watercolor; black border
283 x 397 mm
Signed on right: *J Buys / F. 1763*
Inv. no. 1905:55

The taproom of a village coffeehouse serves as the setting for the denouement of a stage play. The central figure is Rijnaard, a sanctimonious young man who is being confronted with the twins whom he had furtively begotten on Constantia, the unmarried daughter of a rich midwife. He is being reprimanded by his parents, Steven and Dieuwertje, while the woman standing behind his chair may be Sofia, the owner of the coffeehouse, or possibly Constantia's mother Trijntje. The young mother herself is being led in by Zwaantje, the wet nurse. Over by the window a group of villagers look on with undisguised glee, with the exception of Egbertus Styloor, a Quaker, who has no truck with such worldly affairs. Behind the bar stands the serving maid Anna, and seated on a chair to the right, gazing over his shoulder at the audience, is Farmer Goossen, who supplies a running commentary on events as they unfold on the stage.

The plot of this comedy is recorded in editions printed in 1712, 1713, and 1734. A copy of the 1734 script in the Netherlands Theater Institute in Amsterdam is particularly interesting in that it bears the same handwritten date as that of Buys's watercolor (1763), and it also gives the names of the actors. Rijnaard, the young father, was played by "Everts," i.e., Nicolaas Evers (born 1735), Constantia by "Juffer Everts" (Evers's wife, Maria van der Slemp, who was born in 1730), Steven by "Van der Stel" (Willem van der Stel, born 1715), and so on. The role of Farmer Goossen was taken by "Spansier," a misspelling of the name of the celebrated Antonie Spatsier (born 1718). Are the figures in this watercolor portraits of Amsterdam actors? While it is very difficult to say in most cases, an authentic portrait of Spatsier, in the role of Warenar in another play, exists as both a drawing and a print. Both works were executed, once again, by Jacobus Buys, and the man who gazes out at the viewer is unmistakably the "Farmer Goossen" of this watercolor.

It is possible that Buys has here repeated the composition of an oil painting, as he did on other occasions, for on his death he left a painting of another scene from *'t Koffyhuis.*

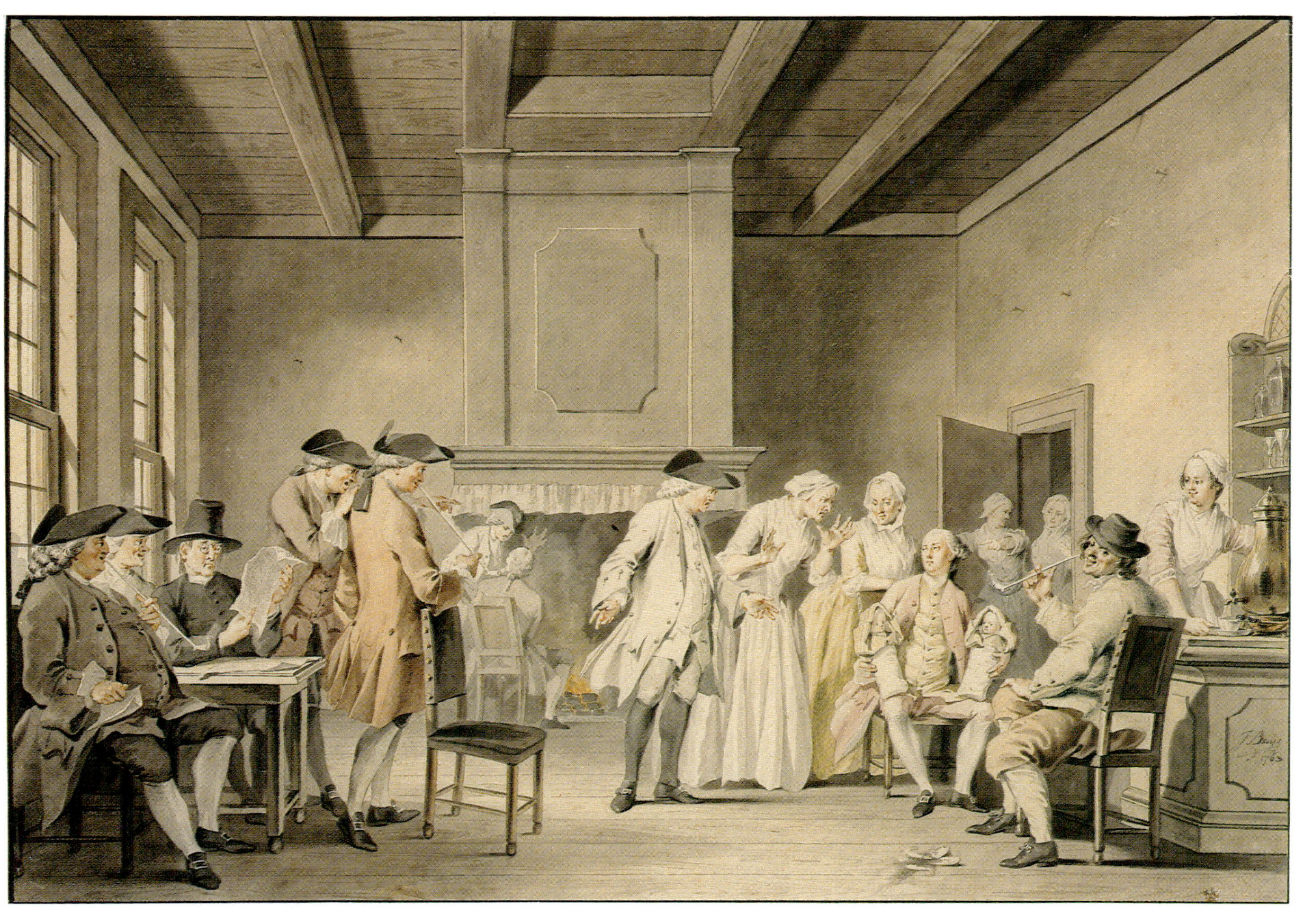

Embarked on a career as a painter of wall-hangings, but later became a celebrated draftsman of landscapes with figures. From the sixteenth century on, many Dutch artists settled in Altona, the town of Jacob Cats's birth, due to the religious tolerance that could be found there. (Altona was incorporated into the city of Hamburg in 1937.)

Cats's parents, too, were Dutch emigrés. They brought him to Amsterdam at an early age, where his first drawing master was the unremarkable Pieter Louw (1725-1800). His second teacher was Gerard van Rossum (ca. 1699/1700-1772), another artist of less than exceptional merit who at least owned a large collection of prints and drawings. In early 1759, Cats found employment in the wall-decoration workshop of Jan Hendrik Troost van Groenendoelen, and in May 1762 he set up a similar business of his own. He was successful from the outset, particularly in Mennonite circles, the religious persuasion that he himself professed. Cats struck up a friendship with Egbert van Drielst (see cat. nos. 17, 18) and collaborated with him by adding figures and animals to Van Drielst's landscapes.

When the demand for painted wall-hangings began to decline, Cats turned to drawing landscapes and townscapes. He peopled them with great ingenuity and variety, and gave them a liveliness that appealed to the taste of Dutch collectors. These collectors were (and still are) prepared to pay high prices for Cats's best work, with its extremely high finish. His seventeenth-century models were Jan van der Heyden and Gerrit Berckheyde for architecture and Adriaan van de Velde for cattle.

12 Street Scene in Beverwijk

Pencil, pen in brown, and watercolor; brown border
312 x 443 mm
Signed on verso, in pen: *Gezigt in de Agterstraat op de Klooster Poort / en kerk, in de steede Beverwijk 1793 / J:b Cats ad viv del.* (View in Achterstraat of the Cloister Gate and church in the town of Beverwijk.)
Inv. no. 1964:58

Even though Cats allowed his love of detail free rein in this work, he skillfully managed to avoid the deadening effect that can attend minute observation through his virtuoso handling of light and shade. This feature was singled out for praise in the catalogue of a public auction held in 1820, which described this watercolor as "treated in great detail in a masterly manner."

The town of Beverwijk lies north of Haarlem, and in the eighteenth century the lofty church spire could be seen for many miles out to sea. At the time Beverwijk was classed as "an open settlement, with borough rights," i.e., an unwalled town. This street scene certainly possesses a rustic appearance. A man drives two bulls down the cobbled street. On the right are seen a few chickens, a man with two pails slung from a yoke across his shoulders, and a small group of townsfolk exchanging gossip. The stocky character on the left has just collected bread from the bakery, which has a sign identifying it as "'T gekroonde Brood" (The Crowned Loaf). Further down the street two men enter the Swan Inn.

Cats's annotation on the back of the sheet is not entirely accurate. His vantage point was in Achterstraat (present-day Koningstraat), looking down to Kerkstraat. What he calls the Cloister Gate had nothing to do with a cloister, but was instead the remains of an old town mansion. All that still stands of this corner of Beverwijk today is the church and the stepped gable between the spire and the tree. Modern apartment buildings occupy the sites of all the other structures. This must have been a particularly popular view in the eighteenth century, for there are two

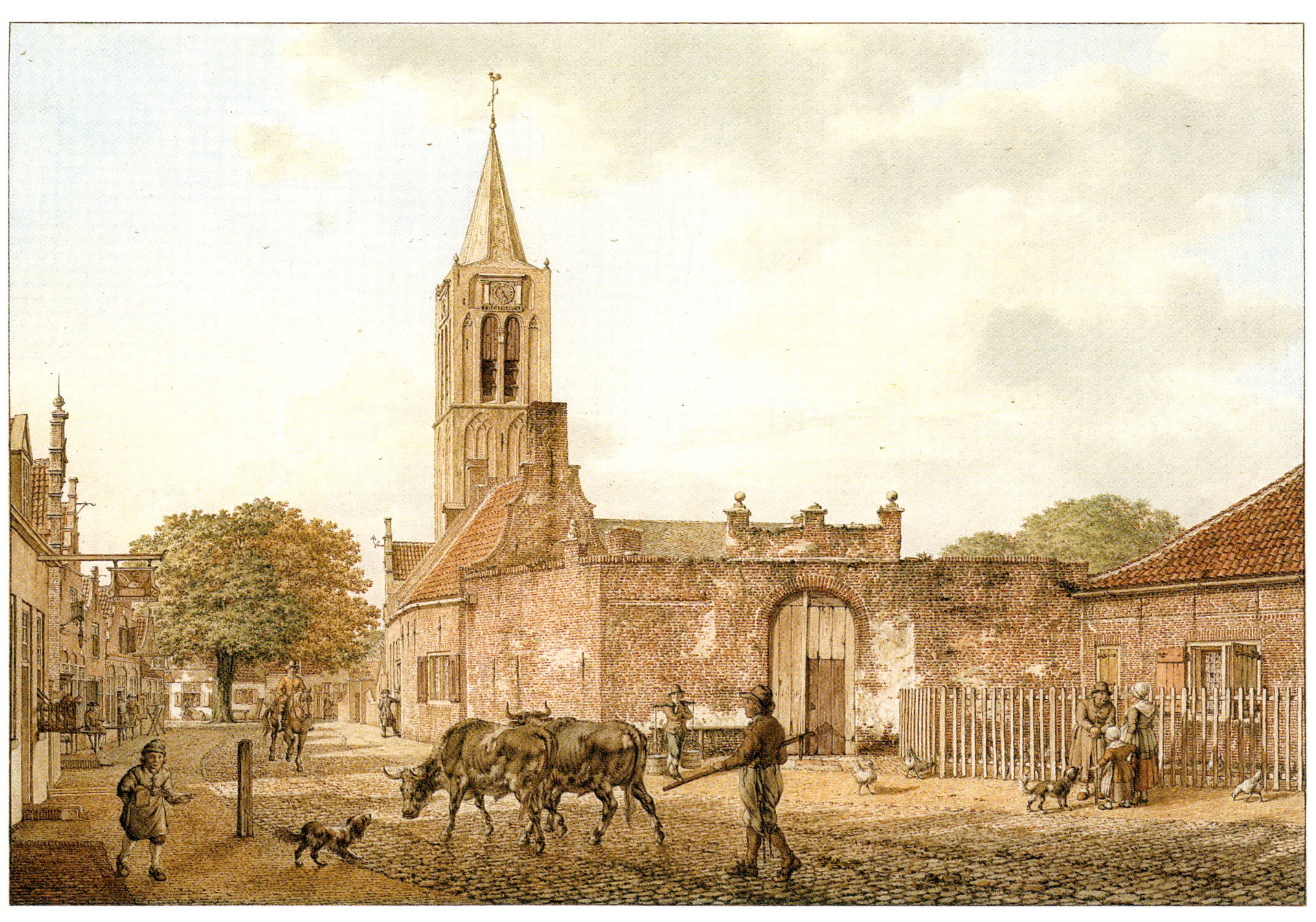

13 **Hilly Landscape with Swineherd and other Figures, a River in the Distance**

Pencil, pen in brown, and watercolor; narrow brown border

295 x 397 mm

Signed on verso, at lower left, in pen: *J:Cats inv et fec.1795*

Inv. no. 1987:50

Signs of autumn are evident in the discolored leaves on the trees, the showery weather, and the activity of picking apples. This watercolor probably belonged to a series of four that depicted the seasons of the year. One such suite, executed earlier than this sheet, was sold in Amsterdam on March 14, 1791, as part of Jan van Dijk's collection (inv. no. I 14-17). *Autumn* of that series contained a number of similar motifs: majestic trees, a countryman driving his cattle, people picking fruit, and a boat on a river.

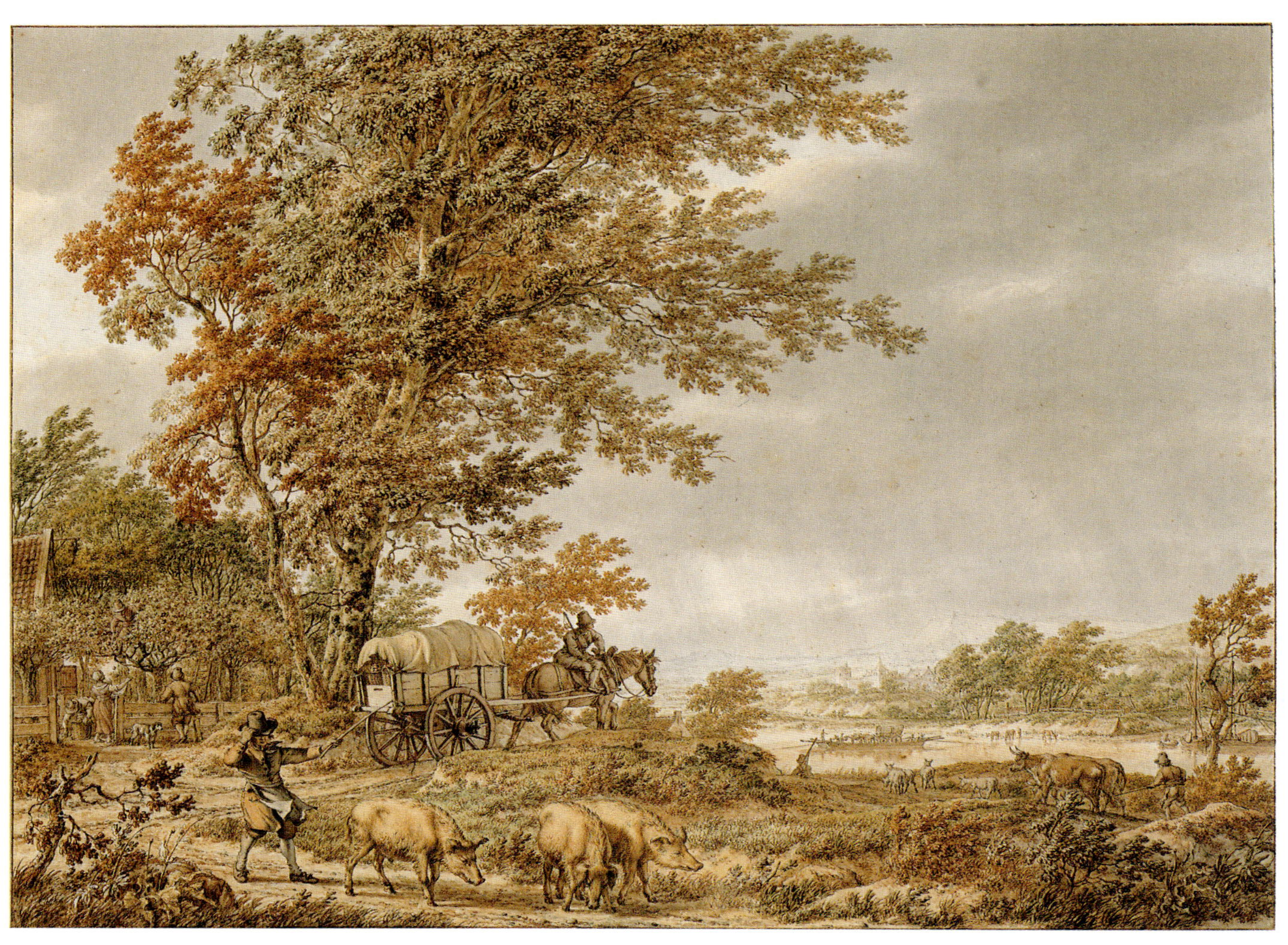

14 Scene on a Frozen River Skirting a City Rampart

Pencil, pen in brown, and watercolor; narrow brown border
187 x 259 mm
Signed on verso, at lower left: *J:Cats inv et fec / 1790*
Inv. no. 1919:36

Two men use tridents to catch eels through a hole that has been hacked in the ice at the foot of a wooden tripod topped by a barrel. The wooden structure, which Cats daringly allowed to dominate the entire scene, is a navigational beacon. Other variants took the forms of a mast surmounted by a basket or lattice, which the captains of vessels could find marked on their charts or mentioned in their pilot books.

Just as the previous watercolor (cat. no. 13) may be a depiction of autumn, so this drawing may symbolize winter. It could also, of course, be a straightforward winter scene. The anecdotal, narrative character of the figures, and the strong sense of action, are typical of Cats's work. The mood differs greatly from that of the *Frozen Canal with Skaters* by his Haarlem contemporary Cornelis van Noorde (cat. no. 46). Cats probably enlivened the composition with the aid of small sketches of one or more figures similar to a sheet in the Amsterdam Printroom (inv. no. 1933:17). His posthumous studio sale, held on April 16, 1800, included a large number of such sketches (see cat. p. 30, no. G).

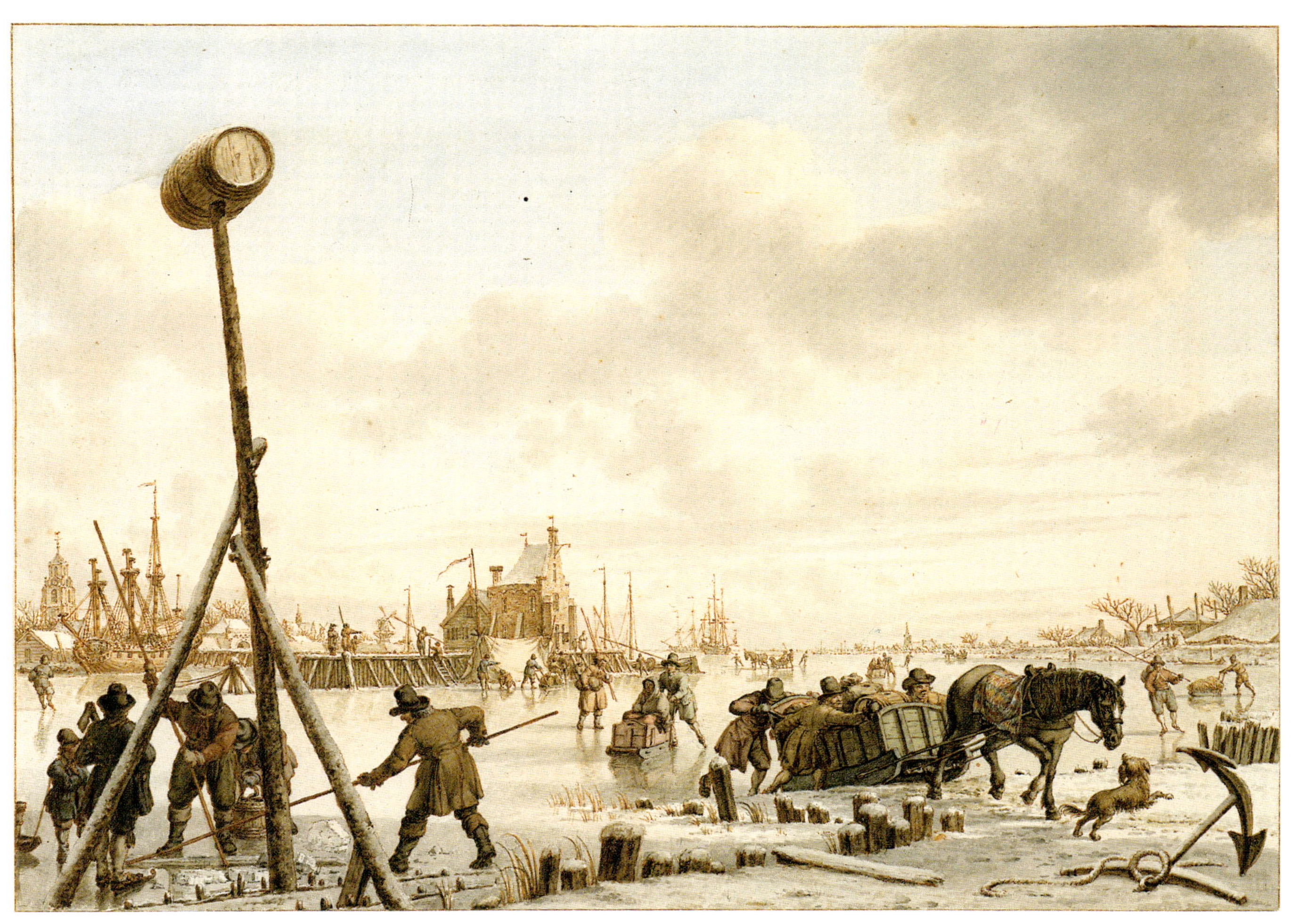

15 Visit to a Nursery Garden

Brush in gray, and watercolor; narrow gray border
131 x 182 mm
Signed on verso: *J:Cats inv et fec / 1791*
Inv. no. 1990:12

Elegant, fashionably dressed ladies and gentlemen stroll among the seed boxes and racks of potted plants in a plainly furnished horticultural nursery. The trees are just coming into leaf, and the sun is still low in the sky. Cats chose this charming scene to depict April in a series of the twelve months that was later reproduced in print by Izaak de Wit Jzn (1744-1809) and published by the latter in 1807. Its title page, by Joannes Pieter Visser Bender (1785-1813), stated that Cats's drawings, including this one, belonged to Jacob Helmolt (1747-1808), town councillor of Haarlem. The artist's studies for the series, which are preserved in the Amsterdam Historical Museum, show that he made only minor changes in the final versions, with the sole exception being this particular month, April, which was originally planned as a scene of a farmer rolling his meadows.

The use of a flower nursery to represent April was by no means uncommon in the traditional program of this series, and it certainly was no more unusual than a farmer in his fields or some other agricultural subject. It is possible, though, that Cats finally settled on a nursery because the series was intended for a member of the town council of Haarlem, a city that served as the center of the Dutch flower industry. In and around Haarlem were the commercial nurseries run by Voorhelm, Schneevoogt, Kreps, and the Van Eedens, as well as numerous smaller establishments and private nurseries on country estates, such as Bosch-en-Hoven, Bosch-en-Vaart, and Velserbeek. Visiting these horticultural gardens was a popular springtime excursion. As a Frenchman recorded at the time, "One went to see the flower gardens. The leisured classes of Amsterdam, Leiden, The Hague, Rotterdam and other towns come to view the gardens at Haarlem, which are the most beautiful of their kind in the entire Seven Provinces." And an English botanist, who was traveling through the region in August 1811, sighed, "In April and May the environs of Haarlem must be truly delightful to the zealous florist."

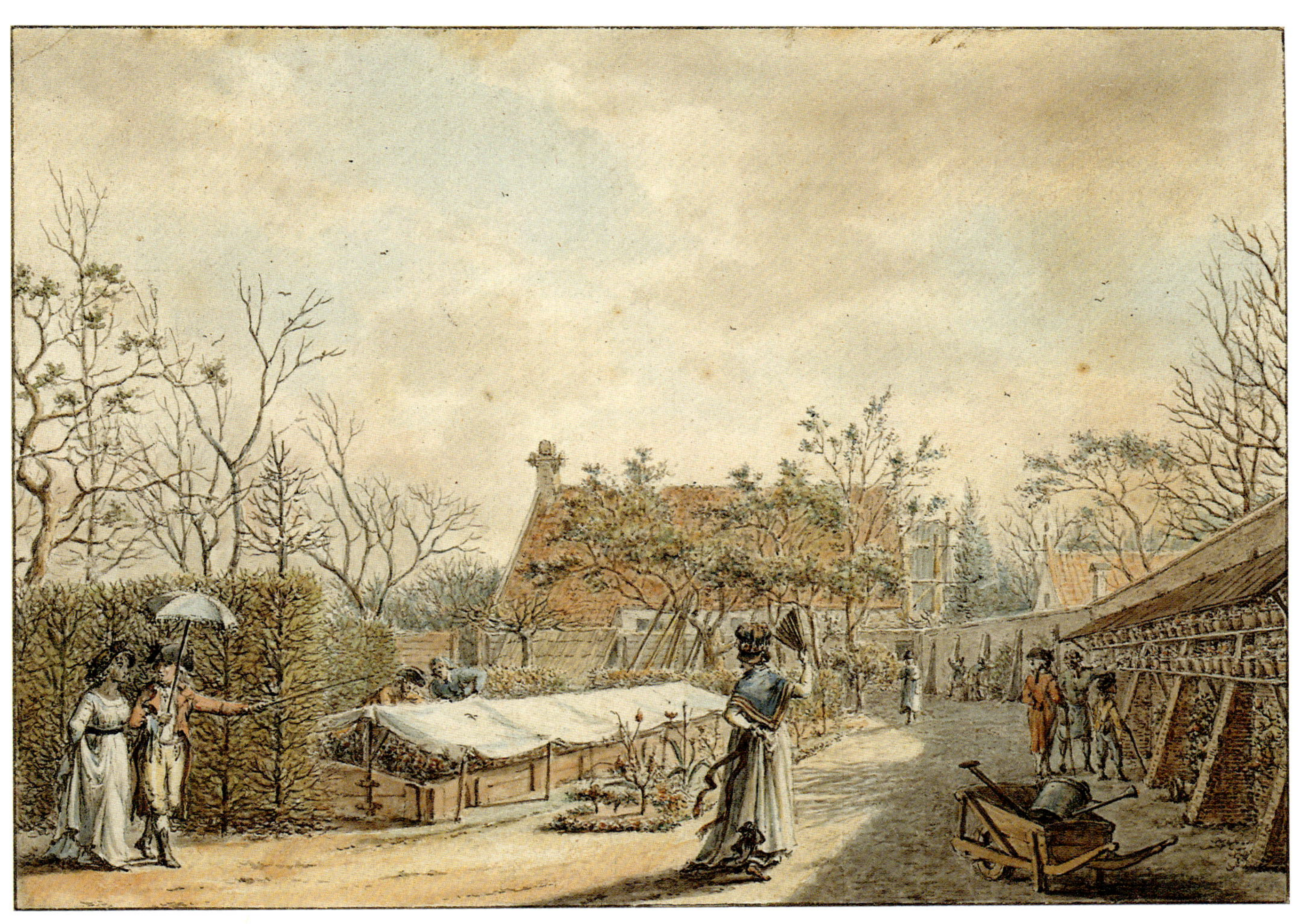

16 Red-and-White Cow in a Landscape

Watercolor; gray-brown border
127 x 158 mm
Signed on verso: *J:b Cats inv et fec. / 1783*
Inv. no. 1953:296

In this *tour-de-force* of brush technique, a well-fleshed cow is observed from a low vantage point, with the artist, who was probably seated in the grass, looking beneath the animal's belly to a farmhouse in the distance. The same device was used in this watercolor's companion, in which a grazing cow faces to the left (inv. no. 1953:295). The seventeenth-century tradition of depicting cattle is still very palpable in this scene, which is especially redolent of the work of Paulus Potter. Numerous etchings of a solitary animal in the fields are also known.

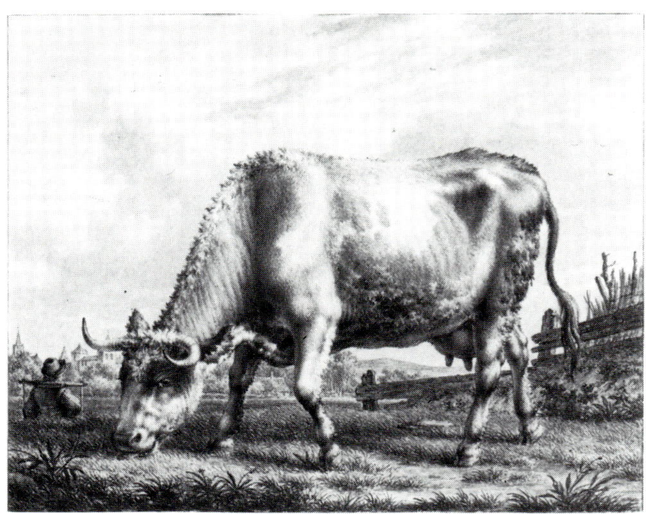

Jacob Cats, pendant to Red-and-White Cow in a Landscape.

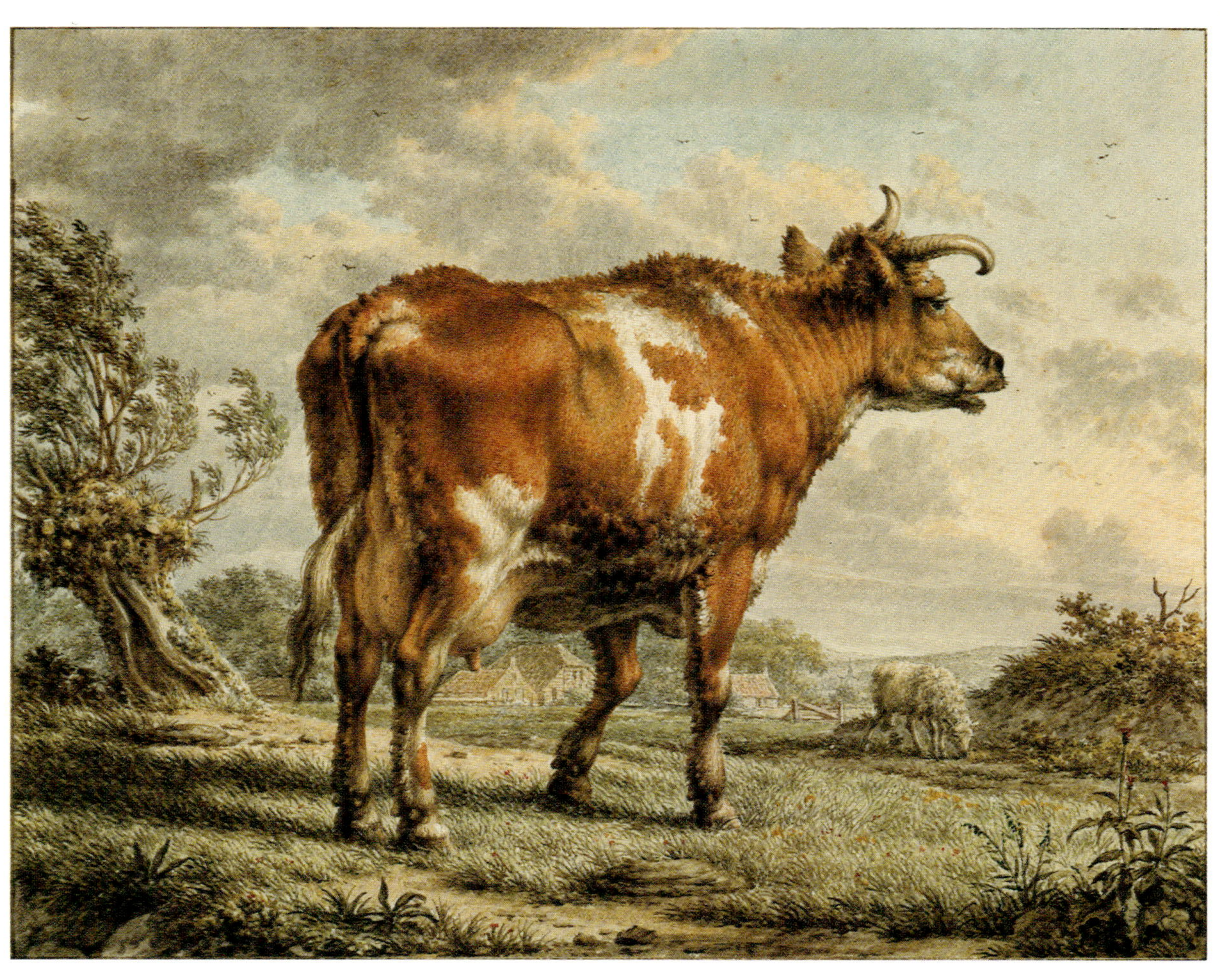

Painter and, above all, a draftsman of landscapes. Egbert van Drielst started his career in his home town of Groningen, where he was employed in a small lacquer-work factory owned by Steven Numan. He and Numan's son Hermanus (see cat. nos. 47, 48) then moved to Haarlem to work with Jan Augustini, also from Groningen, who had taken charge of a studio that produced painted wall-hangings. Van Drielst later entered a similar workshop in Amsterdam and enrolled in the Drawing Academy in 1768. He worked intermittently with Jacob Cats (see cat. nos. 12-16) and, like him, soon abandoned the hidebound and ailing wall-decoration industry to concentrate on landscape drawing. Van Drielst found his main inspiration in sandy plateaus, with their oak copses, picturesque sandy tracks, and low-roofed peasant cottages and barns. The search for these subjects took him to the area around Haarlem, to the Gooi region southeast of Amsterdam, and in particular to the province of Drenthe, not far from his birthplace, which remained largely unspoiled for many years and later attracted Vincent van Gogh. Van Drielst's new approach to nature earned him the reputation as the "Hobbema of Drenthe," the leader of a new current in Dutch landscape art that delivered the coup de grâce to the wall-decoration style around 1800. A stepson, Jan Vuring van Drielst (1789-1813), also trained as an artist but died at the age of twenty-three.

17 The Village of Eext in Drenthe

Black chalk and watercolor; brown-black border
327 x 522 mm
On verso, signed at lower left, in pen: *E. van Drielst 1793 / In den Eext.*
Inv. Felix Meritis no. 32

The village of Eext (or De Eext, as Van Drielst called it) in the northeast of the Netherlands was discovered by artists at the end of the eighteenth century. There they found what was later to attract their French colleagues to Barbizon: unspoiled scenery, picturesque peasant cottages, and generous hospitality. Van Drielst was certainly one of the most regular visitors to the region, which, being from the north, he must have known well from his childhood. He was already making drawings there while he was earning his living as a painter of wall-hangings, which even then, in the closing decades of the century, were beginning to go out of fashion.

When he executed this watercolor, Van Drielst had already made a name for himself as an independent artist, working full-time to meet the demands of numerous collectors. This landscape is not itself the direct product of a day spent out of doors. It is the studio version of a life study, which has also survived and is now in the Musées Royaux des Beaux-Arts in Brussels. Bearing the same date as this sheet, it reveals that all the figures and colors were added in the studio. This was Van Drielst's usual practice, and in some cases he made both summer and winter versions of the same scene.

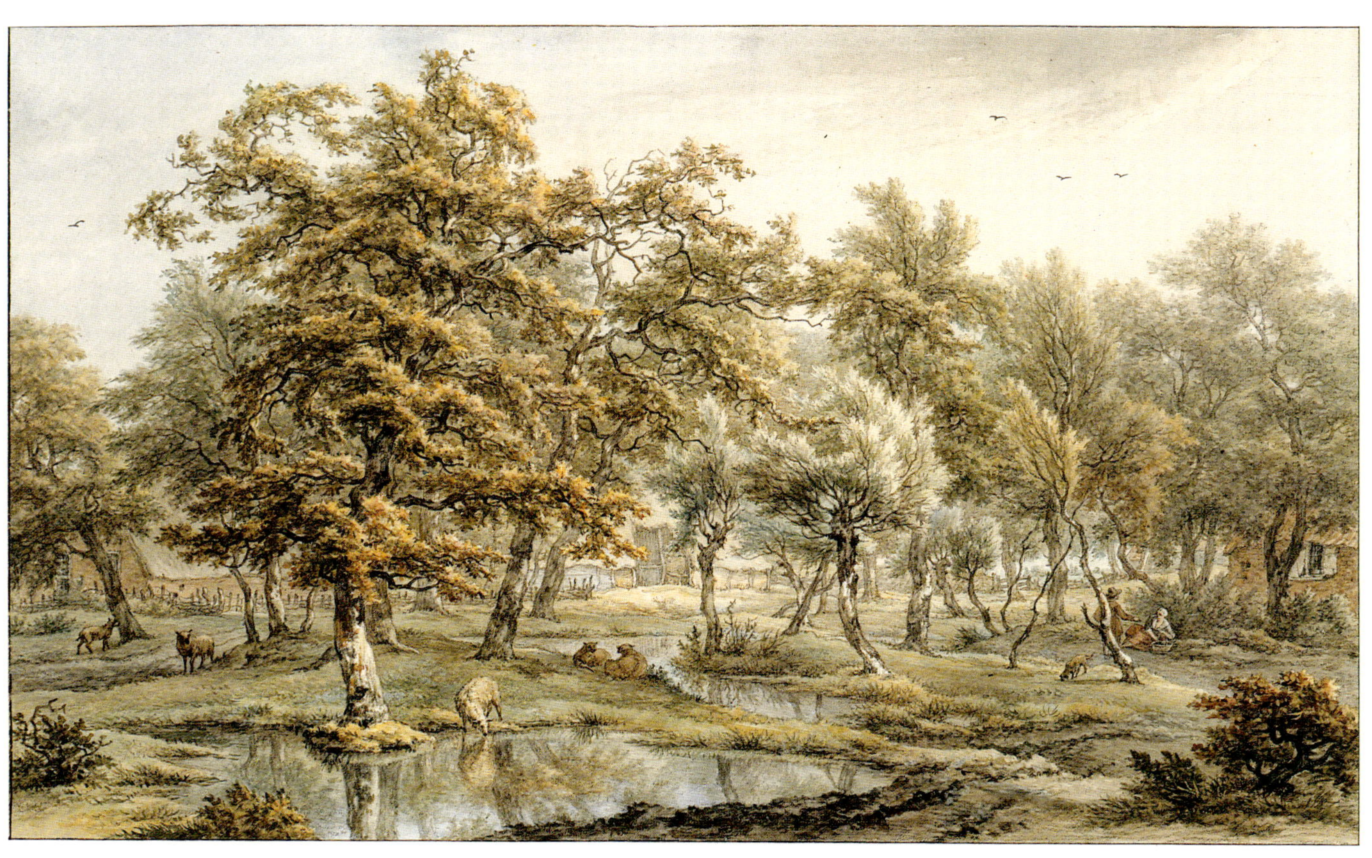

18 The Ruins of De Haer Castle in the Province of Utrecht

Black chalk, watercolor, and some gouache
380 x 515 mm (four pieces of paper joined together)
On verso, signed on left of original sheet, in pen:
het Huijs ter Haar / E van Drielst 1801
Inv. no. 1889 A 1920

The remains of the medieval De Haer Castle, located northwest of the city of Utrecht, provided local artists with a picturesque motif comparable to the ruins of Brederode Castle north of Haarlem, and of Rijnsburg Abbey, near Leiden. Although much of De Haer was destroyed by Louis XIV's troops in 1672, it proved a popular subject in the eighteenth and nineteenth centuries. It is not surprising, then, that it was also a source of inspiration for Egbert van Drielst, who made numerous drawings in this part of the Republic. Thanks to the fact that many of them are dated, it is known that he depicted the ruins of De Haer in the period between 1801 and 1805, so this view from 1801 is one of his earliest – in its original form, anyway. Van Drielst's signature and the date appear on the back of the first sheet he used, but that sheet makes up only a small part of the finished work. He enlarged it by adding strips of paper at top and bottom and on the left, not to show more of the castle, as might be expected, but to develop the landscape element. In doing so, he removed the scene even further from the traditional topographical view that he had first envisaged. Although he may have made the enlargement shortly after finishing the initial sheet, he could also have done it years later, possibly using a sketch that he had made on the spot. What is certain is that the new composition encroached considerably on the first drawing.

Although Van Drielst usually took Meindert Hobbema (1638-1709) as his shining example, on this occasion he seems to have derived his conception from Jacob van Ruisdael (1628/29-1682). Ruisdael's drawings of the ruins of Egmond Castle, which are now in the Amsterdam Printroom, were in the Goll van Franckenstein Collection in Amsterdam in Van Drielst's day. Even closer to this drawing is Ruisdael's superb painting of Egmond (now in the Art Institute of Chicago), although it is not certain that Van Drielst could have seen that work around 1800, since its location at that time is unknown.

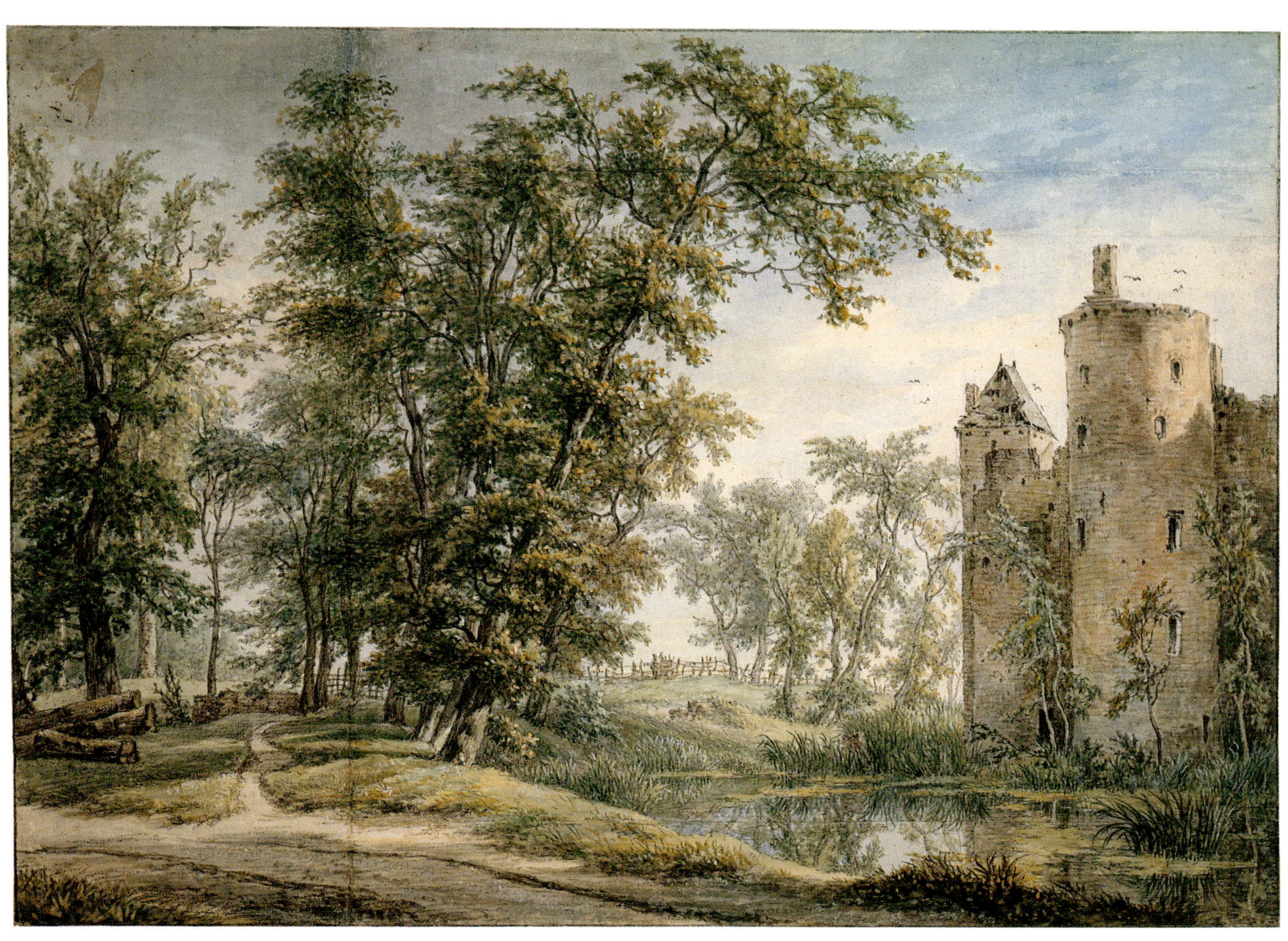

Daniël Dupré (Amsterdam 1751-1817 Amsterdam)

Draftsman, painter, and occasional etcher of highly finished landscapes and topographical views. Daniël Dupré trained with the decorative painter Johannes van Dregt, and from 1767 with Jurriaan Andriessen (see cat. nos. 1-5) at the Amsterdam Drawing Academy. Dupré chose landscape painting as his métier and from an early age traveled abroad in search of subjects. In 1783, after a visit to Switzerland, he made an artistic pilgrimage along the Rhine accompanied by his friends Jan Ekels the Younger (1759-1793) and Jacques Kuyper (1761–1808). From 1785 to 1790 he resided in Italy on a grant from the Holland Scientific Society of Haarlem. Dupré then settled permanently in Amsterdam, and for the rest of his life benefitted from his years of foreign travel. He incorporated southern motifs into his landscape paintings and drew numerous Italian, Swiss, and German views for the albums of collectors. These included Jan Gildemeester (1744-1799), a former owner of the Dupré watercolors seen here, and Dirk Versteegh, a good friend with whom Dupré shared the same birthday. In general, Dupré's style is a little stiff and old-fashioned, but he also produced landscapes that exuded a more dynamic, pre-Romantic look.
Having received the most meticulous training, Dupré belonged to several foreign drawing academies, including the one in Parma. He did not, however, consider it beneath his dignity to do more craft-like work, such as painting small landscapes on lacquered tables and playing-card boxes.

19 People Strolling on a Terrace of the Villa Conti at Frascati
Pen in gray, and watercolor; narrow gray-black border
356 x 498 mm
On verso, signed and dated in pen: *Dl.Du Pré. delt. 1791. Vüe dans la Villa Conti à Frascati*
Inv. no. 1921:141

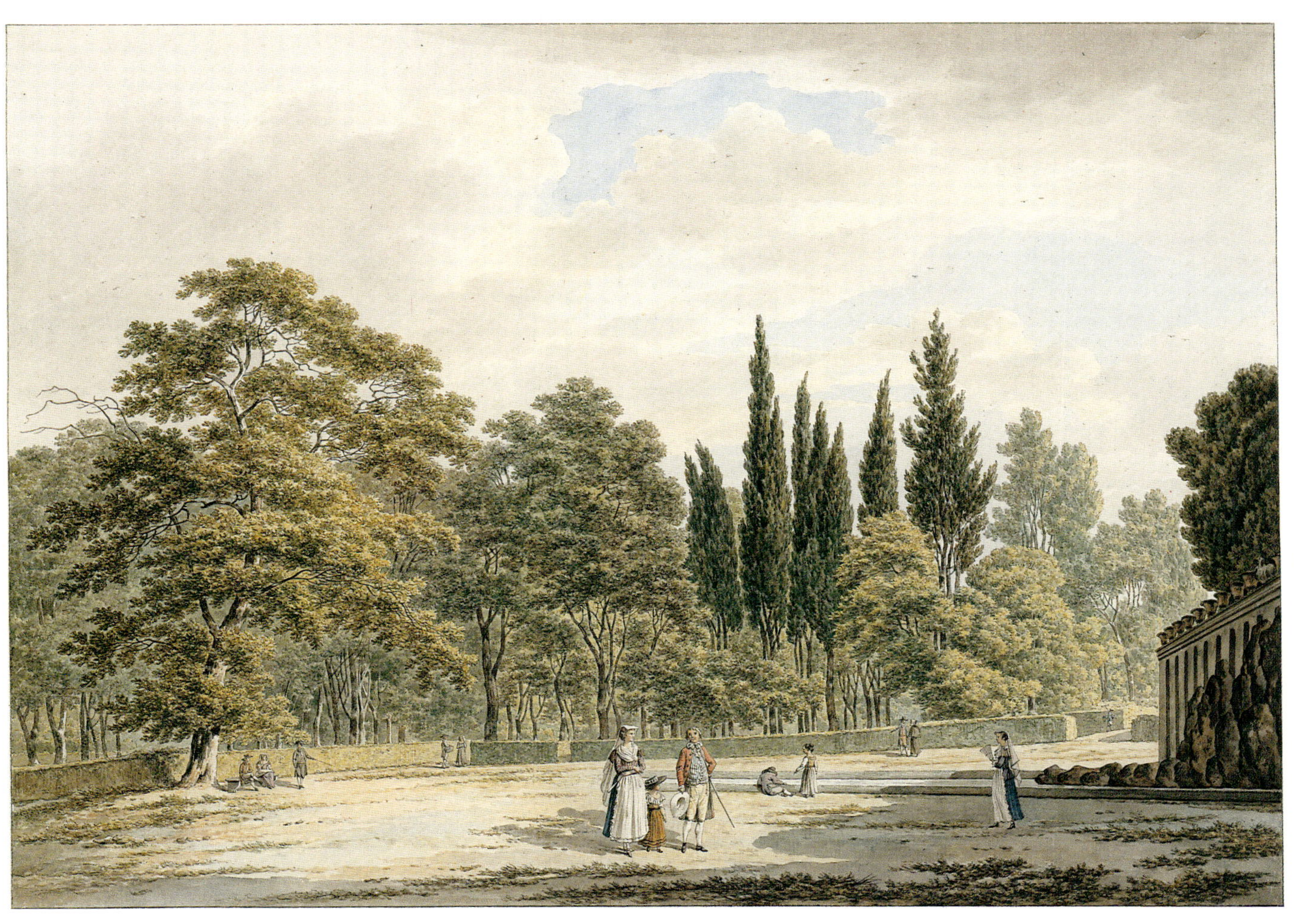

20 **View over the Terraces of the Villa d'Este at Tivoli**
Pen in gray, and watercolor; narrow gray-black border
359 x 500 mm
On verso, signed and dated, in pen: *Dl.Du Pré. delt 1791. Vüe dans la Villa d'Este à Tivoli.*
On verso, annotated with a key to numbers in drawing: *1. la ville de Rome / 2. le Sépulcre de Plautius*
Inv. no. 1921:142

This and the previous drawing (cat. no. 19) are companion views depicting the parks of two famous villas in the hills to the east of Rome: the Villa d'Este (see also cat. no. 45) and the Villa Conti. The latter is also known as the Villa Ludovisi or the Villa Torlonia, in association with its earlier and later owners.

The date 1791 on each watercolor indicates that the two works were executed after Dupré had returned from Italy the previous year. He undoubtedly based them on sketches that he had made on the spot. For the figures, too, he would have used life studies of the kind found in great numbers among his possessions after his death in 1817. (One is now in the Amsterdam Printroom.) In the first image (cat. no. 19) is seen the southwestern terrace of the Villa d'Este, which looks out over the valley of the River Anio towards Rome. The faint outline of the dome of St. Peter's Basilica in the far distance can be made out between the trees.

The other park view (cat. no. 20) is closed off on the right by a wall inset with niches, behind which a waterfall splashes onto some rocks beside a large pond, on the edge of which a young boy is sitting. This is the Teatro del Acque, which still exists today. Designed by Carlo Maderno (1556-1629), it was built in the seventeenth century. In both watercolors, but especially in that of the Villa d'Este, Dupré made great play of the contrast between verticals and horizontals.

The two dozen drawings by Dupré in the Amsterdam Printroom include several other views of Tivoli, but these are uncolored.

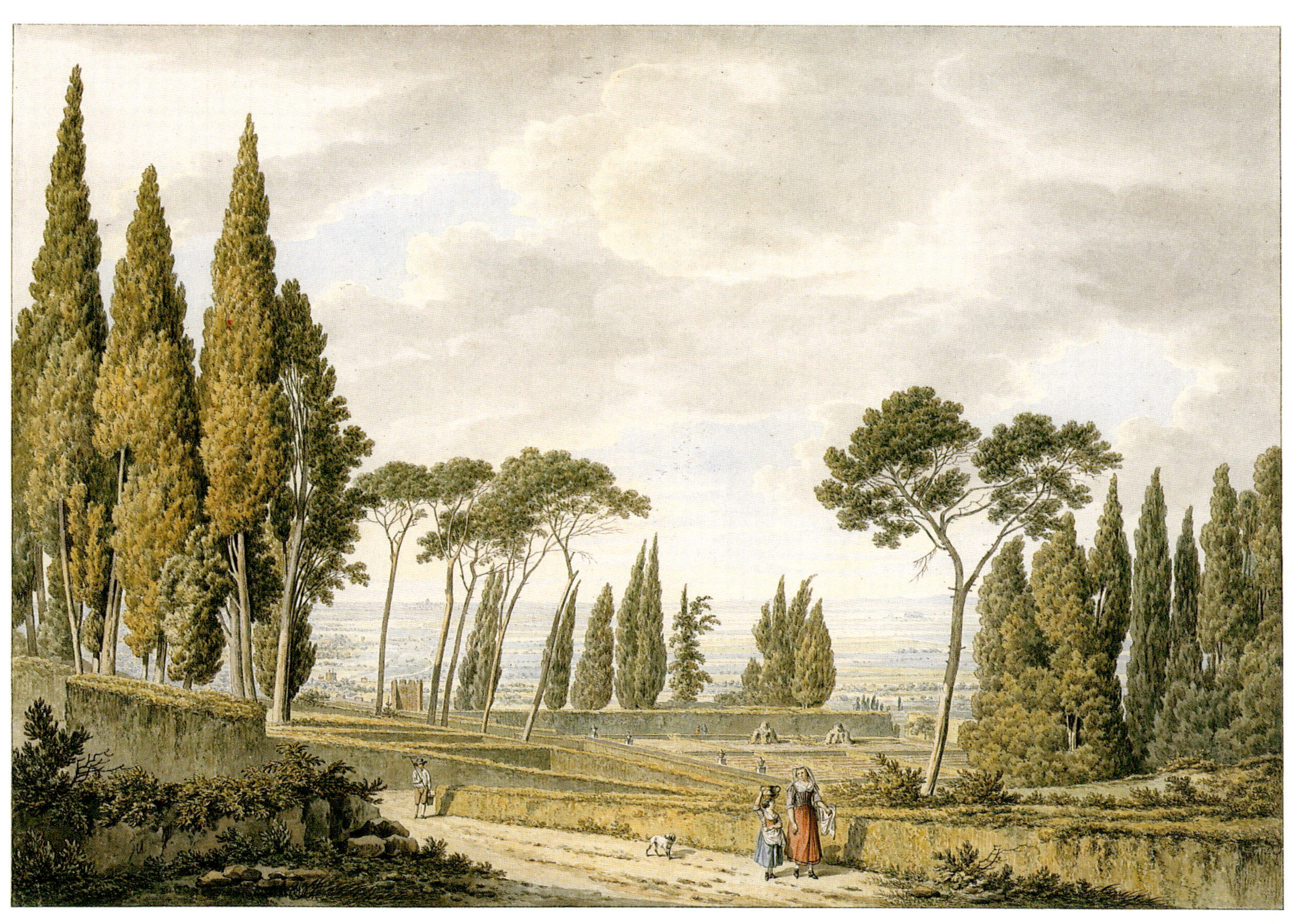

21 The Arch of Titus in Rome

Watercolor over outline etching, reinforced in parts with tempera or gum; broad border with pen and brush in brown
441 x 308 mm
Inv. Prenten no. 1973:3

Some twenty years ago this sheet was presented at auction as "*The Triumphal Arch of Vespasian*, a watercolor by Jules Dupré." The staff of the Rijksprentenkabinet in Amsterdam, realizing that the nineteenth-century painter of French landscapes had been confused with the eighteenth-century Daniël Dupré of Amsterdam, decided to buy this brightly colored sheet. It was soon discovered that the monument must, in fact, be the Arch of Titus and that there was a cursory etching beneath the watercolor. In 1888, the Printroom had acquired two other Italian views by Dupré done in the same technique. They depicted the waterfalls of Terni and Tivoli, each of which was *dessiné d'après Nature, gravé et Colorié par Dl.DuPré*, according to the nineteenth-century inscriptions on the reverse, which were evidently based on contemporary and possibly autograph annotations.

Dupré was in Italy from 1785 to 1790, shortly after the series of watercolored etchings, produced in the same technique by Louis Ducros and Giovanni Volpato, were published (1780-84). In addition to scenes of the waterfalls of Terni and Tivoli, the series also included a view of the Arch of Titus. A strikingly close similarity between Dupré's depictions and those by Ducros is evident – not only in vantage point, scale, and framing of the image, but also in the figures. It looks as if Ducros provided a model upon which Dupré eagerly seized. And he was not the only one to do so, for similar scenes were executed by Franz Kaisermann (1765-1833), Johann Heinrich Wilhelm Tischbein (1751-1829), and other artists.

All that remained of this triumphal arch in Dupré's day was a ruin hemmed in by medieval ramparts. By the beginning of the nineteenth century, the entire structure had become so dilapidated that Pope Pius VII had it torn down and rebuilt in its full, original form in 1822 by the architect Giuseppe Valadier (1762-1839). That free-standing structure can be seen on the site today.

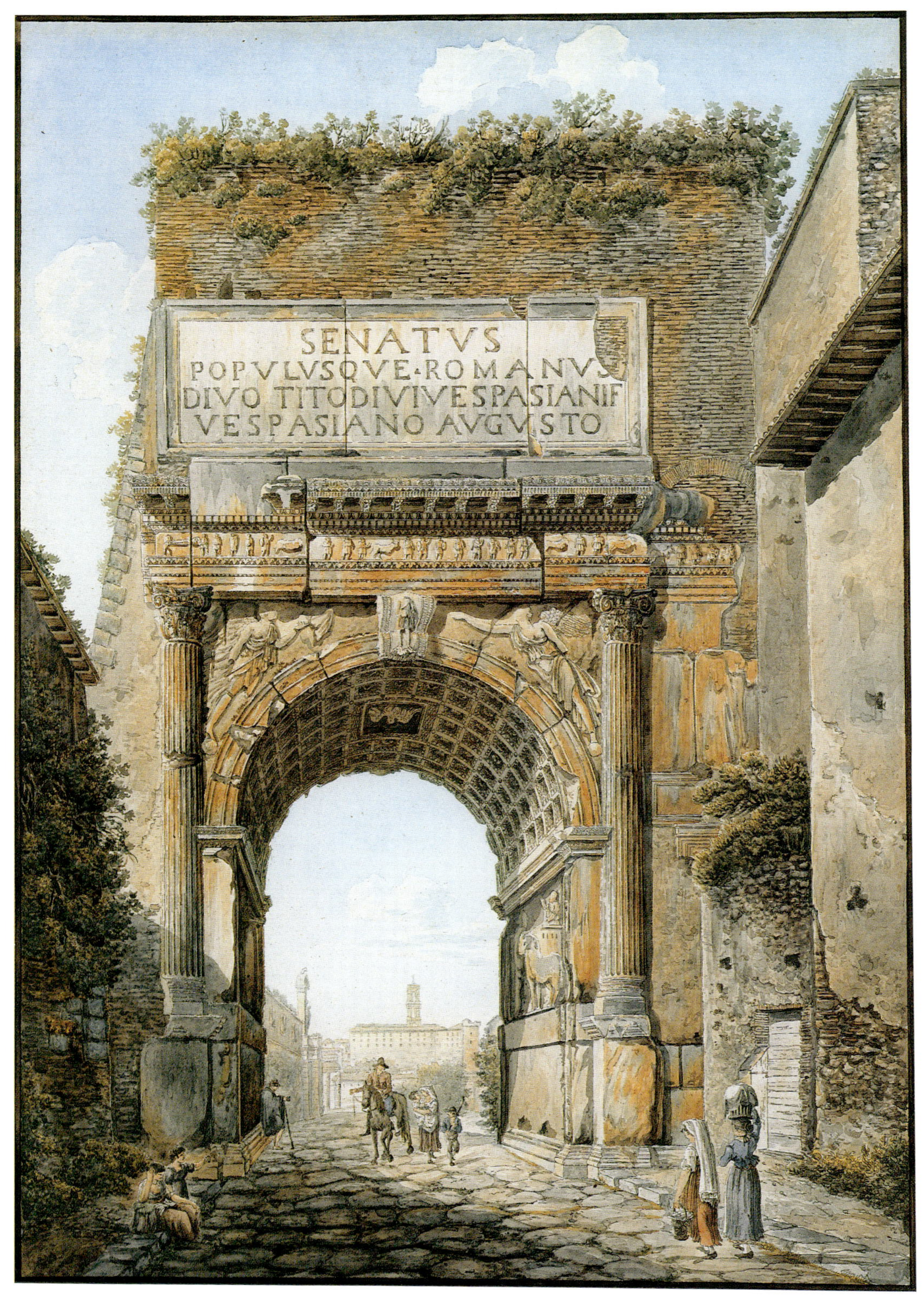
SENATVS
POPVLVSQVE·ROMANVS
DIVO TITO DIVI VESPASIANI F
VESPASIANO AVGVSTO

Jean Grandjean (Amsterdam 1752-1781 Rome)

Painter and draftsman of figures and landscapes who died tragically young. Jean Grandjean's real artistic development began in 1771, when he was admitted to the wall-decoration workshop of Jurriaan Andriessen (see cat. nos. 1-5). That same year Grandjean enrolled in the Amsterdam Drawing Academy, and he also practiced drawing from the live model in one of the many private societies that were then flourishing in Amsterdam. He was particularly fond of subjects taken from classical history and mythology. Six years later, in 1777, he was one of the founders of the Felix Meritis Society. The young Grandjean's talent and ambition came to the notice of a number of wealthy connoisseurs, chief among them being Jan Tersteeg and Dirk Versteegh. Thanks to their financial support, the artist was able to set sail for Italy in June 1779, where he continued his studies in Rome. This revived the tradition, moribund for more than sixty years, that had taken so many artists to Italy in the Golden Age of Dutch painting.

This firsthand experience of the great works of Italian art, and his companionship with the inspired German Romfahrer, made a profound impression on Grandjean and added a new dimension to his style. Drawings from this Italian period show how swiftly his horizons expanded. In all probability he would have become one of the Netherlands' most important neoclassicists had not death put an end to his career before he reached the age of thirty.

22 Arcadian Landscape

Pen and watercolor; black border
354 x 283 mm
Inv. no. 1921:67

Grandjean was one of the forty or so young artists who received their training, for varying lengths of time, in the studio of Jurriaan Andriessen. That influence is well illustrated in this watercolor, which, in its subject matter, composition, and handling of foliage, is very close to that of his teacher, although it lacks Andriessen's fluency. It can safely be assumed that it dates from the 1770s, before Grandjean's departure for Italy. Two similar watercolors – companion pieces – with the same dimensions as this sheet and dated 1775 and 1776, respectively, were exhibited in 1958 at the Delft Art and Antiques Fair.

The first known owner of this sheet was Jan Tersteeg, who supported Grandjean and provided him with funds to undertake his trip to Italy. In the auction catalogue of Tersteeg's estate, this drawing is described at length under the title given to it here. Considering, however, the striking contrast between the lighter side of the drawing, with its carefree scene of women bathing and playing with festoons, and the shaded side, with its lurking menace of satyrs posed among broken masonry and toppled vases, might this be an allusion to the transience of human life?

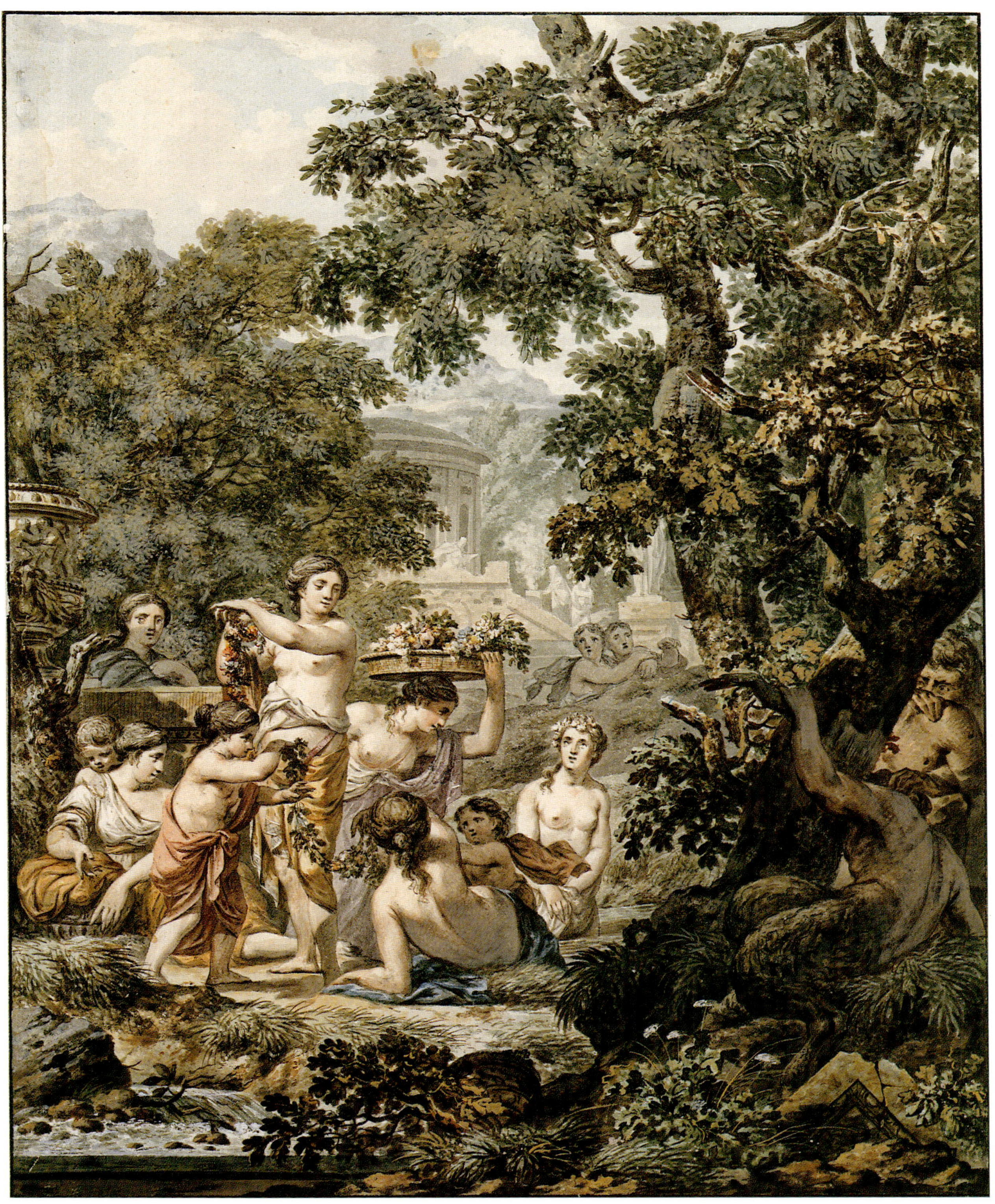

Tethart Philip Christiaan Haag (Kassel [Germany] 1737-1812 The Hague)

Painter of horses and horsemen, attached to the stadtholder's court in The Hague. After living for a few years in Leeuwarden, in the northern province of Friesland, where his father, Johan David Christiaan Haag, was employed as painter to Princess Marie Louise of Orange-Nassau, who also came from Kassel, the future artist moved to The Hague with the court when he was age ten. After his father died there in 1760, Haag succeeded him as a portraitist with special ties to the court. (It is doubtful whether he was a court painter in the usual sense.) He was also appointed director of the stadtholder's collection of paintings.

As time passed, Haag's practice of producing portraits of people gradually gave way to depictions of animals. He was a friend of the bird and animal painter Aart Schouman (see cat. nos. 55-60) and worked in a related genre. Both he and Schouman supplied drawings of the stadtholder's menagerie for a series of works that was published by Arnout Vosmaer between 1766 and 1784. Haag also had his own collection of stuffed birds. In 1771 he visited Paris.

Haag is best known for his paintings and drawings of horses, either alone or with royal or patrician riders, and sometimes with grooms in attendance. He was a respected figure in The Hague as a member of the board of the Drawing Academy and as warden, and later dean, of the Pictura artists' society. The French occupation in 1795 put an abrupt end to the public life of this loyal servant of the House of Orange.

23 Stable Interior

Pen in gray, and watercolor; narrow brown border
329 x 265 mm
Signed on left, in pen: *TPCH* [interlaced] *aug / 1780*
On verso, at lower center, in pencil: *N4032* [Goll];
Deensch paard (Danish horse)
Inv. no. 1957:170

The annotation on the back of this drawing refers to a type of horse that was bred at the royal stud attached to Frederiksborg Castle in Denmark. Originally a heavily built animal, this breed of horse was gradually refined in the seventeenth century by crossing it with Polish and Spanish bloodlines. The prominent position and pose of this horse, as well as the individualized features of the groom, might suggest that these are portraits. That this is not the case can be deduced from a variant of this watercolor in the Musées Royaux des Beaux-Arts in Brussels (De Grez Collection, no. 1475). In that image, the horse and groom are absolutely identical to the ones seen here (albeit in a different stable), except the horse has a completely different coat – one that is not dappled. That drawing, which bears the inscription *Cheval Danois*, dates from 1780, the same year as the Amsterdam sheet. Haag depicted the same horse five years later, in a small painted panel and, once again, in a new setting. The latter picture, which is in Cannenburch Castle in the northeastern province of Gelderland, has a gilt frame with the words *Cheval Danois* in a cartouche at the top. It is one of a series of ten devoted to breeds of horse that Haag painted between 1785 and 1789.

This kind of equine scene, which was so common in England, was virtually unknown in the Dutch Republic before Haag's day. Judging by the signature on a small painting in the collection of A. Staring, it seems that Abraham van Strij (see cat. no. 62) also tried this genre, which was later continued, almost unchanged, by Anthonie Oberman (1781-1845). Two canvases by Oberman in the Rijksmuseum, both dated 1828, show horses from the stables of the banker Adriaan van der Hoop. It is not that the Dutch were uninterested in horses. Writing slightly later, a tourist from horse-loving England remarked, "I was much struck with the kind treatment and careful attention which horses in particular meet with throughout Holland."

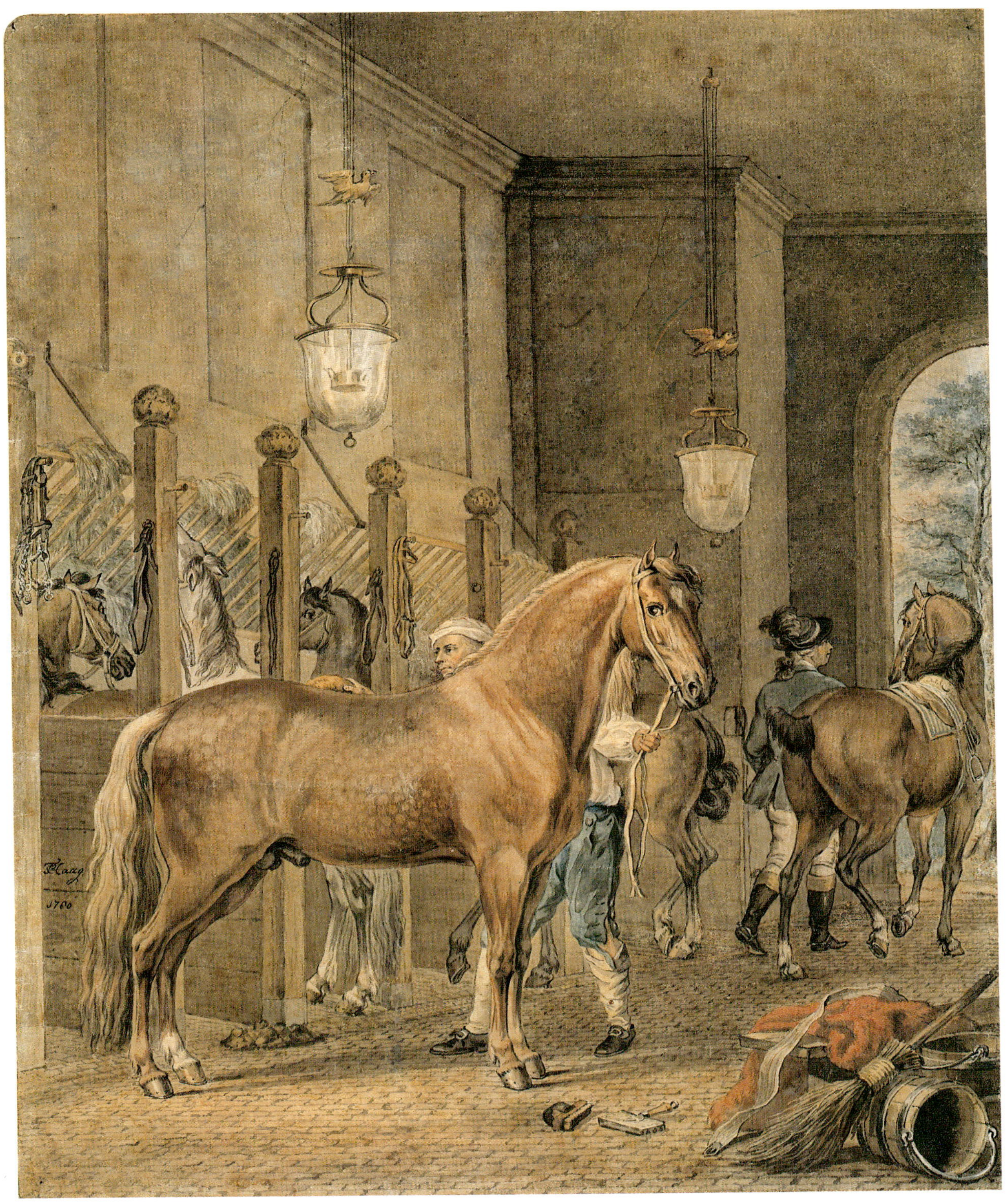

Wijbrand Hendriks (Amsterdam 1744-1831 Haarlem)

An important painter and draftsman who created a varied oeuvre of portraits, landscapes, genre scenes, townscapes, and still lifes. Like so many artists of his generation, Wijbrand Hendriks began his career in a wall-decoration shop – the one run by Johannes Remmers in Amsterdam. There he met Willem Joseph Laquy (see cat. no. 40), who became his friend and frequent collaborator. Hendriks then operated his own wall-hangings shop for a few years, before he moved to Haarlem in 1778. It was around then that he and Hendrik Meyer (see cat. no. 44) journeyed to England together, although Wijbrand fell ill and hastily returned to Holland. From 1777 to 1782, he acted as director of the Haarlem Drawing Academy, and then worked for four years in the province of Gelderland. In 1785 he was appointed curator of the Teylers Foundation in Haarlem, a post he held for nearly thirty-five years. He served in several other public capacities, which testifies both to his social conscience and to his gifts as an administrator. As a portrait painter, he was the ideal interpreter of the stylistic ideals of the Mennonite élite of intellectual democrats. One of his hallmarks was a strong characterization that was often enlivened with a hint of humor. After 1800, Hendriks's art took on a markedly simple and natural realism. He continued to produce watercolors well into his old age.

24 Barn in Gelderland

Black chalk, brush in gray, and watercolor; brown border
258 x 383 mm
On verso, signed in pen: *in 't Buurtschap Maanen* (In the hamlet of Maanen) / *W.H*[S] *ad vivum 1783*
Inv. no. 1894 A 2873

Hendriks made many drawings out of doors during the summers of the few years that he spent in the east of the country. During that time his style gained in immediacy and freshness. In this scene in a Gelderland hamlet, sunlight plays on the tree trunks and the slightly unkempt barn. The convincing evocation of natural scenery and peaceful atmosphere was achieved by integrating the black chalk with the shades of watercolor. Hendriks handled his materials more freely than did others at a time when chalk still served primarily for sketching the initial design and watercolor was used to add tonality.

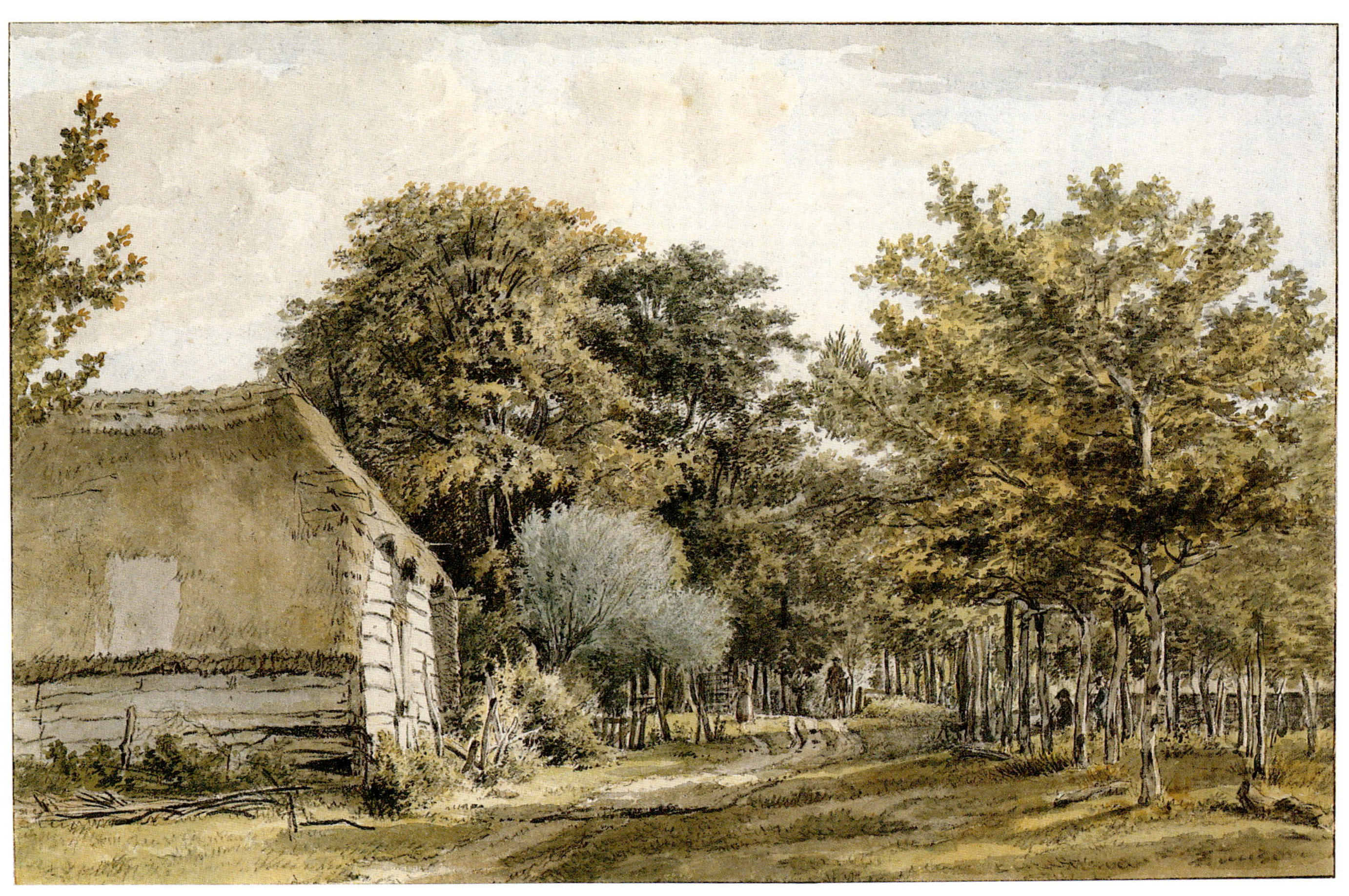

25 **Head of a Roebuck**

Black chalk and watercolor; gray-black border
322 x 345 mm
On verso, in pencil: *W.Hendriks / ad vivum*
Inv. no. 1958:13

Watercolors of the head of a single animal – other such works can be found in the Teyler Museum in Haarlem and the Boymans-Van Beuningen Museum in Rotterdam – can be dated in the final years of the eighteenth century. The animal portrayed here was probably dead, lying on the ground with glazed eyes. The dun color of its coat suggests that this drawing was done in winter, for in summer the coat would have been a reddish brown. The velvety growth on the six-point antlers, which are almost fully grown, indicates the period before February or March.

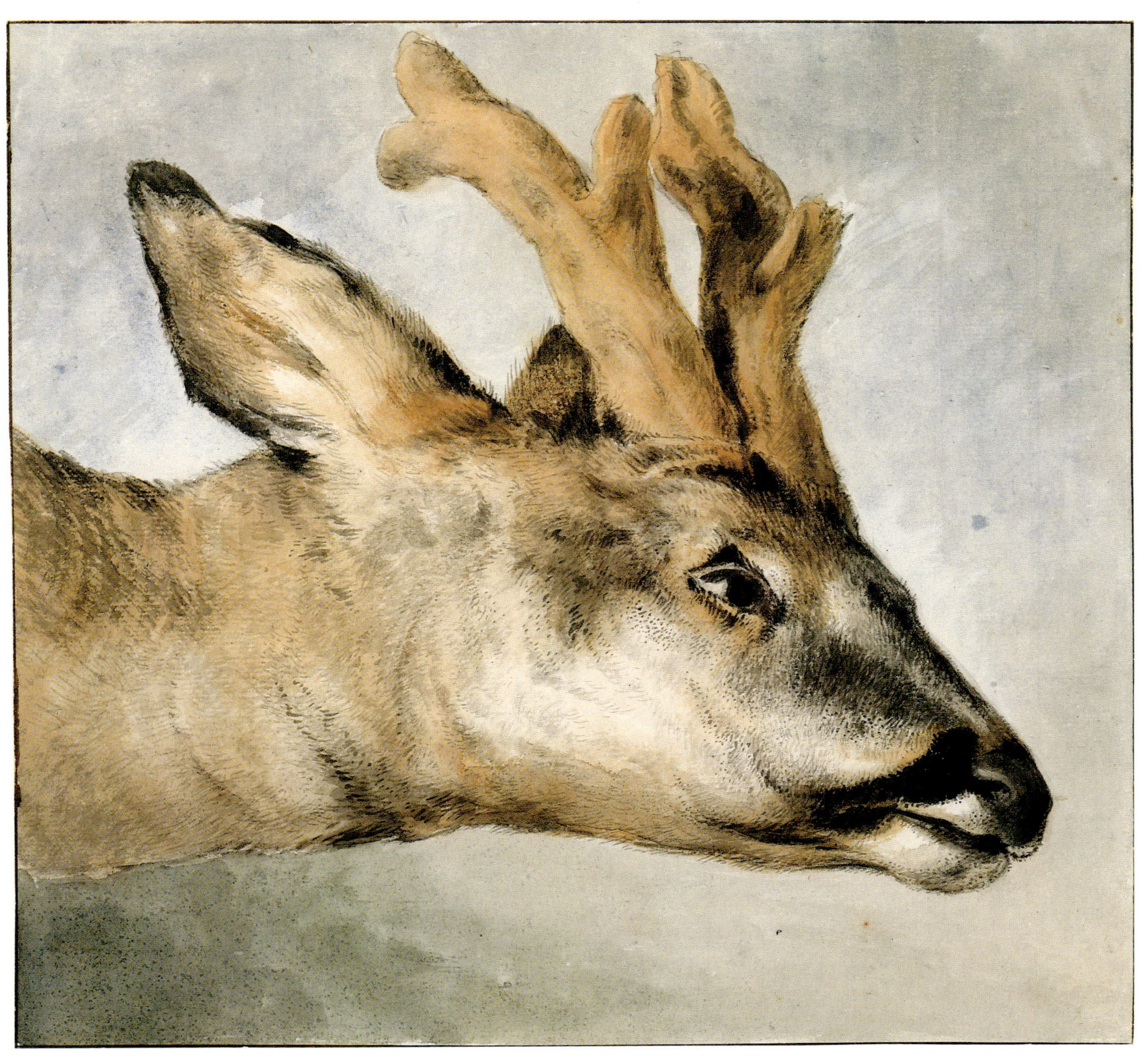

26 Landscape with Ruined Castle, after Hobbema

Pencil, pen in brown, and watercolor; black border
250 x 250 mm
On verso, signed at lower left, in pen: *N° 9 M:Hobbema Pinxit / WH* [later expanded to *Hendriks*]
At upper left, in pen: *N° 95*
Inv. no. 1932:2

Here, Hendriks copied the left half of a well-known picture by Meindert Hobbema (1638-1709) that is now in the Wallace Collection in London. In Hendriks's day, however, it was still in Haarlem, among the paintings that belonged to the Hoofman family, which had built a special exhibition gallery to house its collection. In Hobbema's painting, the landscape continues much further to the right, with a man and a dog walking on a path between the trees. Hendriks may have left this out because he was more interested in the ruins. They were part of a larger complex that made up Egmond Castle, also known as the Castle on the Hoef, west of Alkmaar. The structure shown here was the southwestern tower of the outer bailey. Jacob van Ruisdael had also depicted this distinctive, hexagonal tower from the same vantage point in two drawings now in the Amsterdam Printroom. In paintings, such subjects drawn from life were often inserted into invented compositions, which is what Hobbema did. This section of the outer bailey at Egmond does not, in fact, stand alone: ruins of a massive square tower should have been included in the left foreground. Hobbema's painting also inspired the Dutch Romantics. Wijnand J.J. Nuyen (1813-1839) painted a landscape with ruins, now in the Gemeentemuseum in The Hague, which has a very similar central motif.

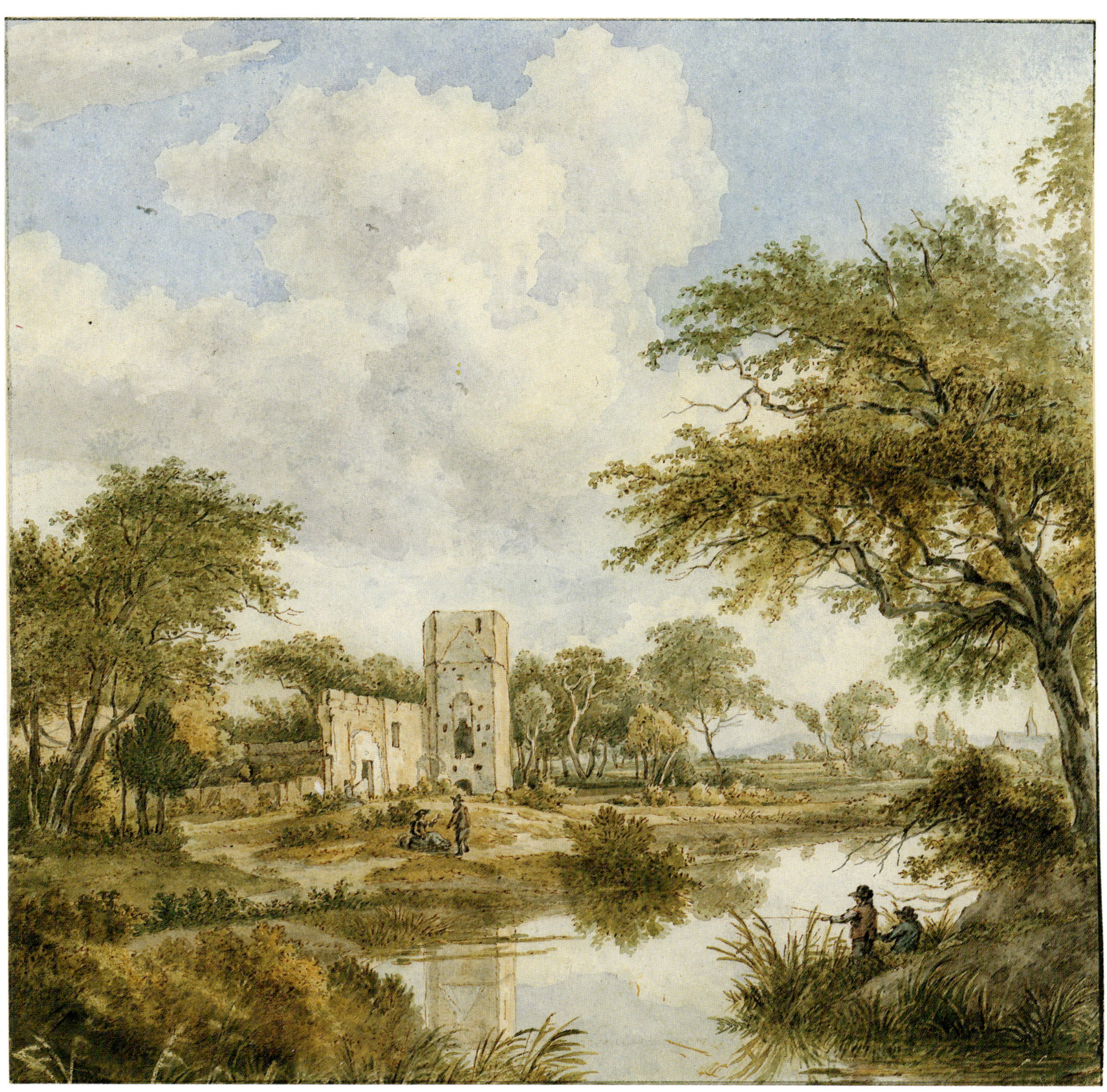

Herman Henstenburg(h) (Hoorn 1667-1726 Hoorn)

Painter of birds, insects, flowers, and fruit on vellum. Herman Henstenburgh was completely self-taught until 1683, when he became the pupil of the local artist Johannes Bronkhorst (died 1727), who, in addition to giving him lessons in art, trained him in his own trade as a pastry cook. This also became Henstenburgh's occupation, and he practiced it until he died, one year before his teacher.

Henstenburgh's choice of subject, drawing style, and use of materials were largely shaped by the example of Pieter Holsteyn, whose drawings provided him with his first models, and of Johannes Bronkhorst. Due to his residency in Hoorn, which was somewhat outside the artistic mainstream, Henstenburgh's art retained a rather old-fashioned look. It was through the celebrated Mattheus Terwesten, who met him by chance in Hoorn, that Henstenburgh gradually built up a small clientele, which even included a few English collectors. One of his great admirers was the Middelburg connoisseur Pieter van den Brande, whose heirs, around 1750, still owned a "considerable number of flower, fruit and other pieces, all most ingeniously wrought." The remains of that collection were dispersed at a sale in Amsterdam in 1972. According to his biographer, Johan van Gool, Henstenburgh perfected a special kind of watercolor paint which was so bright and robust that it rivaled oils. His son Antonie followed in his footsteps, as both a pastry cook and an artist, and he signed copies after his father's work with his own monogram, AHb.

27 Fruit with a Butterfly and a Snail

Gouache and watercolor (?), gum, and tempera on vellum; broad black border
269 x 220 mm
Signed at lower left, in pen: *H.henstenburg fec.*
Inv. no. 1898 A 3501

In 1695, after specializing chiefly in birds and insects, Henstenburgh broadened his repertoire to include flowers and fruit. This fact, recorded by Van Gool (vol. 1, p. 250), places this drawing around or after the turn of the century. The brilliantly detailed objects, which Henstenburgh had formerly depicted either in isolation or dispersed at random across a sheet, are here grouped into a coherent composition. This kind of design apparently appealed to collectors and brought the artist some measure of fame. After he died there was a great demand for his accomplished still lifes. Van Gool, the artist's biographer and art dealer, saw someone pay 105 guilders for a similar watercolor of three peaches and a bunch of grapes. When painting his "watercolors," Henstenburgh very probably followed the suggestions given by Willem Goeree in his popular handbook. The grapes in this sheet are rendered exactly as advised by Goeree: lay in with purple, shade with ash blue, and heighten with white.

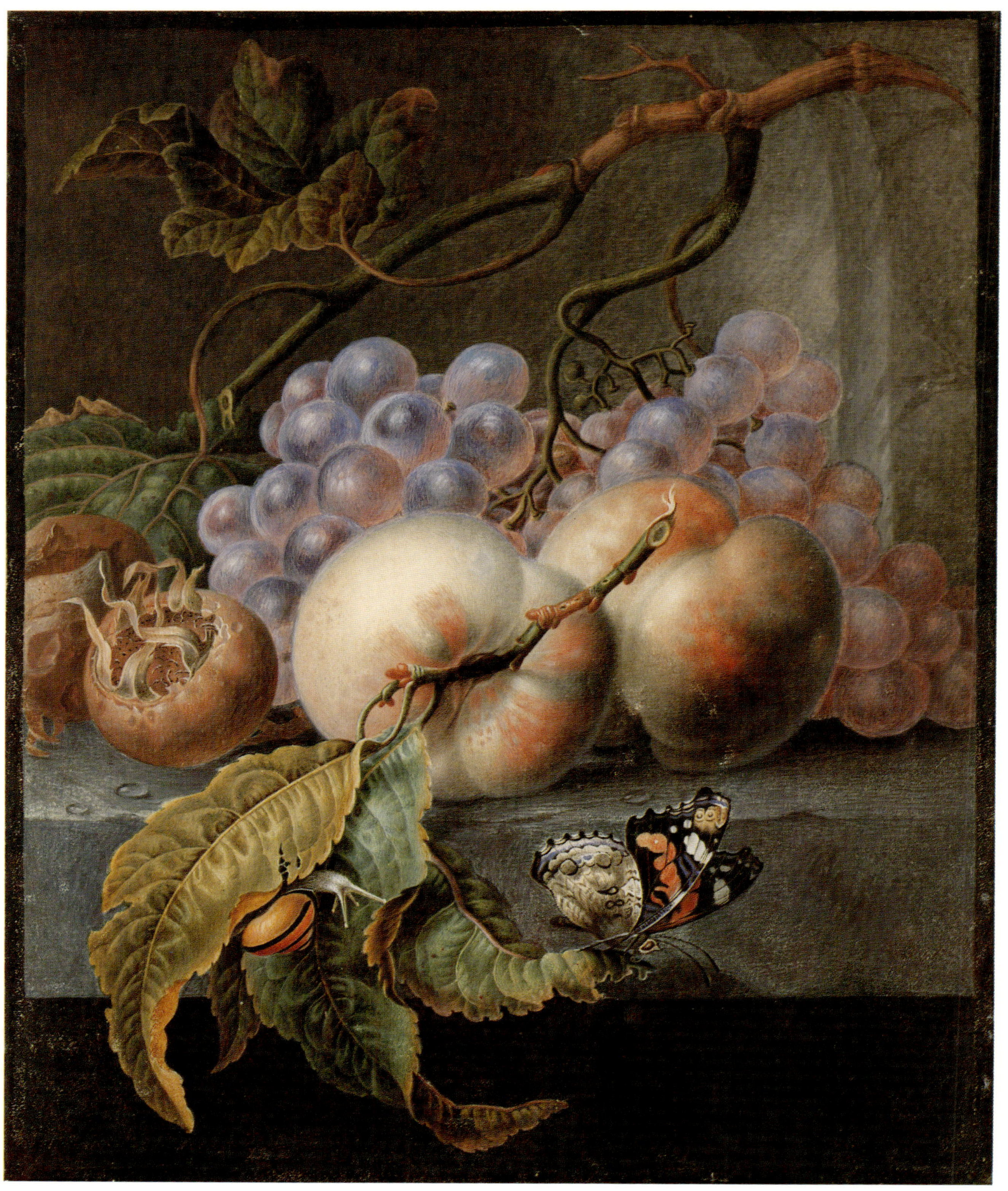

Painter, but above all watercolorist, draftsman, and etcher who started out as a silversmith. Later Warnaar Horstink became the pupil of Cornelis van Noorde (see cat. no. 46), who was also from Haarlem, and briefly of Wijbrand Hendriks (see cat. nos. 24-26). Horstink emulated Hendriks's style whenever he could find the time to produce original work between his engagements as a drawing master, which kept him fairly busy in an artistic town such as Haarlem. In 1778, Horstink became a member of the artists' Guild of St. Luke. He left a varied oeuvre, consisting of many topographical views in and around Haarlem, as well as more freehand landscapes, portraits, and watercolor copies of paintings. Horstink was a friend of Jordanus Hoorn (1753-1833), and it may have been through Hoorn that he came to know the Haarlem burgomaster G.W. van Oosten de Bruyn, who commissioned from him paintings for Randenbroek, his country seat near Amersfoort. An active member of the Haarlem Drawing College, Horstink was widely respected by his many pupils and associates as being a quiet, respectable man, qualities that are also reflected in his drawings.

28 The Artist and His Family

Pen in gray, watercolor, on two sheets of paper joined along an irregular line and pasted onto cardboard
395 x 360 mm
Signed and dated at bottom, in pen: *Wr Horstink / inv.et ft.1796*
Annotated by artist on separate sheet:
Warnaar Horstink geboren [born] *1757.den 1 Nov: / Martijntje van der Zee.1757 den 31 July / Barend Horstink gebooren 1782 den 9 maart* [March] / *Adriana Petronella gebooren 1785 den 16 febr: Overled.* [died] *2 Maart 1785 / Adriana Petronella gebooren 1786 den 4 augus: / Nicolaas Willem gebooren 1793 den 20 Maart / door Warnaar Horstink / naar het Leeven getekend* [drawn from life by Warnaar Horstink] *1796.*
Inv. no. 1964:12

The annotation "drawn from life" applies only to the sitters and not to the setting. Such a massive framed opening would never have been found between two rooms in Haarlem at the end of the eighteenth century. This visual device has a long history in art, being popularized in the Dutch Golden Age mainly by Gerard Dou (1613-1675) and Frans van Mieris (1635-1681) in the form of a stone niche rather than the wooden aperture seen here. Nevertheless, Horstink's composition displays considerable affinity with works by Leiden artists, who often depicted half-length figures behind a waist-high parapet and with a variety of objects displayed on the ledge. Time and again, a potted plant is seen in the righthand corner.
A curtain that partially closes off the background is another popular motif in seventeenth-century painting, as in the work of Dou and his school. In a sort of illusionistic miscalculation, Horstink has placed the top of the curtain in front of the arch but has allowed the bottom to hang not only behind the ledge but also behind his own standing figure, which it would not have done naturally.
That is not the only spatial incongruity in the composition. If the model horse is indeed standing on the floor, as would seem logical, there is not enough space between the ledge and the floor to accommodate the lower bodies of the husband and wife. Even if the horse rests on a low table or on some other item of furniture, the draftsman still seems very short in relation to his seated wife and their fourteen-year-old son. Despite these shortcomings, Horstink's portraits succeed in conveying an authentic and convincing picture of a middle-class Dutch family in the late eighteenth century.

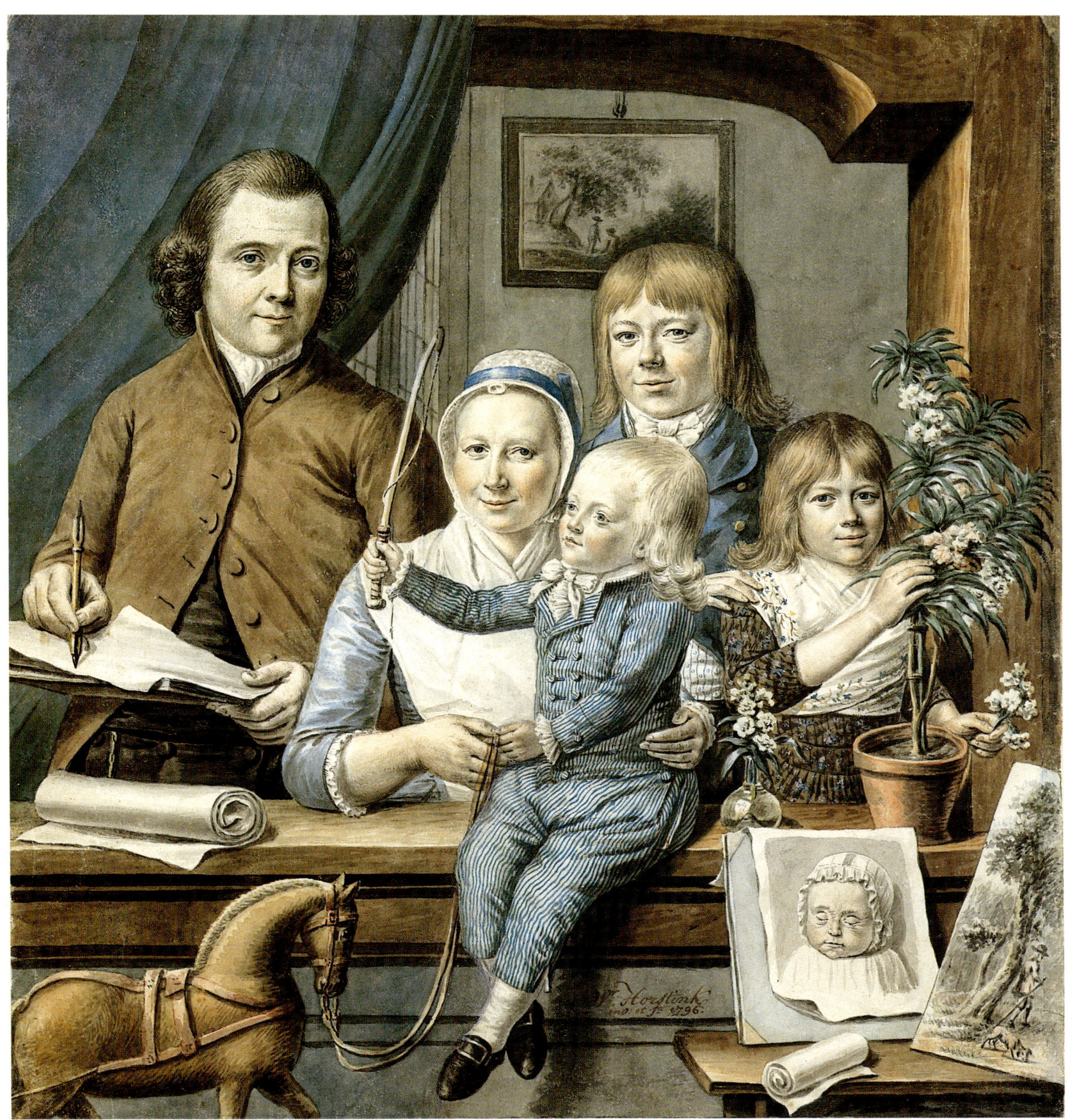

Jan van Huysum (Amsterdam 1682-1749 Amsterdam)

A famous painter and draftsman of sprigs bearing flowers and fruit. Jan van Huysum was the eldest son of the artist Justus van Huysum, whose own father left the village of that name (now called Huizum) in the northern province of Friesland to seek his fortune in Amsterdam. Jan van Huysum became an independent master after his marriage in 1704. Although he also painted classicist landscapes, he was most successful with his still lifes. Virtuosity in arranging his flowers and fruit, a meticulous technique, and an unrivaled ability to depict nature made him famous throughout Europe and allowed him to charge staggeringly high prices for his work. This "phoenix of flower painters," as his biographer Johan van Gool called him, outstripped older colleagues such as Coenraet Roepel (1678-1750), and even Rachel Ruysch (1664-1748).

His contributions to the development of the flower-and-fruit still life include the masterly freedom with which the blooms are strewn throughout the compositon and, even more important, the light backgrounds that he gave his scenes. He often prepared his pictures with broadly executed sketches, and then painted the final work from real flowers and fruit. By his own admission, a picture was sometimes left unfinished for several months because a particular kind of rose was not available or a species of flower had not yet bloomed. Although he was very secretive about his art – he never let anyone into his studio, except for one pupil, Margaretha Haverman, with whom he later had a furious argument – Jan van Huysum did become the father of a school. Jan van Os (1744-1808), Willem van Leen (1753–1825, see cat. no. 42), Paulus Theodorus van Brussel (1754-1791), and the brothers Gerardus and Cornelis van Spaendonck (1746-1822 and 1756-1840, respectively) can be regarded as his followers.

29 Sketch for a Still Life with Fruit and Flowers

Charcoal soaked in oil, and watercolor; black border
408 x 320 mm
Inv. no. 1899 A 4272

In his flower-and-fruit pieces, Jan van Huysum was first and foremost a painter. Drawings merely served as preparation for a new canvas or panel. That is also the function of this sketch, which was swiftly and loosely laid down using the material that had been prescribed for this kind of work back in the seventeenth century: small sticks of charcoal soaked in linseed oil, which prevented the lines from rubbing off. Here, the celebrated flower painter displayed his virtuosity in filling a composition with his standard studio props (which are also featured in other works) of an urn, a plinth, and a square basket that provides the framework for a profusion of fruit and flowers. His skillful touch is evident in the way the main colors are applied with transparent watercolor.

Jan van Huysum's career spanned almost half a century, and it is difficult to arrange his undated works in a clear, chronological order. A similar sketch in the British Museum is quite evidently a preliminary study for a painting that bears the date 1730. A related drawing in the Louvre is associated with a painting that has the dates 1732 and 1733, and a drawing (Paris, Louvre, Dutuit Collection), with the same motifs as this sheet, is itself dated 1733. These similarities invite a dating of this work in the same period of the early 1730s.

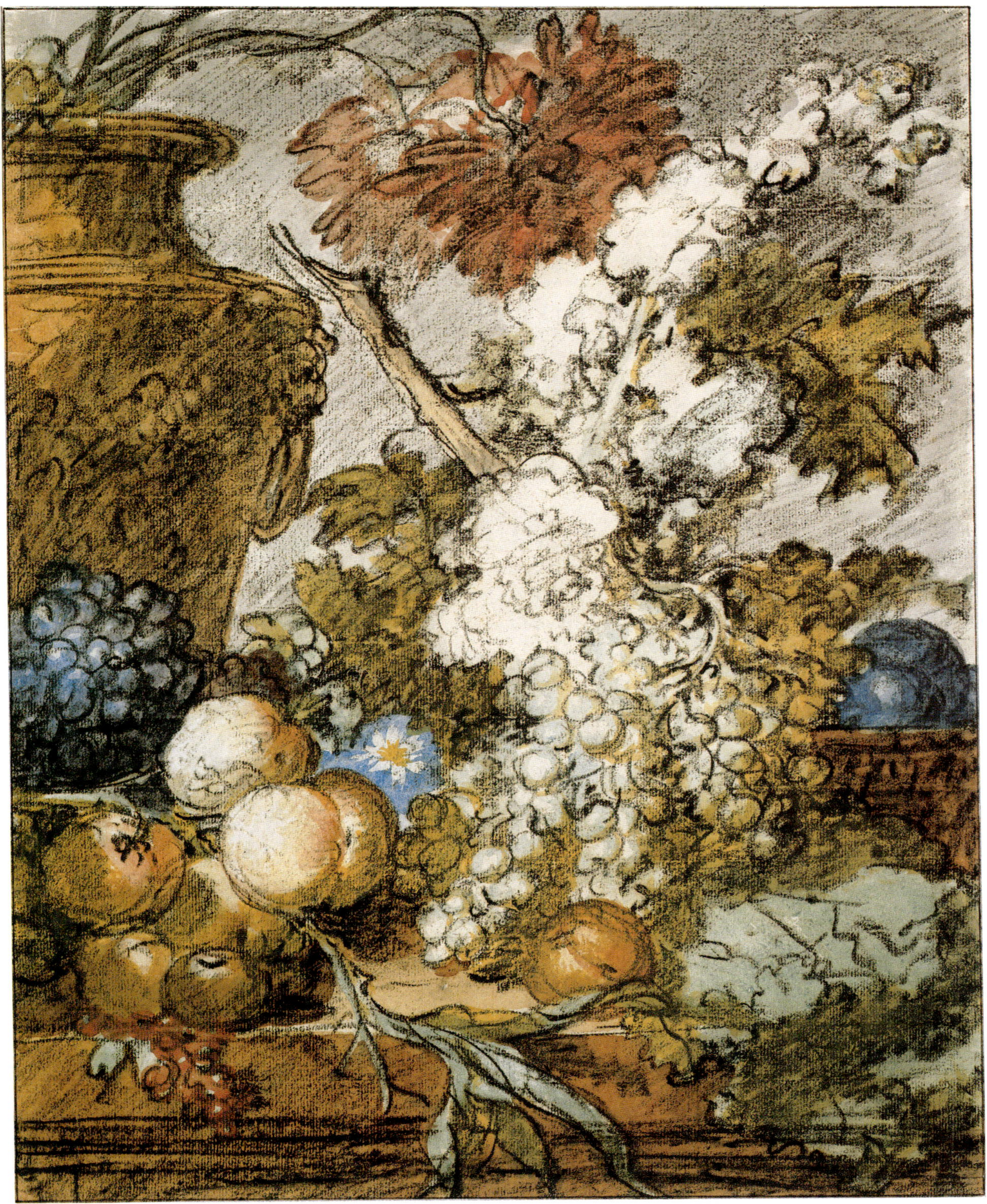

Chiefly known as a draftsman of flowers, fruit, and Arcadian landscapes. Michiel van Huysum was a much younger half-brother of Jan van Huysum (cat. no. 29), and like him lived and worked in Amsterdam. He lacked Jan's natural genius, but he compensated by depicting his subjects with the utmost realism. According to the catalogue of the famous collection of drawings that belonged to Jan Gildemeester (1744–1799), which was sold at auction in November 1800 and contained dozens of works by Michiel van Huysum, the artist specialized in individual fruit, as in this sheet, and in compositions with flower vases, bowls, pedestals, birds' nests, and other objects. Like his half-brother Jacob (who died destitute in London in 1740), Michiel made copies after the work of Jan van Huysum and supplemented his income by giving drawing lessons to prominent figures, among them members of such patrician Amsterdam families as Bicker, Cruys, and Van Lennep, and also to Nicolaas Faas, director of the Amsterdam Drawing Academy, and to the merchant and collector Jan Gildemeester Jansz.

30 A Melon, Bunches of Grapes, a Lemon (?), and a Hazelnut

Watercolor, coated in parts with gum or tempera; remnants of brown border
249 x 377 mm
Signed at bottom, in pencil: *MVHuijsum*
Inv. no. 1953:293

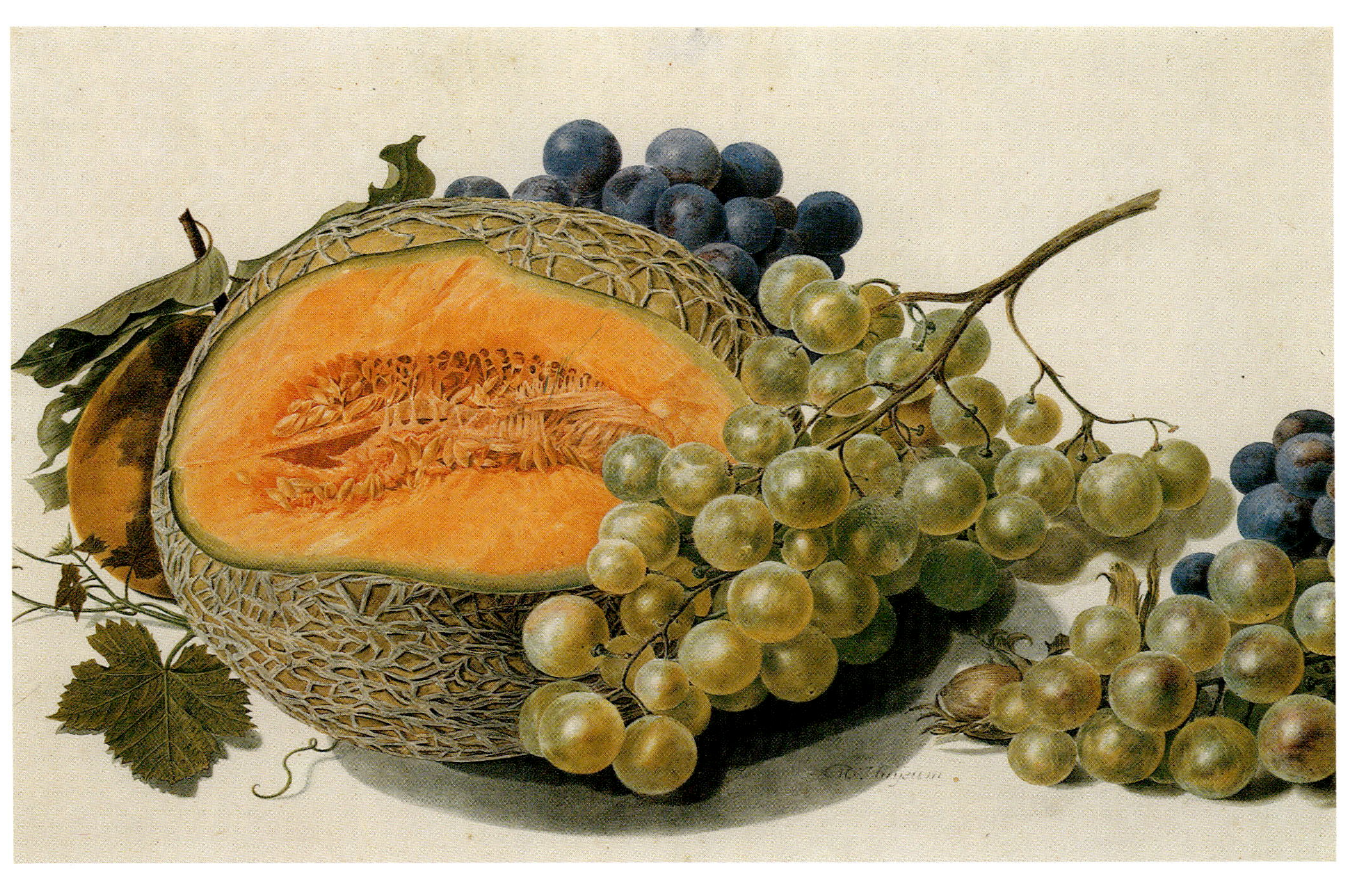

31 A Calabash, Two Peaches, and a Walnut

Watercolor, possibly with light, local coating of gum or tempera; remnants of brown border
259 x 365 mm
Signed at lower left, in pencil: *MVHuijsum*
Inv. no. 1953:294

Van Huysum used a stunningly delicate brush to render this life-size depiction of the fruit that he had arranged in front of him. These watercolors had to rival the natural objects and rise above the limitations imposed by working in just two dimensions. Signed with a calligraphed flourish, they left the studio as finished works of art to grace the pages of collectors' albums. Modern research has increased awareness that fruit and flowers in still-life pictures may have one or more symbolic connotation. Grapes can stand for Christ, for physical or spiritual fecundity, or both; the peach for earthly love or even lust; and the walnut for the Trinity. In other contexts they can symbolize the seasons, the transience of life, or friendship. Here, however, there is no reason to accord any symbolic meaning to the fruit in this or the preceding watercolor (cat. no. 30). They are presented in isolation, devoid of any thematic framework.

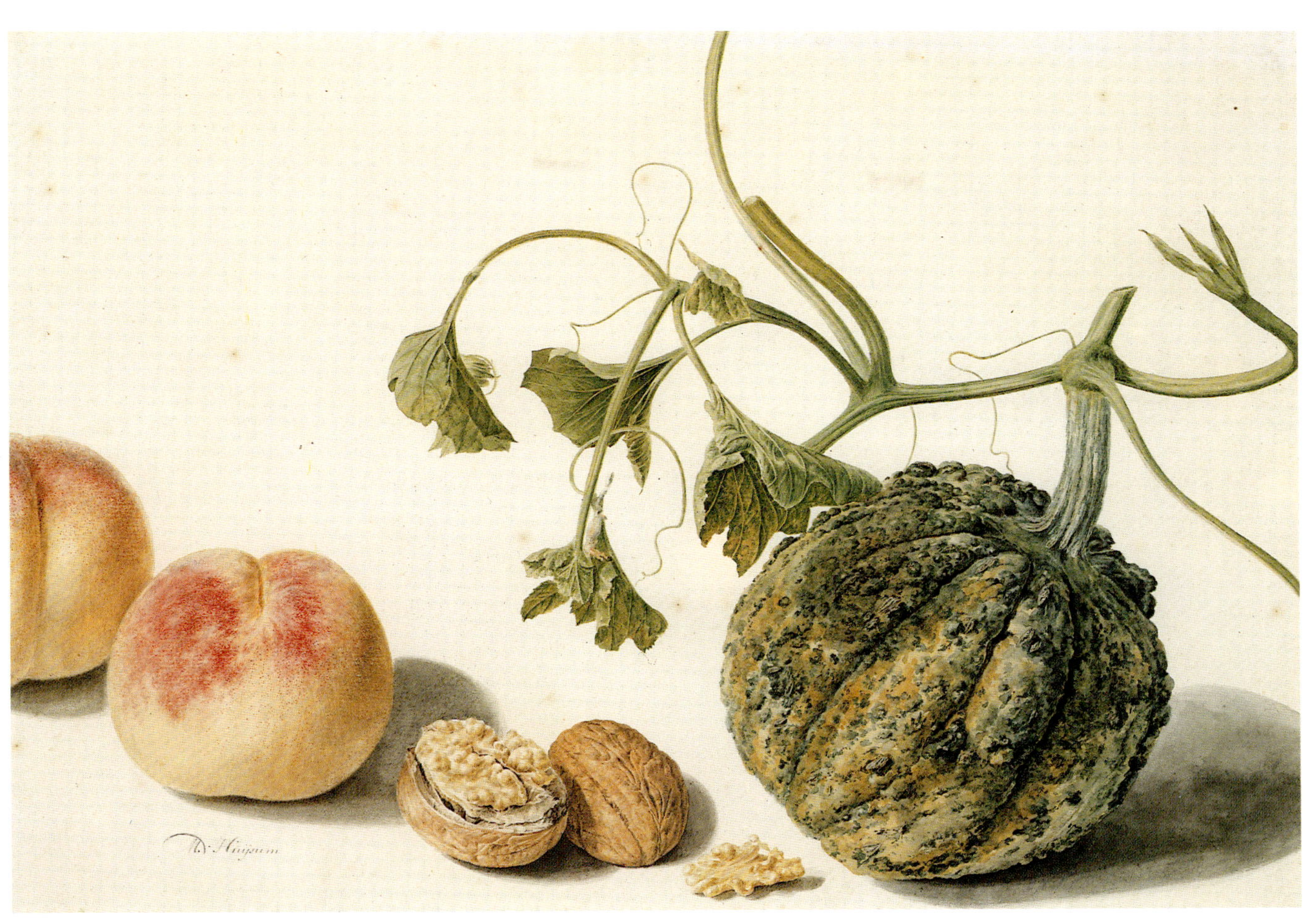
M. v. Huijsum

Rienk Keyert (Leeuwarden 1709-1775 Leeuwarden)

Regional painter of portraits and decorative pieces. Little is known of Rienk Keyert's origins or early life. He seems to have trained in The Hague from 1727 to 1731, where he is recorded as a pupil of the Pictura artists' society. In 1732 he was painting decorations in his native Leeuwarden. Twenty-four years later he advertised himself as a painter of domestic wall-hangings, overmantels, bas-reliefs, and portraits. He served as a town councillor from 1750 until his death in 1775. The Fries Museum in Leeuwarden possesses noteworthy examples of his painting. These works reveal that, despite the years he spent in the cosmopolitan atmosphere of The Hague, Keyert remained a somewhat provincial artist.

32 Design for a Wall Decoration with Neptune and His Retinue

Pen in brown, watercolor, and gouache;
fragmentary brown border; squared for enlargement
248 x 393 mm
Signed on one panel, in pen: *R:Keyert / fecit / 1751*
Inv. no. 1906:10

This drawing, by an artist who could by no stretch of the imagination be counted among the avant-garde of eighteenth-century Holland, has nevertheless been included here on its own merits. As Keyert's only known watercolor, it offers an idea of how the "chamber hangings" mentioned in his advertisement of 1756 might have looked.

This kind of decoration, which is not divided into compartments but stretches unbroken across the entire surface of the wall, was old-fashioned even by the time of its execution. The exuberant tonality, too, may have appealed more to the provincial Frisian's love of gay colors than to the taste of fashionable circles in the large cities.

The unusual wainscoting with the abbreviated panels might indicate that the artist made this drawing for a specific room. The marine theme points to a shipowner's house or, if the client was a public institution, an office of a Board of Admiralty. Yet even if Keyert's design was actually executed, as the squaring suggests, the finished painting has perished.

Designing such a scene placed heavy demands on an artist's imagination, and Keyert must have been happy to rely on the examples in the so-called *Drawing Book* of Abraham Bloemaert (1564-1651), which appeared in a deluxe edition under the supervision of Bernard Picart in 1740. The entire righthand group of Neptune's retinue is copied directly from plate 147 in that book, and Keyert used other prints for motifs, such as the cherub over the door and probably the Triton on the far left as well (plates 109 and 98, respectively).

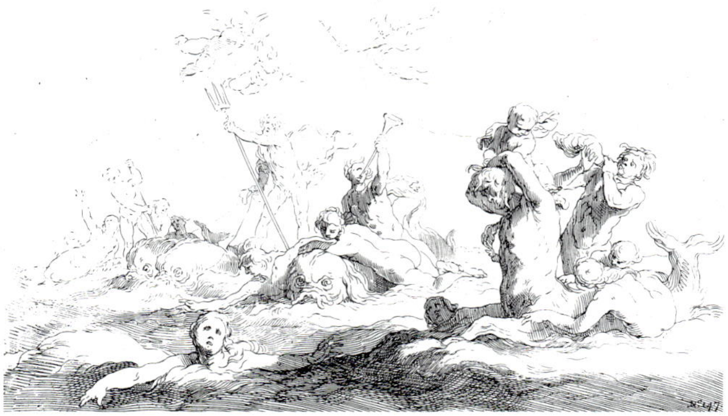

Etching no. 147 from Abraham Bloemaert's Konstrijk tekenboek (1740 edition).

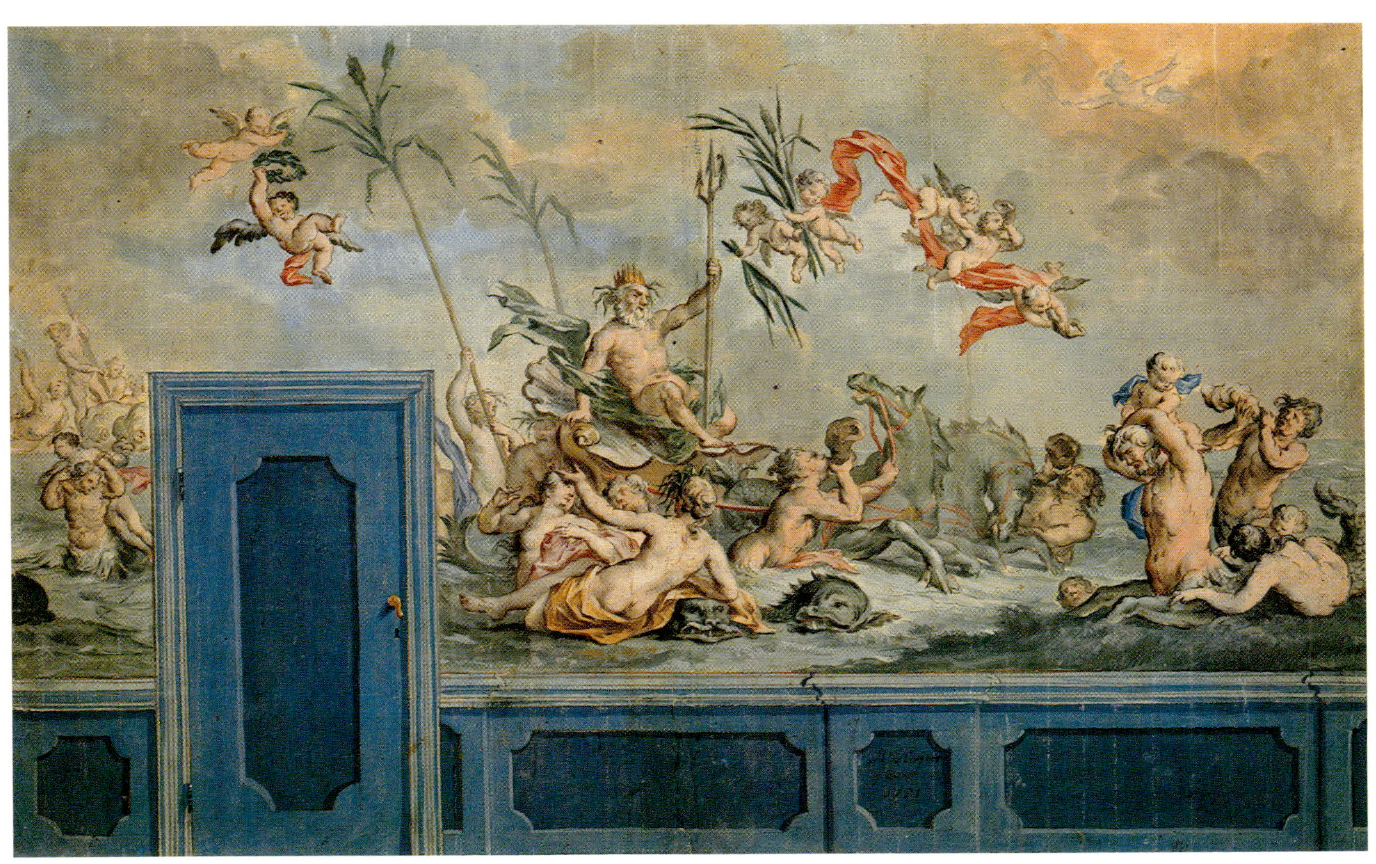

Hendrik Kobell (Rotterdam 1751-1779 Rotterdam)

Draftsman and etcher who died at an early age, a specialist in views of rivers with scenes of shipping and commerce. His father, who came from Frankfurt-am-Main, was related to the German painters Ferdinand, Franz, and Wilhelm Kobell. Hendrik's brother Johannes (1756-1833) was also a painter, draftsman, and etcher, and Hendrik's son Johannes Baptist (1778-1814) became a celebrated painter of cattle in the tradition of Paulus Potter.

A precocious talent, Kobell enrolled in the Amsterdam Drawing Academy in 1771, where he listed among his previous teachers Xavery (probably Franciscus Xavery, born 1740) and Ferdinand Kobell, his cousin who was living in Mannheim at the time. Kobell had already visited England and had exhibited paintings there, some of which were made into prints. After a journey to France, Kobell eventually settled in Rotterdam. There he became friendly with Dirk Langendijk (see cat. nos. 38, 39), corresponded with Cornelis Ploos van Amstel in Amsterdam, and became a confidant of Wilhelm Tischbein during the German artist's visit to Holland in 1772. He married in 1774. A few years later he began to suffer from mental illness, and he was committed to an asylum when his rages became uncontrollable. He died insane, as did his son, Johannes Baptist Kobell.

33 Strollers and Skaters on a Frozen River with Ships

Pencil, pen in gray, and brush in watercolor; black border; in an old mount (probably eighteenth-century)
188 x 265 mm
Signed at lower left, in pen: *H.Kobell.f.1773*
On verso, signed at lower left, in pencil: *H:Kobell / 1773*
Inv. no. 1952:11

Ice scenes were a popular theme in Dutch art from the seventeenth to the nineteenth centuries. Here, Hendrik Kobell combined this subject with his true specialty – depictions of the large, oceangoing ships that regularly entered the port of his native Rotterdam. This view might, then, be of the River Maas, which flows through the city, although the catalogue of the eighteenth-century collection from which this work probably comes merely mentions "a frozen river." Beyond the topographical question, the scene was very probably set in the bitterly cold winter of 1771. On January 11, horse-drawn sleighs were traveling along the River Amstel in Amsterdam, and on March 31, people were cooking eggs on the ice. These Arctic conditions lasted into April.

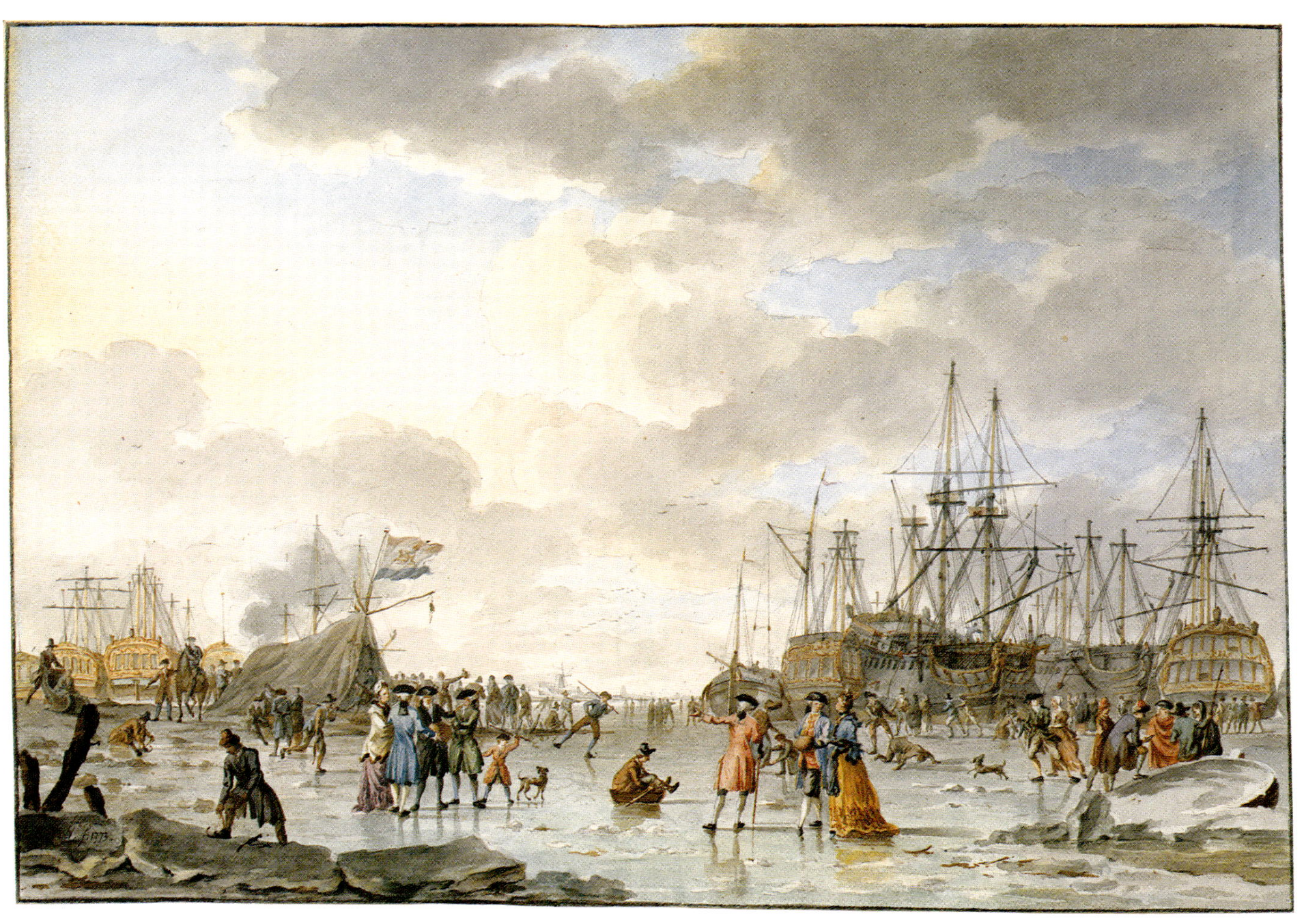

Simon Andreas Krausz (The Hague 1760-1825 The Hague)

An eccentric, nonconformist artist who received his first training while only just in his teens from the Belgian painter Léonard de France, who was living in The Hague in 1773-74. His practice of drawing from the live model at the Pictura Academy in The Hague later gained Krausz a gold medal from the hereditary stadtholder, Prince Willem V, in 1782. In 1784 the artist married Adriana Everdina Boers in nearby Scheveningen. The marriage was childless.

Somewhat unexpectedly, given its unconventional and highly personal nature, Krausz's work was much in demand, and in 1806 he was described as one of "the most celebrated painters, draftsmen and engravers in the Kingdom of Holland."

One document that records Krausz's own judgment of his contemporaries, and of a younger generation of artists, is his critique of an exhibition held in The Hague in 1817. (The manuscript is now in the Fondation Custodia in Paris.)

On July 25, 1825, after Krausz's death, the contents of his studio were sold at auction in The Hague. That catalogue is one of the prime sources of information on his work. It lists 56 paintings, which are extremely rare today. His drawn studies remained together as groups for a long time; approximately 150 were included in the sale of Graafland, Geisweit van der Netten, and others (The Hague, 1884), and 190 were pasted into an album that was sold at auction in Amsterdam on May 8-10, 1900. In 1952, the Amsterdam Printroom acquired a miscellany containing 120 drawings.

34 **Covered Wagon**
Brush in gray, with touches of color; brown border
136 x 177 mm
At lower right, below border, remnants of an inscription or signature
Inv. no. 1910:18

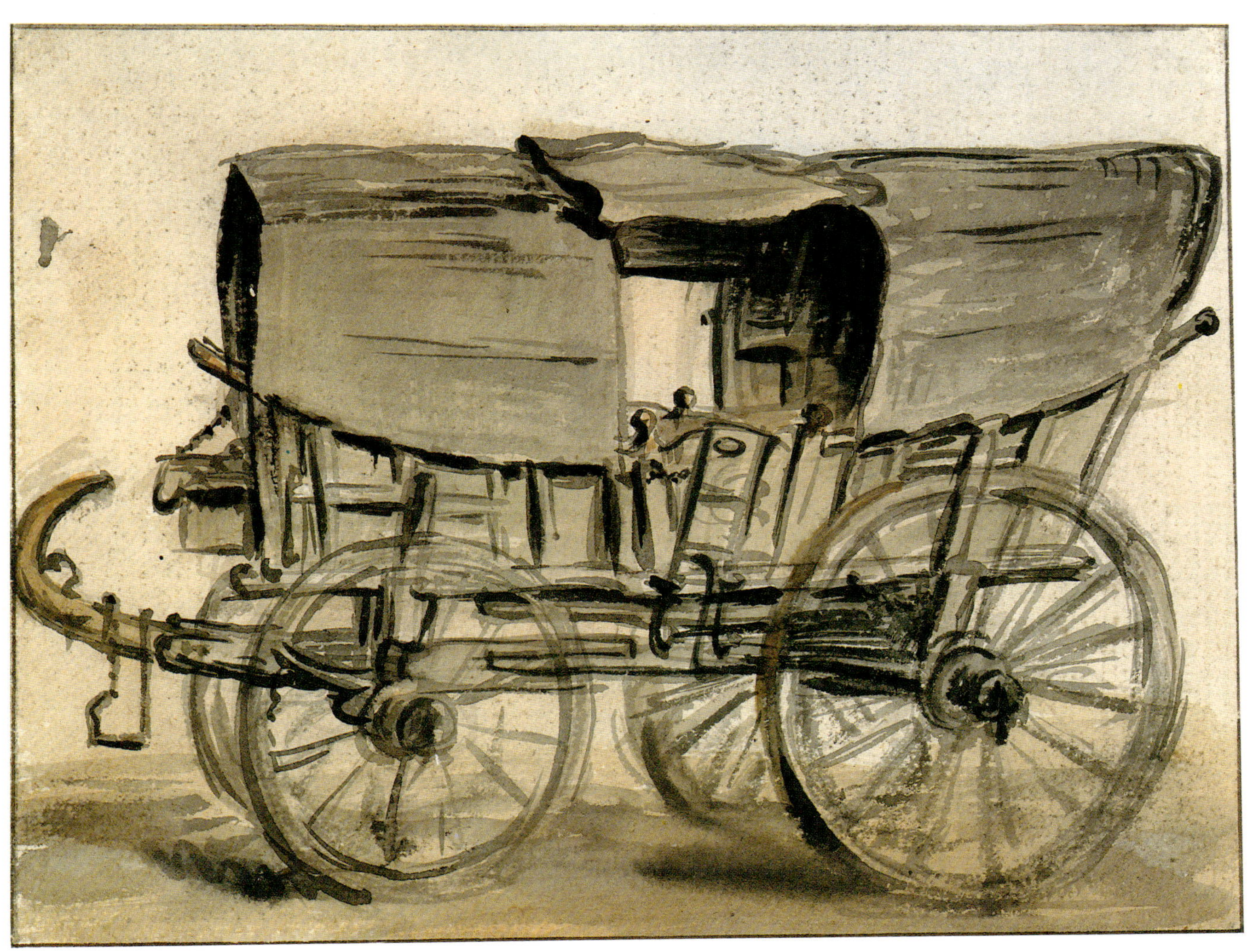

35 The Back of a Four-Wheeled Wagon

Brush in gray, with touches of color; brown border
142 x 162 mm
At upper right, a faded signature, in pen:
S.A Krausz ft
Inv. no. 1910:21

Despite their apparent differences, these two sheets may well be of the same wagon – with and without its hood. The second sheet shows it with a rack to increase its carrying capacity. A third drawing in the Printroom is largely devoted to the structural elements and wheel attachment of this rural form of transportation, and it may even illustrate the same wagon. This type of cart, solidly built and unsprung, had changed very little since the sixteenth century, and it was still being used in country areas in the early decades of the this century.

With his drawn studies of wagons – the Printroom has one image of a three-wheeled specimen, while studies of a stagecoach were auctioned with the Lannoy Collection in 1925 – this otherwise unconventional artist was, unintentionally, following in a long tradition. From the seventeenth century are similar studies by Willem Buytewech (in Berlin), Jan van de Velde (Amsterdam, Rijksprentenkabinet; Bayonne; and the former Beets Collection), Adriaan van de Venne (V.d.S. Collection, Vorden), Izaak van Ostade (Amsterdam, Rijksprentenkabinet), and Rembrandt (London, British Museum). Since only a handful of Krausz's paintings are still known today, it is difficult to say whether these two studies were actually used in a finished composition (as Buytewech, for instance, did with his, which reappears in a hawking scene that was engraved by Jan van de Velde under the title *Aer* [Air]). The artist may have done so in a panel that measures 350 x 400 mm, entitled *Wagon Passing a Flock of Sheep on a Forest Track* (location unknown) and dated 1809, which was auctioned in Dordrecht on November 6-7, 1951.

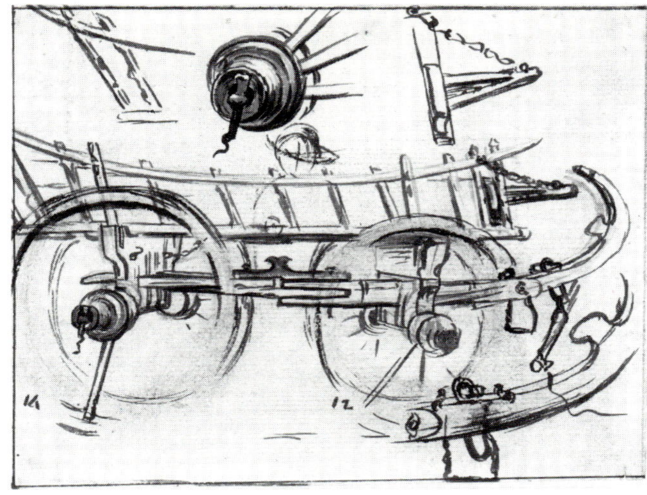

Simon Andreas Krausz, Parts of a Wagon. Amsterdam, Rijksprentenkabinet.

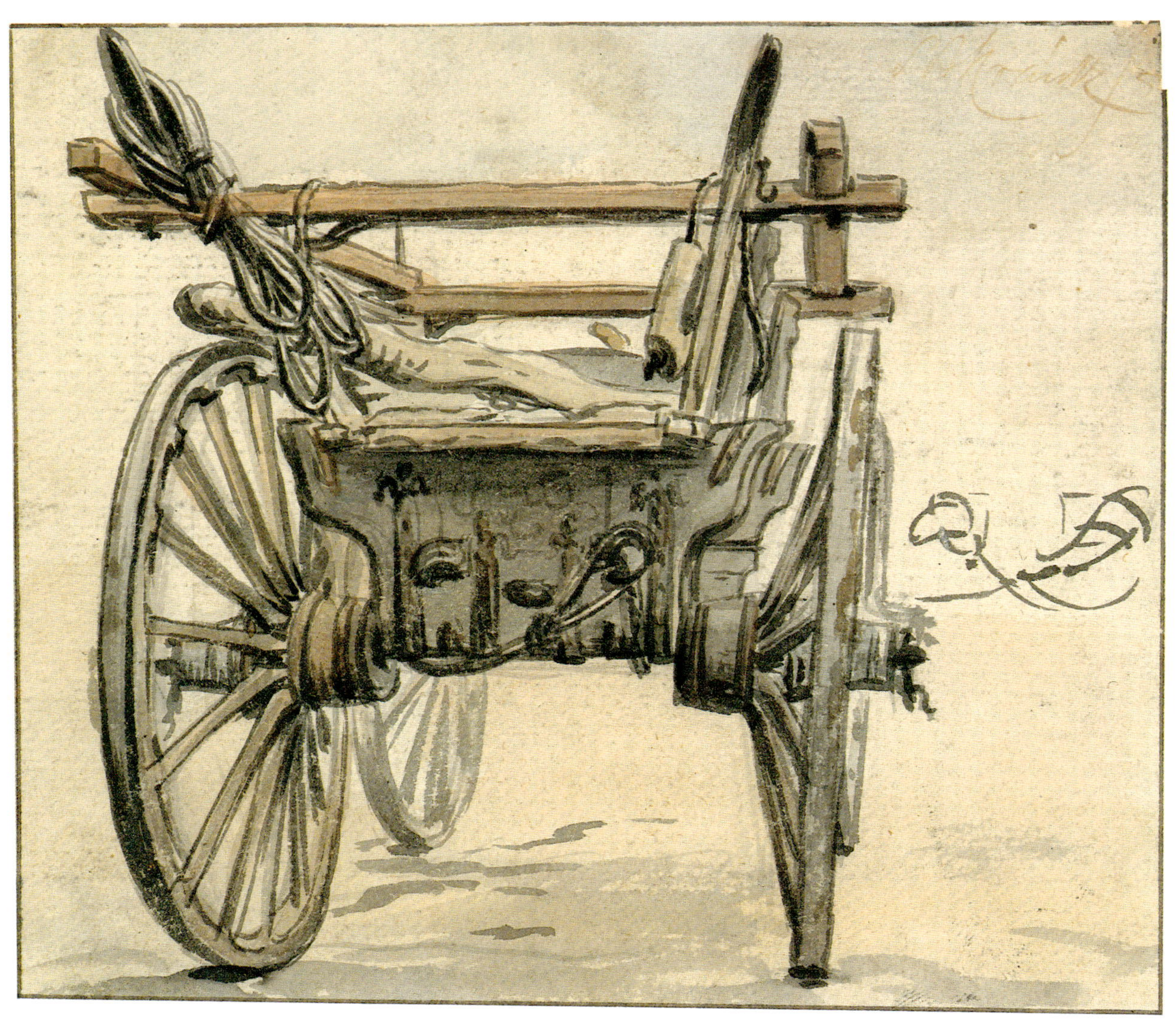

Paulus Constantijn La Fargue (The Hague 1729-1782 The Hague)

The most gifted and enterprising member of a family in which four brothers and one sister became artists. A painter, draftsman, and etcher, mainly of topographical views, who was probably self-taught, La Fargue started his career as a painter of wall-hangings. Together with one or more of his brothers, he decorated rooms for the art dealer Gerard Hoet, Jr., and for the French and English ambassadors in The Hague. Late in life, in 1771, he enrolled as a student in the University of Leiden, where he also belonged to a poetry society, but by 1776 he had moved back to his home town of The Hague. La Fargue's topographical work took him throughout much of the modern province of South Holland, where he focused in particular on the area around The Hague, Leiden, and Rotterdam. He also produced several views a little further afield, with scenes of Amsterdam, Haarlem, and the seaside town of Zandvoort.

In La Fargue's drawings, penwork defines the forms. His brushwork is less accomplished, betraying its shortcomings chiefly in the skies that hang over his views of towns and villages.

36 Country Waterway near Voorburg

Pencil, pen in brown, and watercolor; brown border
143 x 167 mm
Signed at lower left, in pen: *P.C. la Fargue fc*
On verso: *A Mounted Officer*, pen in brown, signed in pen: *gezight aan de Broeksloot bij voorburg. La Fargue* (View on the Broeksloot near Voorburg)
Inv. no. 1975:90

This small watercolor does not entirely do justice to the artistic significance of P.C. La Fargue, who also made some extremely beautiful, large colored views in and around his native city of The Hague. Unfortunately, the Amsterdam Printroom does not have any of these particular works in its collection. This colorful, rustic scene has nevertheless been included here as an example of an unpretentious impromptu drawing that was jotted down in a sketchbook and then probably colored back in the studio before it was signed and annotated on the verso.

Its inscription identifies the location as Broeksloot, a small waterway in Voorburg. The draftsman, a longtime resident of nearby The Hague, had a special tie with Voorburg, for he had spent six of his childhood years there. Broeksloot, which still exists, although it is now canalized, was a very long watercourse. It would have been well-nigh impossible to identify this precise spot had there not been a version of the scene (much larger, more skillfully executed, and uncolored) with an inscription stating that the spire in the distance is that of Rijswijk village church. This places the vantage point in the western part of Broeksloot, probably not far from the Bethlehem farm estate (also known as Vrijburg, or Quarles House, after its owner). Several drawings of that estate are in the Amsterdam Print Room and elsewhere. All these views along Broeksloot date from 1757, in other words, from La Fargue's early period.

Above the top of the tree in the center of this sheet floats the ghostly head of a man wearing a cocked hat. This is part of what appears to be an army officer mounted on a horse, which was drawn on the back of the sheet. Horsemen are common in La Fargue's work, both individually and as part of a larger composition, such as a parade, a horse market, or a funeral procession. No direct connection, however, has been found between this sketch and any of those scenes.

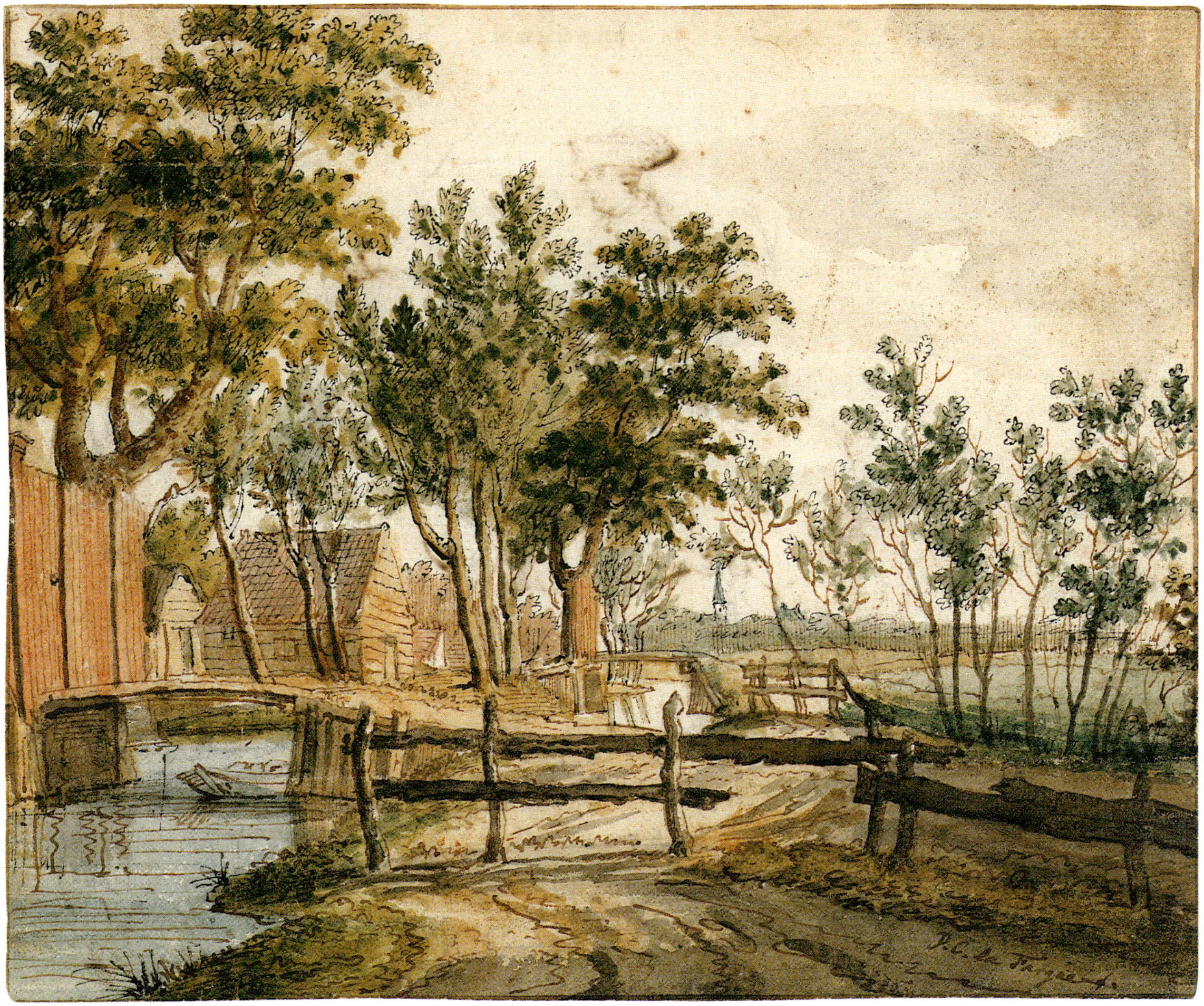

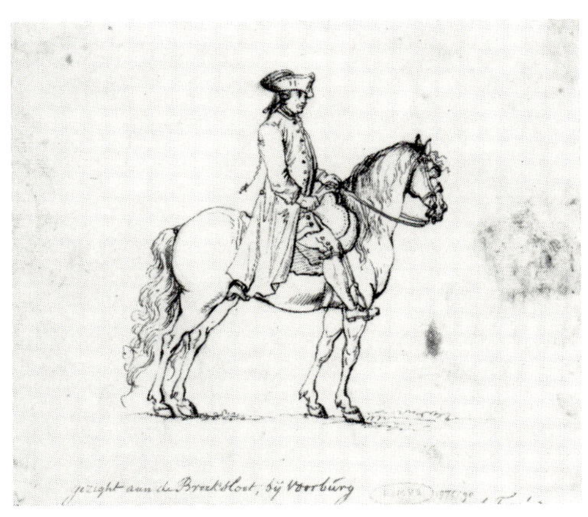

Paulus Constantijn la Fargue, verso of Country Waterway near Voorburg.

Ary (Arie) Lamme ('s-Heerjansdam 1748-1801 Dordrecht)

Draftsman and painter of Dordrecht, mainly of decorative pieces and landscapes. While he was still a child, Ary Lamme's parents moved to Dordrecht, south of Rotterdam, where an artistic community flourished. There Lamme became the pupil of Joris Ponse (1723-1783), a decorative painter of middling ability, who had himself been taught by Aart Schouman (see cat. nos. 55-60). Lamme then embarked on a career as an independent artist of decorative wall-hangings. He married at the age of twenty and was the father of a daughter, Cornelia, who in 1795 gave birth to Ary Scheffer, the world-famous artist. Lamme's son Arnoldus was a painter and art dealer, as was his son, Arie Johannes Lamme, and grandson, Dirk Arie Lamme.
A cultured man, Ary Lamme also wrote poetry and plays. Politically, he espoused the Patriot, anti-stadtholder cause. It is difficult to form a clear idea of his activity as an artist, since very few of his paintings, watercolors, or drawings have been identified.

37 A Park with a Peacock and Poultry Startled by a Dog

Pencil, watercolor, gouache, and some gilding; black border
339 x 244 mm
Inv. no. 1900 A 4481

The traditional attribution of this drawing has been retained, even though there is no signature or inscription, nor a provenance that would securely associate it with the person or oeuvre of Ary Lamme. In subject, composition, and technique, it is closely allied to the work of Aart Schouman, who was also a citizen of Dordrecht but was more than a generation older than Lamme. The barking dog, a spaniel, that has these birds all aflutter also causes a commotion in several of Schouman's works, and the gold paint in the peacock's plumage is found in Schouman's works as well. Lamme departs from Schouman, however, by accentuating the foliage of the trees with a network of pencil lines. The swirling mass of feathers and flowers in the foreground is also far less structured than in Schouman's compositions.
Lamme is known as a painter of landscapes and interior decorations, and it is possible that this is a sketch for a wall-hanging. If so, this would explain why it is unsigned, since it would not have been intended for sale.

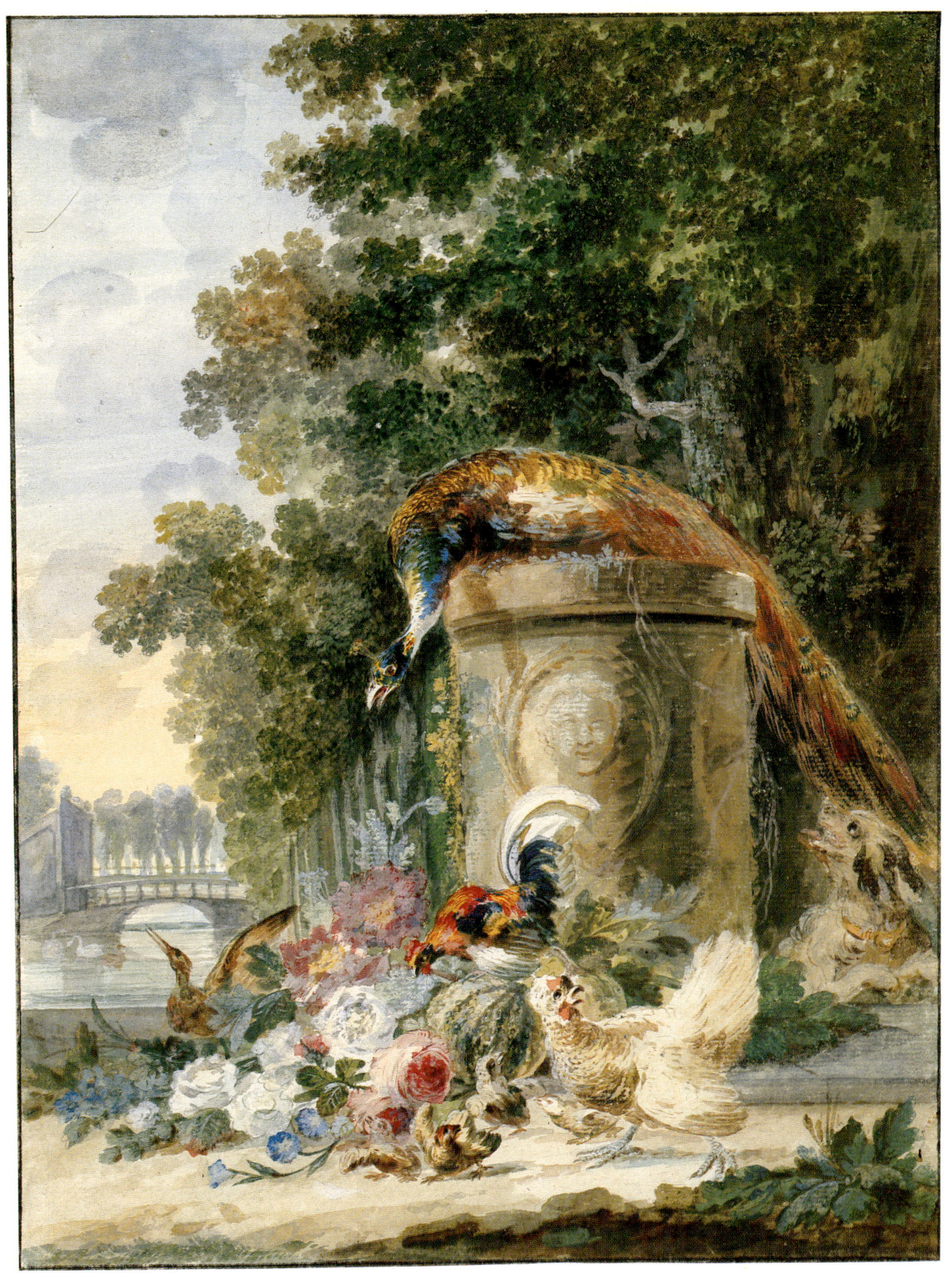

A prolific draftsman of army scenes and depictions of current events. In his native Rotterdam, where he lived all his life, Dirk Langendijk trained with the coachwork painter Dirk Anthonie Bisschop. In the 1770s and 1780s, before he specialized as a draftsman, Langendijk also made easel paintings, often of views that recall works by Philip Wouwermans (1619-1668). His son, Jan Antonie (born 1780), also took up drawing, and his early work is virtually indistinguishable from that of his father. In the turbulent years after 1785, when the Dutch Republic found itself divided into royalist and republican camps, Langendijk gave his allegiance to the latter party, to which his chief patrons in Rotterdam also belonged. As a result, his drawings often exhibit an anti-English or pro-French bias. Langendijk's contemporaries attributed his taste for scenes of battle, shelling, and conflagrations to his impetuous and fiery nature, and the minute detail that informs many of his works to his shortsightedness. It remains a moot point whether it was due to this disability or to intoxication that he fell into the water and drowned in December 1805.

Many of Langendijk's drawings were translated into prints by such artists as Reinier Vinkeles, Joannes Bemme, Johannes C. Bendorp, Theodorus de Roode, Franciscus Sansom, and Cornelis Brouwer. In 1784, Matthias de Sallieth made an etching of his interpretation of Admiral de Ruyter's raid on Chatham, a military strike that resulted in the destruction or capture of part of the English fleet. That large history print confirmed Langendijk's reputation.

38 The Battle of the Pyramids, July 21, 1798
Pen in brown and watercolor
540 x 840 mm
Signed at lower right, in pen: *Dirk Langendijk delin et fecit 1803*
Inv. no. 1954:74

After capturing Alexandria on July 3, 1798, during his Egyptian campaign, Napoleon occupied the Nile delta. There he came up against the far larger army of the Mamelukes, the rulers of Egypt, commanded by Murad Bey. After only a few hours, however, it became clear that they were no match for the well-trained French troops. They were slaughtered by the thousands, or driven into the Nile and drowned. The news of Napoleon's victory unleashed such a wave of rapture in France that litle heed was paid to Nelson's devastating rout of the French fleet at the Battle of the Nile on August 1. Napoleon was fêted on his return to Paris a year later and was proclaimed First Consul.

Napoleon's Egyptian campaign was described and illustrated in a deluxe publication (1802) by Vivant Denon, who had accompanied the French army. The following year, the first part of the three-volume Dutch edition appeared, with the second and third volumes following in 1804 and 1805. Although the print of the *Battle of the Pyramids* in the French edition does not correspond to this watercolor (it was not included in the Dutch translation), that book may nevertheless have given Langendijk the idea for the various versions of the subject that he produced. In addition to one work on paper, of approximately the same size, in the collection of Princess Juliana of the Netherlands, there are five smaller watercolors by Langendijk in the Musées Royaux des Beaux-Arts in Brussels.

Here, too, Langendijk has tinkered with the facts in order to create a dramatic scene. The battle did not take place at the foot of the pyramids at all, but some fifteen kilometers away, and there were not five of them, as shown here, but three.

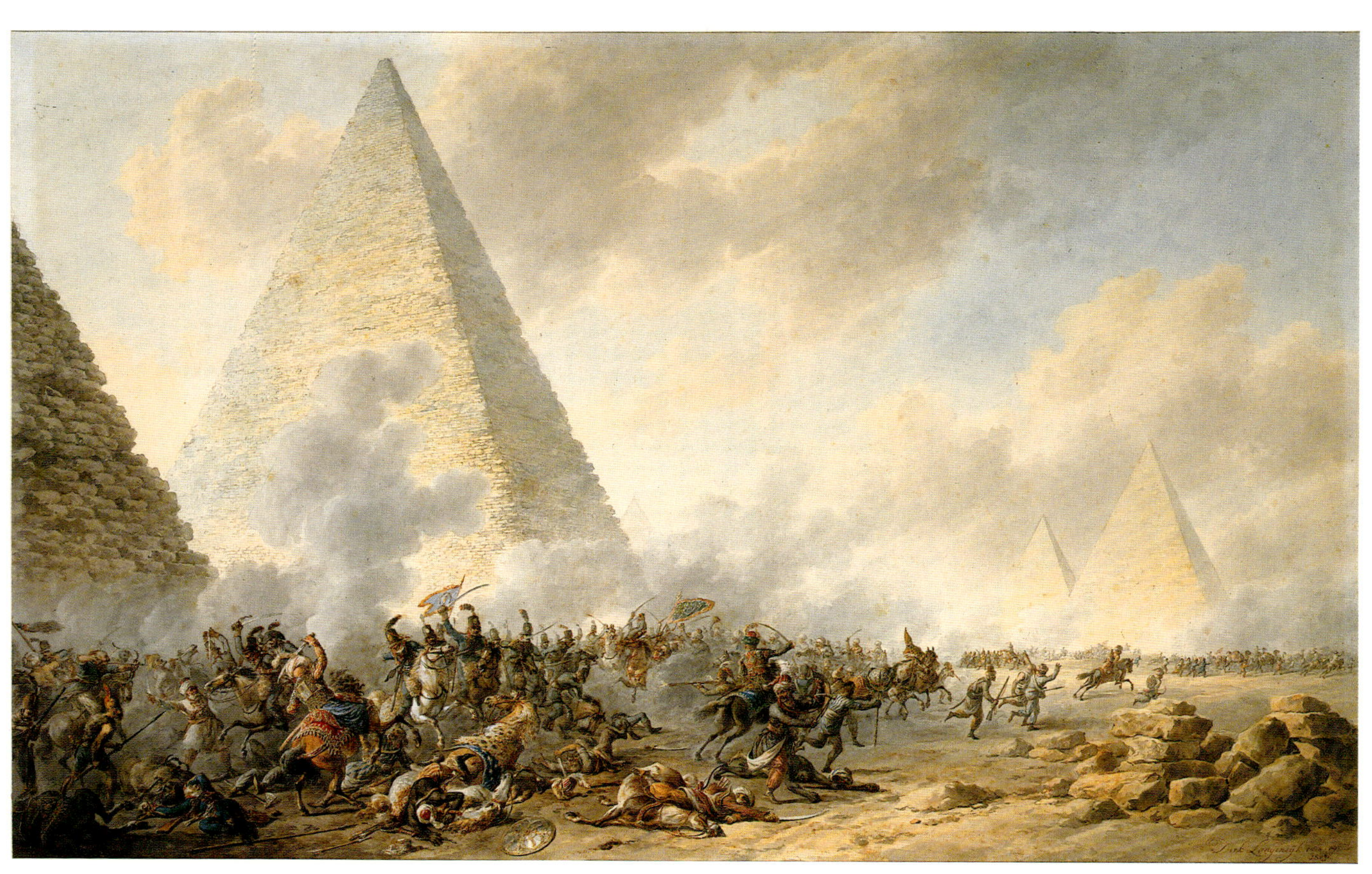

39 French Troops Capturing a City

Pen in brown, brush in watercolor; black border
244 x 343 mm
Signed at lower left, in pen: *Dirk Langendijk [. . .] 1801*
Inv. no. 1892 A 2619

When this watercolor was bequeathed to the Amsterdam Print Room almost one hundred years ago, it was described simply as "the taking of a city under shellfire." The burning church was later recognized as St. John's in Arnhem, and it was assumed that Langendijk had depicted the capture of that city by the French army in January 1795. He based his watercolor on a large drawing with gray washes that he had made that year (until recently in the collection of H. van Leeuwen in the Netherlands). The battle rages fiercely in both of those sheets, as it does in a third variant in the Teyler Museum in Haarlem. That watercolor, like this one, is dated 1801. There is every reason to believe, however, that Langendijk was allowing his imagination to run riot. The city of Arnhem capitulated after the French had fired only a few shells, and the scale of the devastation could not have approached that shown in this drawing. The church stood unscathed; when one of its towers was torn down in 1809, it was due to its dangerous state of dilapidation. It was followed by the razing of the rest of the structure in 1817.

Exactly the same situation applies to another drawing by Langendijk, yet this one depicts the capture of Bergen op Zoom in 1795. Fires burn out of control amid a shell-shattered church and houses in ruins. In reality, the townspeople had surrendered to the French without putting up the slightest resistance. Here again, Langendijk based his townscape on prints by other artists. For the scene in Bergen op Zoom, he used an engraving in an album titled *Vaderlandsche gezigten* (Views of the Fatherland; vol. 2, no. 348). His probable source for this particular view of the Church of St. John was Hendrick Spilman's etching in *Het verheerlijkt Nederland* (The Netherlands Glorified; vol. 1, 1745, no. 85). The etching on the next page of that book shows another of Arnhem's medieval churches, St. Walburga's, which Langendijk also incorporated into a battle scene in his series of forty-eight prints on warfare (now in the Teyler Museum). The unavoidable conclusion is that in each of these cases, the artist had little interest in a faithful account of a historical event. Instead, he used topographical prints to supply the setting as he embroidered on the truth to stir the viewer's emotions.

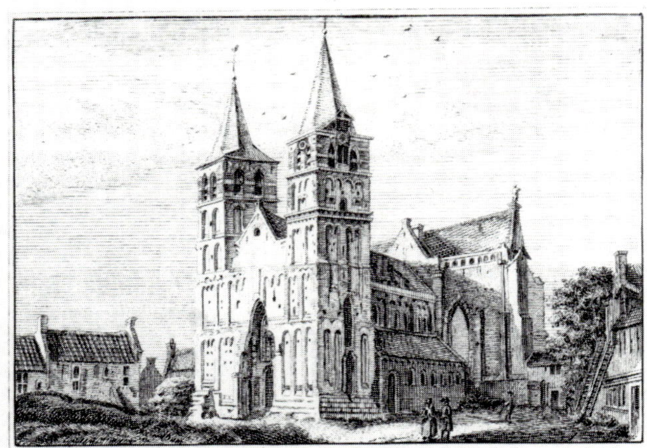

Hendrick Spilman, etching in Het verheerlijkt Nederland.

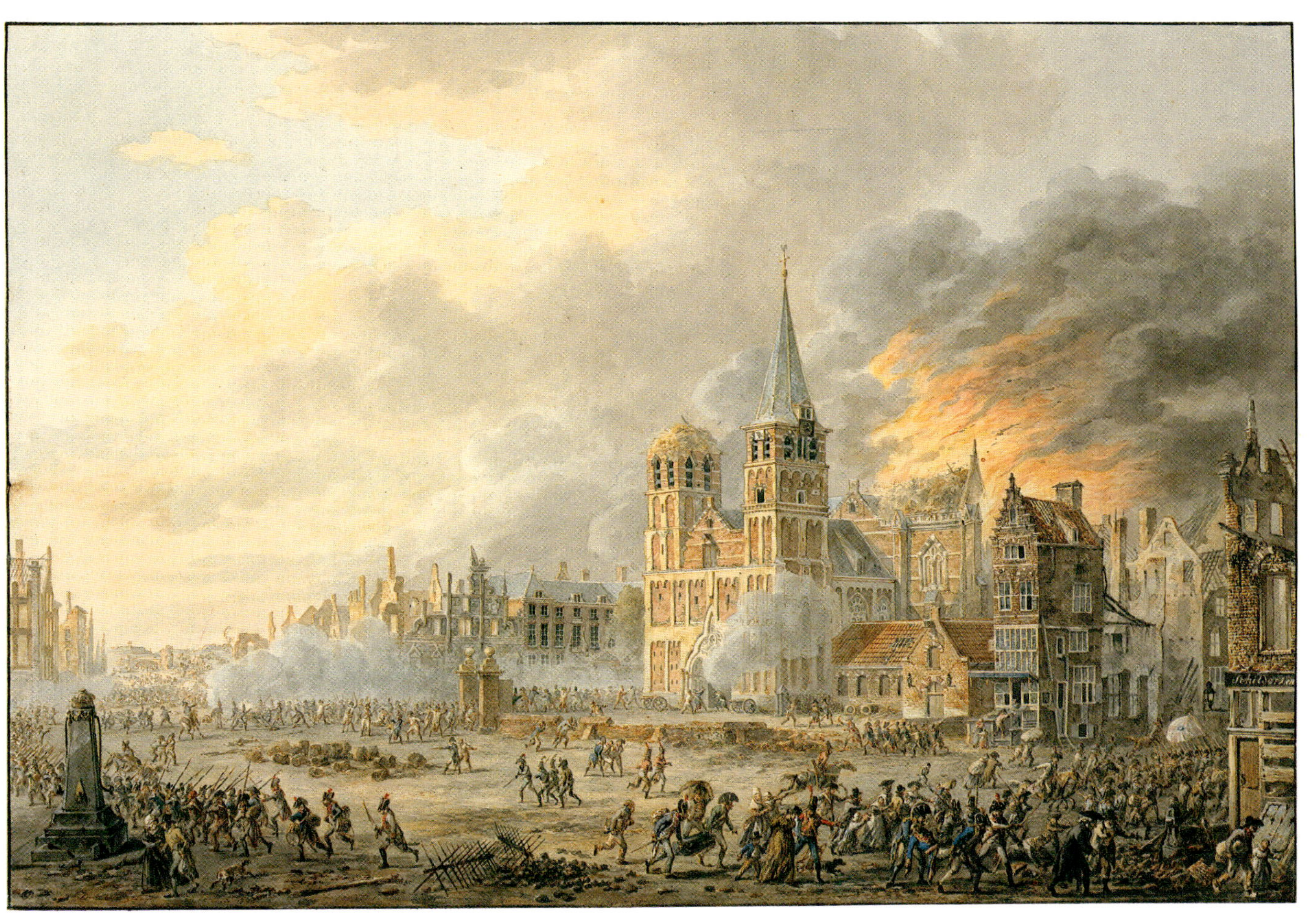

Willem Joseph Laquy (Brühl, near Cologne, 1738-1798 Cleves)

Painter and draftsman of genre scenes. In his native Germany, Willem Joseph Laquy studied as a pupil of a painter whose name he gave as "Bildieu" when he enrolled in the Amsterdam Drawing Academy in 1765. Nothing else is known of Bildieu. After completing that apprenticeship, Laquy traveled to Amsterdam, and then worked briefly in The Hague. In the 1760s, he was back in Amsterdam, where for many years he was attached to the flourishing wall-decoration studio run by Johannes Remmers and his son. There he became friendly with Wijbrand Hendriks (see cat. nos. 24-26), and he often painted the figures in Hendriks's landscapes. After a disagreement with his employer, who was delighted to have him as a painter but balked at the idea of having him as a son-in-law, Laquy established himself as an independent artist, and very soon he came under the patronage of the famous collector Gerrit Braamcamp (died 1771), who was probably a fellow Roman Catholic. In 1783, Laquy settled in Cleves, in Germany, where he married. He continued to sell his paintings and drawings in Amsterdam through a network of friends and acquaintances. In addition, he received commissions from the stadtholder's court, which was located at Nijmegen, in the east of the Republic from November 1786 to September 1787. Laquy also painted portraits, but it seems that he was not always able to capture a good likeness. He had more success with his interiors: some contain figures reminiscent of the old, seventeenth-century manner of Dou, De Hooch, and Metsu; others are populated with contemporary washerwomen and fishwives, or members of the upper classes playing checkers or chess, or making music. (Laquy was himself a first-rate violinist.) He was sometimes accused of not adhering to the truth due to his mixing of elements and fashions from different periods.

40 **Young Woman at Her Toilet**
Pen in brown, watercolor, and gouache; black border
363 x 276 mm
Signed on right, in pen: *W:Jos: / Laquij / 1771*
Inv. no. 1921:245

The prominent date confirms that Laquy, who lived and worked in various towns, executed this watercolor while he resided in Amsterdam. Elegant scenes such as this are relatively rare in eighteenth-century Dutch art. It has the look of a seventeenth-century composition that has been translated into a French Rococo idiom, in the manner of artists such as Lavreince and Freudeberger. This may relate to Laquy's apprenticeship to an artist with the French-sounding name of Beldieu or Bildieu.

This decorous scene actually possesses a strong, erotic undertone, due to Laquy's use of the same metaphors as those employed by his seventeenth-century forerunners Adriaen van de Venne, Jan Steen, and the Leiden *fijnschilders*: the open curtain around the bed, the lapdog, the candle, and the mules. The relief over the fireplace, with the goat barely being restrained by *amorini*, should clearly be interpreted as an "allusive accessory."

Broadly painted passages alternate with meticulous details that are occasionally executed in a hatching technique, a method that found little favor with the influential critic Adriaan van der Willigen in 1817.

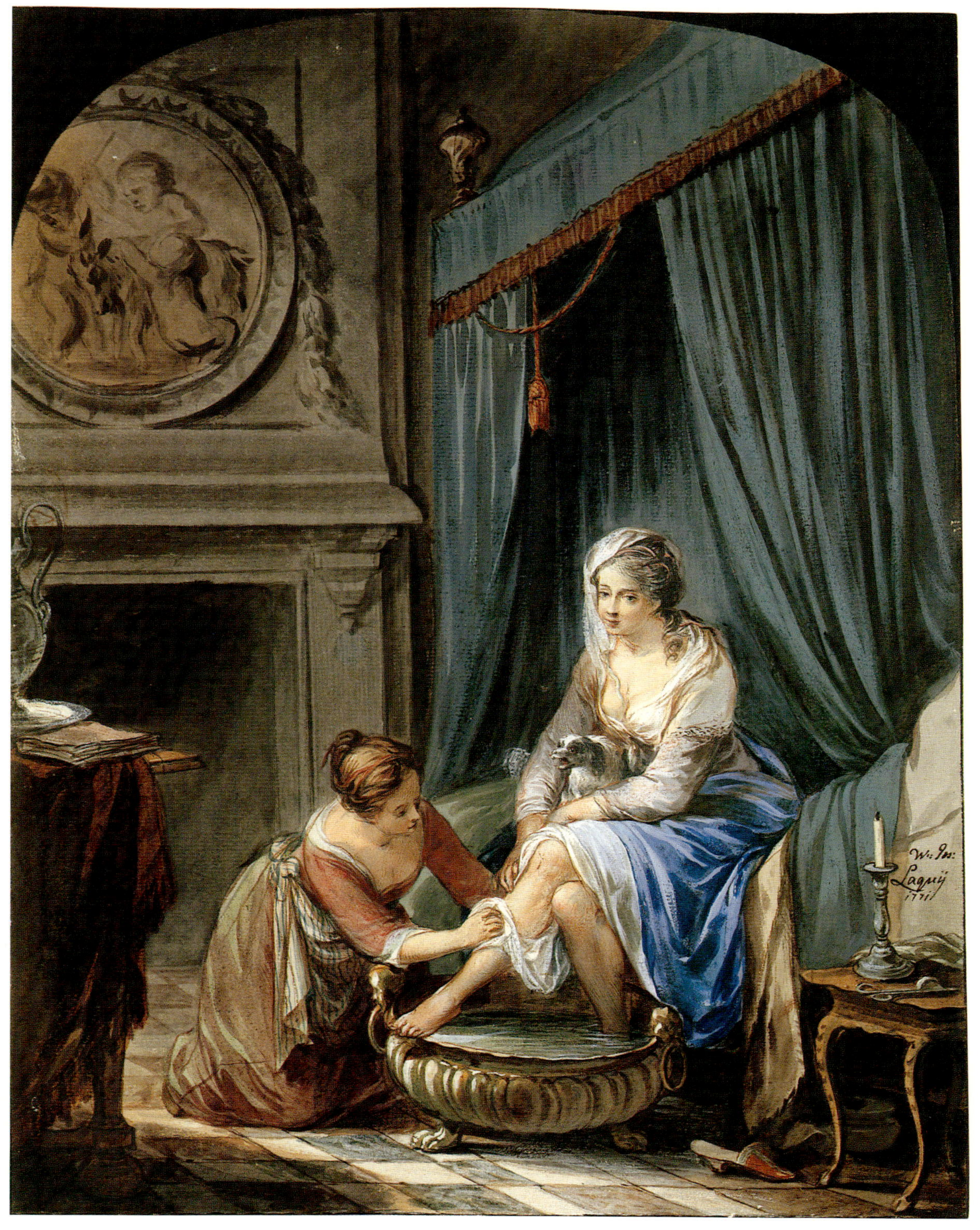
W: Jos:
Laquy
1771

Jacobus Johannes Lauwers (Bruges [Belgium] 1753-1800 Amsterdam)

A Flemish figure painter and draftsman who moved to Amsterdam around 1780 and married Maria de Frey, whose sister Ann and brother Johannes Pieter were also artists. Prior to this, Lauwers spent some time in Rome, where he and André de Muynck, an older artist from Bruges, were taught by Jean Baptiste Suvée, also a native of Bruges and later director of the Académie de France. While in Rome, Lauwers painted the portraits of several priests. It is believed that he and De Muynck left Italy in 1777 and that they lived for a while in Paris, although there is little substantive information about this period of Lauwers's life. In Holland he specialized mainly in genre scenes in the manner of Dou and other seventeenth-century masters, and he also made copies of their works. In addition, he painted the figures in monumental wall-hangings by Barbiers (see cat. nos. 6, 7). Shortly before his death, Lauwers restored a large number of paintings that were to be hung in a museum that was to be opened in Huis ten Bosch Palace in The Hague. Known as the National Art Gallery, this formed the nucleus of what is now the Rijksmuseum in Amsterdam.
The Rijksprentenkabinet has an elegant portrait drawing of the artist by Wijbrand Hendriks (see cat. nos. 24-26).

41 Drawing from the Live Model in an Old Building

Pencil, pen in brown, and watercolor; black border
450 x 525 mm
Signed at bottom, in pen: *J:Lauwers delin*
Inv. no. 1988:111

Several artists are drawing from a male nude, in the presence of two young women, in an impromptu studio set up in a building with a high, vaulted ceiling. The studio was evidently used for painting as well, judging by the presence of the palette laden with pigments and the two easels bearing stretched canvases, one painted with an image of a seated Bacchus.

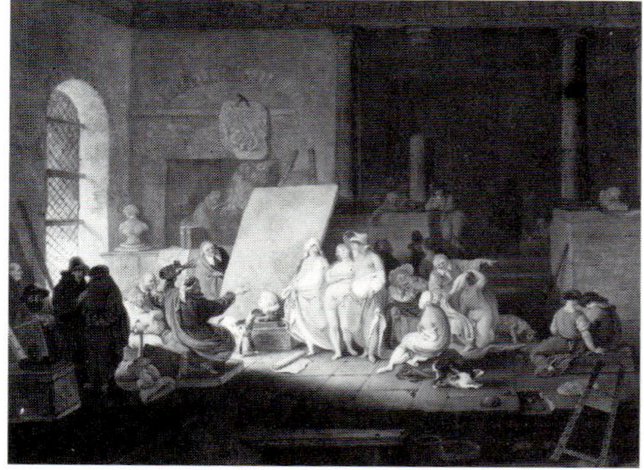

Jacques-Albert Senave, Parody of Zeuxis. Brussels, Musées Royaux des Beaux-Arts.

It is very unlikely that this depicts a real event, considering the archaic-looking figures in the background, the man sketching in the dark passage, the staged jumble of objects in the foreground, and above all, the two ladies in Greek dress who casually stroll near the nude man. It is an idealized scene that the artist probably drew in the 1790s, a time when he incorporated into his drawings memories of his years in Rome and Paris. The mid-ground observer seems to have been inspired by one of the merry cavaliers that appears in many portraits by Frans Hals. He is particularly reminiscent of *Man Holding a Branch*, a portrait that is now in Ottawa but was sold in Amsterdam in 1773 as part of the Van der Marck Collection as the supposed portrait of the painter Frans Post.
While the point of this scene is elusive, it can be no coincidence that Jacques-Albert Senave, Lauwers's compatriot, contemporary, and fellow-pupil with Suvée, produced two paintings of studios, one of which bears a remarkably close resemblance to this imaginary setting. That work is titled *Parody of Zeuxis*, while its companion allegorizes the saying *Ne sutor ultra crepidam* (Let the cobbler stick to his last).

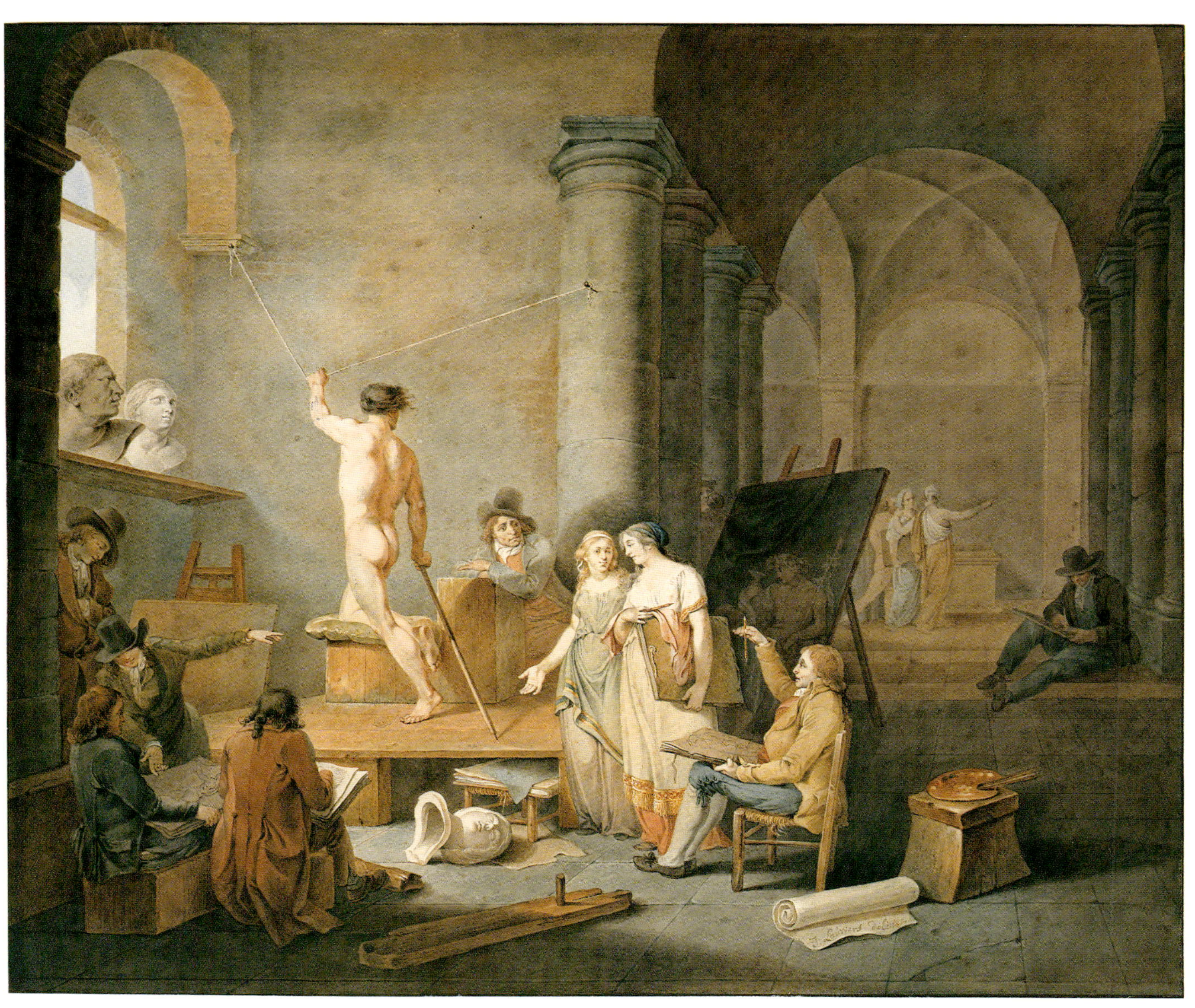

Willem van Leen (Dordrecht 1753-1825 Delfshaven)

A still-life painter and draftsman. As the son of the studio director and art dealer Jan van Leen, Willem received his first training from local artists. He then left for Paris, where he studied with his compatriot Gerard van Spaendonck, who, as the court painter of miniatures, had apartments in the Louvre. After three years Van Leen returned to Holland, but he was back in Paris in 1788-89. Driven out by the French Revolution, he settled in the township of Delfshaven, not far from Rotterdam. There, in 1801 and 1804, he published a series of six outline etchings that were watercolored by his Coebergh nieces, who lived in his house. With the exception of a few months in Paris in 1808, he spent the rest of his life in Delfshaven. Van Leen's watercolors of flowers, fruit, and birds continue a form of art that had been brought to a pitch of perfection by Van Spaendonck, Van Huysum, and Schouman. Like Van Spaendonck, Van Leen was forced to realize that as the nineteenth century advanced, demand declined for elegant, baroque heaps of roses, lilac blossoms, honeysuckle, and lilies. Around 1812 his health failed, but he nevertheless zealously continued drawing fresh blooms that were sent to him.

Van Leen was also a noted art dealer. In that capacity, the king of Holland sent him to Antwerp and Malines in 1808 in search of possible purchases for the newly founded museum in Amsterdam, the forerunner of the present-day Rijksmuseum.

42 Study of Vine Leaves

Pencil and watercolor; border in pencil
441 x 324 mm
Signed at lower right, in pen: *Willem van Leen. Del.1796.*
Inv. no. 1976:68

This large, decorative sheet should not be regarded as a study for the artist's own use, but as a finished work, legibly signed and dated, and intended for sale. When he drew it, Van Leen had just moved to Delfshaven after his return from Paris, where he had made a successful career for himself. It is not clear whether these are six different vine leaves or just a few drawn from different angles.

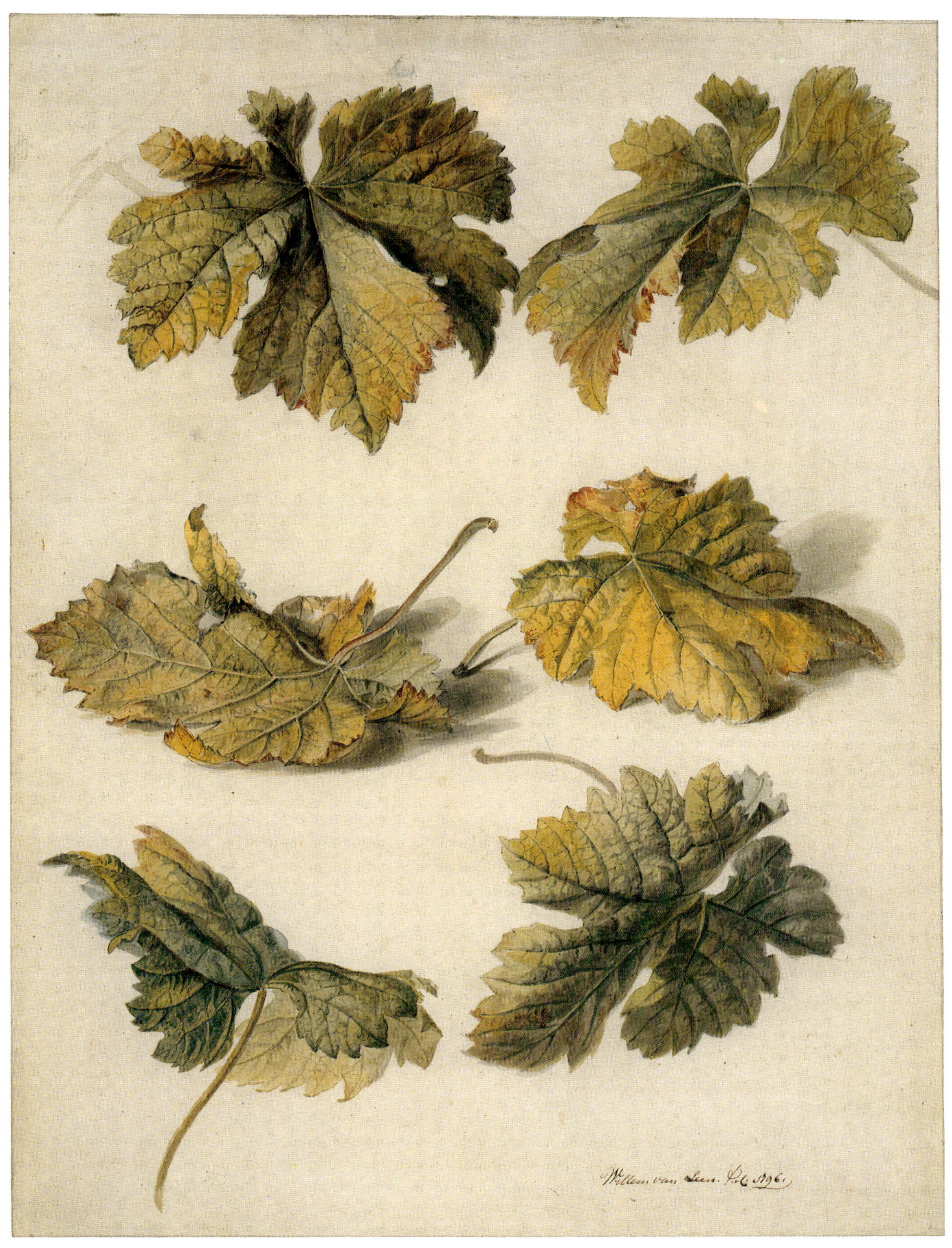

Paulus van Liender (Utrecht 1731-1797 Utrecht)

Draftsman and etcher of town and village scenes. Paulus van Liender and his elder brother, Pieter Jan (1727-1779), learned the basics of their craft from their uncle, Jacob van Liender (1696-1750), an Utrecht physician, amateur draftsman, and art collector. Paulus decided on a career in art, and accordingly moved to Amsterdam, where he was trained further by the draftsman Cornelis Pronk (see cat. nos. 52-54). It was possibly through Pronk that Van Liender was introduced to Jan de Beijer (see cat. nos. 8-10), who became his friend and traveling companion. Between 1758 and 1762, Van Liender produced more than one hundred small etchings after topographical views by De Beijer for the multipart Kleefsche outheden en gezichten (Antiquities and Views of Cleves), which was renamed Gezichten van Cleefsch-land (Views of the Land of Cleves) from volume 3 and reissued in 1785 as Het verheerlijkt Kleefschland (The Land of Cleves Glorified). He also made prints of some of De Beijer's Amsterdam townscapes.

In the 1760s, Van Liender moved to Haarlem, where in January 1765 he and Cornelis Ploos van Amstel bought a sawmill and lumberyard, of which the artist became sole owner three years later. He was also appointed receiver of the excise duties on wine. Van Liender did not, however, allow his business ventures to interfere with his art. In 1772 he became one of the overseers of the Haarlem Drawing Academy, of which he was also treasurer, and in 1774 he was appointed to the important post of "poser of the model." He taught Hermanus Petrus Schouten (see cat. no. 61), Jacob Elias van Varelen (1757-1840), and Franciscus Andreas Milatz (1764-1840). Towards the end of his life Van Liender returned to Utrecht, where he died a bachelor.

Drawings by Van Liender show the influence of both Pronk and De Beijer. His most original contribution to the art of drawing in eighteenth-century Holland was provided by his fanciful woodland scenes, which are washed with the brush and offer sharp contrasts of white and black.

43 View in the Town of Montfoort

Pen in gray and brown, and watercolor; double border in gray (the wash frame that Van Liender applied around drawings of this type has been trimmed off)
206 x 262 mm
On verso, signed in pen: *Paul v: Liender fec: 1775*; and also in pen: *Montfoort*
Inv. no. 1882 A 1652

After a study trip to Paris, which he undertook when he was already well into his forties, Van Liender returned to the work at which he was so expert: making drawings of towns, villages, and castles in the central regions of the Netherlands. Montfoort, in Utrecht province, was a small, medieval borough that had seen better days. From left to right are the town's principal church, which was dedicated to St. John, the town hall with its monumental staircase, and a complex that was founded in 1544 as the Commandery of the Knights Hospitalers. By Van Liender's day, its grand function had long ceased, and the chapel (the section towering over its neighbors in the watercolor) now housed a corn chandler. The signboard on the next building announces that it is the home of a surgeon.

This drawing illustrates one aspect of Paulus van Liender's oeuvre: a peaceful, sunlit view executed with a pointed brush in delicate, light shades of color. The majestic tree presages his later specialty of fanciful woodland scenes, generally built up of gray tones, that are filled with gnarled tree trunks and dense foliage, of which the Amsterdam Print Room has a fine example. With this genre Van Liender foreshadowed the nineteenth-century Romanticism of Barend Cornelis Koekkoek.

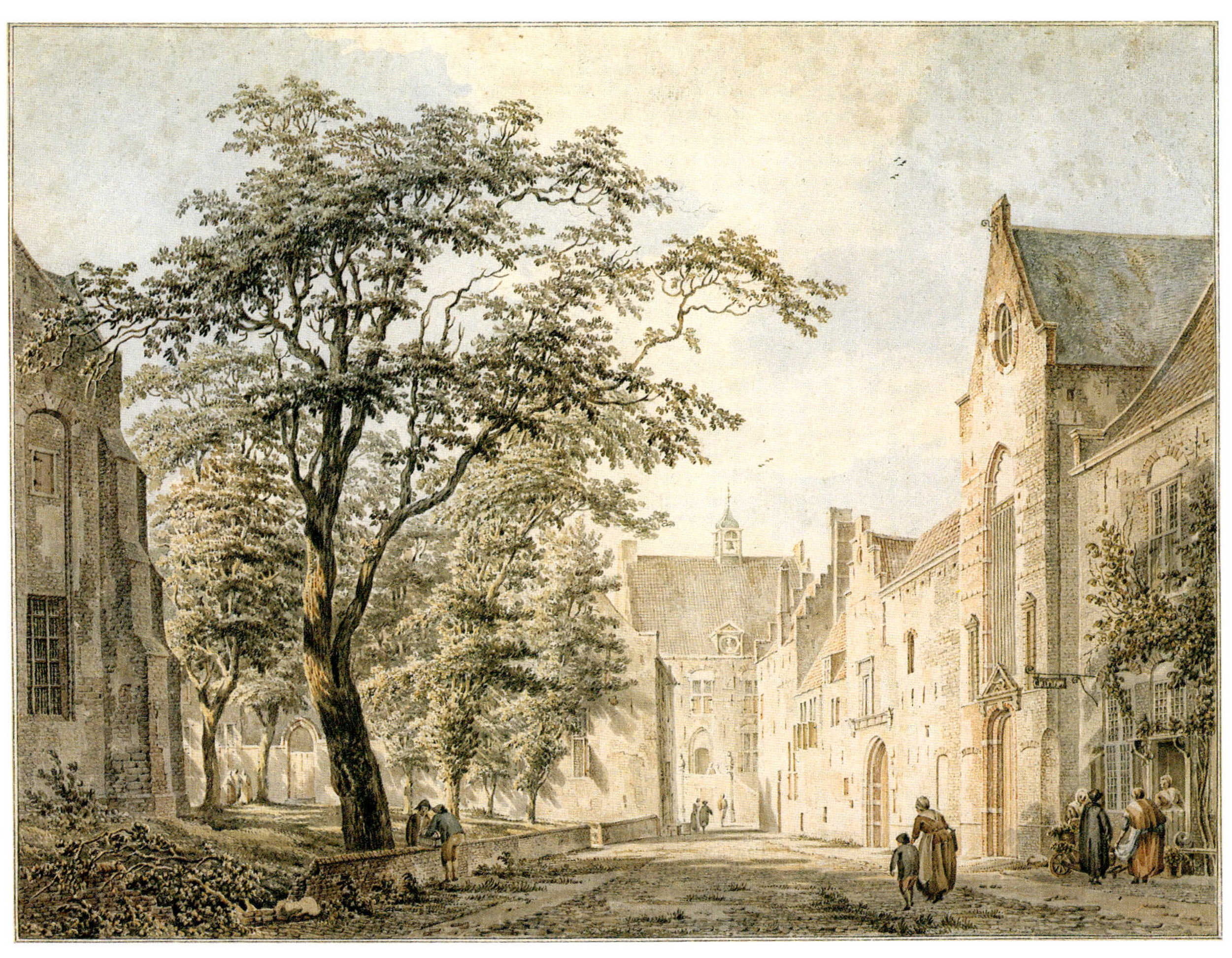

Initially a painter, but later an etcher and above all a draftsman of figured landscapes. At the age of twenty, Hendrik Meyer began studying at the Drawing Academy in Amsterdam, where he remained for four years. On his enrollment he gave the name of his first master as David Coenraadts, who is now completely unknown. After leaving the Academy in September 1768, Meyer moved to Haarlem, where he set up a wall-decoration shop and became a member of the board of the local drawing academy. At some time, probably around 1774, he and his contemporary, the Haarlem artist Wijbrand Hendriks (see cat. nos. 24-26) made a trip to England.
On his return, Meyer lived in various towns, including Leiden, where he enrolled in the university in April 1775, and painted a series of wall-hangings in or shortly after 1776 (now in the city's Lakenhal Museum). Three years later, in 1779, he was still in Leiden, but he then left for London, where he worked with Timothy Sheldrake on a series of twelve landscapes in etching and aquatint that were intended as drawing models. In contrast to the images in that print series, which are very vigorous and unfettered in style, Meyer's drawn work is fairly conventional and often extremely detailed. His weakness for theatrical effects, however, manifested itself in his love of paraphrasing sixteenth-century architectural forms in his buildings.

44 Harvest near a Village in a Hilly Landscape
Pen in brown, gouache, reinforced in parts with tempera or gum; broad black border
435 x 545 mm
Dated on tree trunk at right, in pen: *1767*
Inv. no. 1968:93

It is remarkable that Hendrik Meyer executed this microscopically fine-brushed landscape at a time when he was mainly working as a painter of wall-hangings – a branch of art that often seduced its practitioners into the loosest of touches. Only in the beautiful and painterly cloud formations did the artist allow his brush to flow across the paper. Meyer was twenty-three years old at the time. Through highly detailed, densely populated landscapes such as this, rendered in opaque watercolor, Meyer perpetuated an old tradition that had been kept alive by Gerrit Battem (ca. 1636-1684) and Dirk Dalens the Younger (1658/59-1688) and was then continued by Abraham Rademaker (1675-1735), Louis Chalon (1687?-1741), and Willem Troost (1684-1752). Chalon and Troost were, respectively, the stepfather-in-law and uncle of the famous Cornelis Troost, who himself executed many works in gouache.
As seen with Jacob Cats (cat. nos. 13-16), it is possible that this harvest scene represented autumn in a series documenting the four seasons. The lack of a signature may also indicate that it had a signed pendant. The work known as *Village in Winter*, which is almost the same size and does bear Meyer's signature, would have made a fitting companion piece from a compositional point of view. That gouache appeared several times at auction in the 1970s, but its location is now unfortunately unknown.

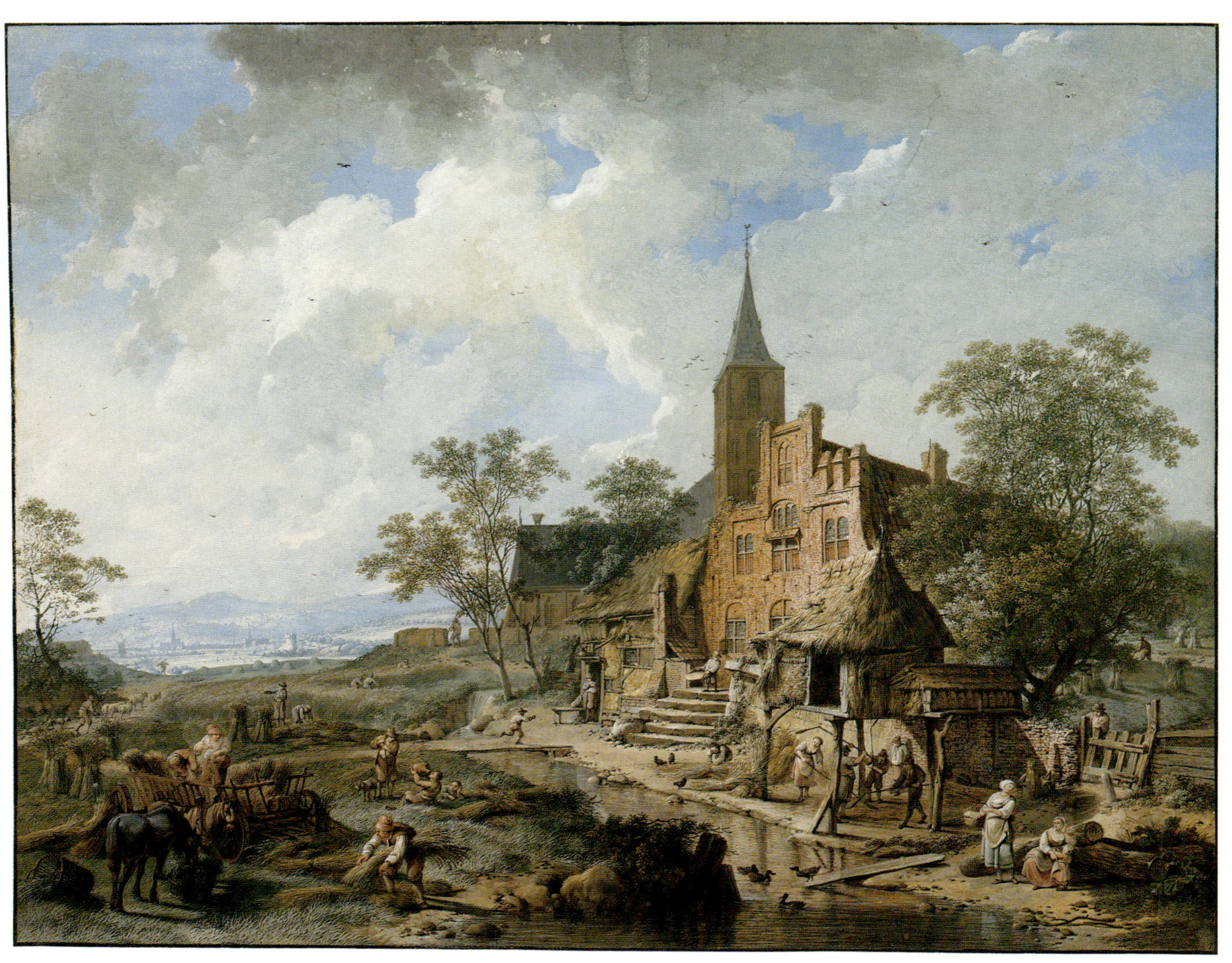

Isaac de Moucheron (Amsterdam 1670-1744 Amsterdam)

A versatile painter, draftsman, and etcher of vedute and courtly classicist landscapes; he was also active as an architect and landscape designer. Descended from a distinguished Norman family, Isaac de Moucheron was christened after his maternal grandfather, Isaac de Jouderville (1613-between 1645 and 1648), who was a pupil of Rembrandt. Isaac received his first introduction to art from his father, the landscapist Frederik de Moucheron (1633-1686), who died when Isaac was sixteen. From then on he was self-taught.

In 1695 de Moucheron traveled by way of Bologna to Rome, where his skillful compositions earned him the nickname Ordonnantie ("the Arranger"). He was back in Amsterdam by August 1697, where he was immediately inundated with commissions. In 1700 he joined forces with Daniël Marot (1663-1752) to decorate the main staircase in Voorst Castle. He also collaborated with other artists, among them Jacob de Wit (see cat. nos. 70-72) and Nicolaas Verkolje (1673-1746), and he befriended the much younger Cornelis Ploos van Amstel (1724-1798). De Moucheron was so highly rated as a colorist that many collectors asked him to add color to their seventeenth-century drawings.

Architecture plays a vital role in De Moucheron's entire oeuvre, and in this, too, he was an autodidact. He should be regarded as an exponent of an international classicism, an artist who practiced the "grand style" in the Franco-Italian mode.

45 Villa d'Este, Tivoli

Pencil, pen in brown, and watercolor; brown border
228 x 341 mm
Signed at bottom, in pen: *IMoucheron.Fecit* [I and M interlaced]
Inv. no. 1898 A 3571

The Villa d'Este, built between 1550 and 1570 as a country seat for Cardinal Ippolito d'Este, was (and still is) one of the most popular tourist attractions of Tivoli, located not far from Rome. When De Moucheron was working in Rome around 1695, he must have visited the little town many times. On one of those occasions he made the sketch that later formed the basis for this idealized *vedute*.

The main subject is not so much the villa itself as it is the majestic Dragon Fountain (Fontana dei Draghi) that stands on a terrace on one of the axes radiating from the main building. He allowed himself considerable license, particularly in the vegetation, which was by no means so luxuriant and asymmetrical at the time. The elegant figures and the hunting dogs, together with the wind-tossed branches, heavy with leaf, and the *repoussoir* trees, lend the scene a festive grandeur.

The grayish blue green tonality of this watercolor is borne by an extensive framework done in pen and ink. Another drawing by De Moucheron in the Rijksprentenkabinet, also of a subject from Tivoli, the Rocca Pia Fort (inv. no. 1948:121), was executed throughout in this finely detailed penwork. It serves as testimony to the artist's mastery of this technique.

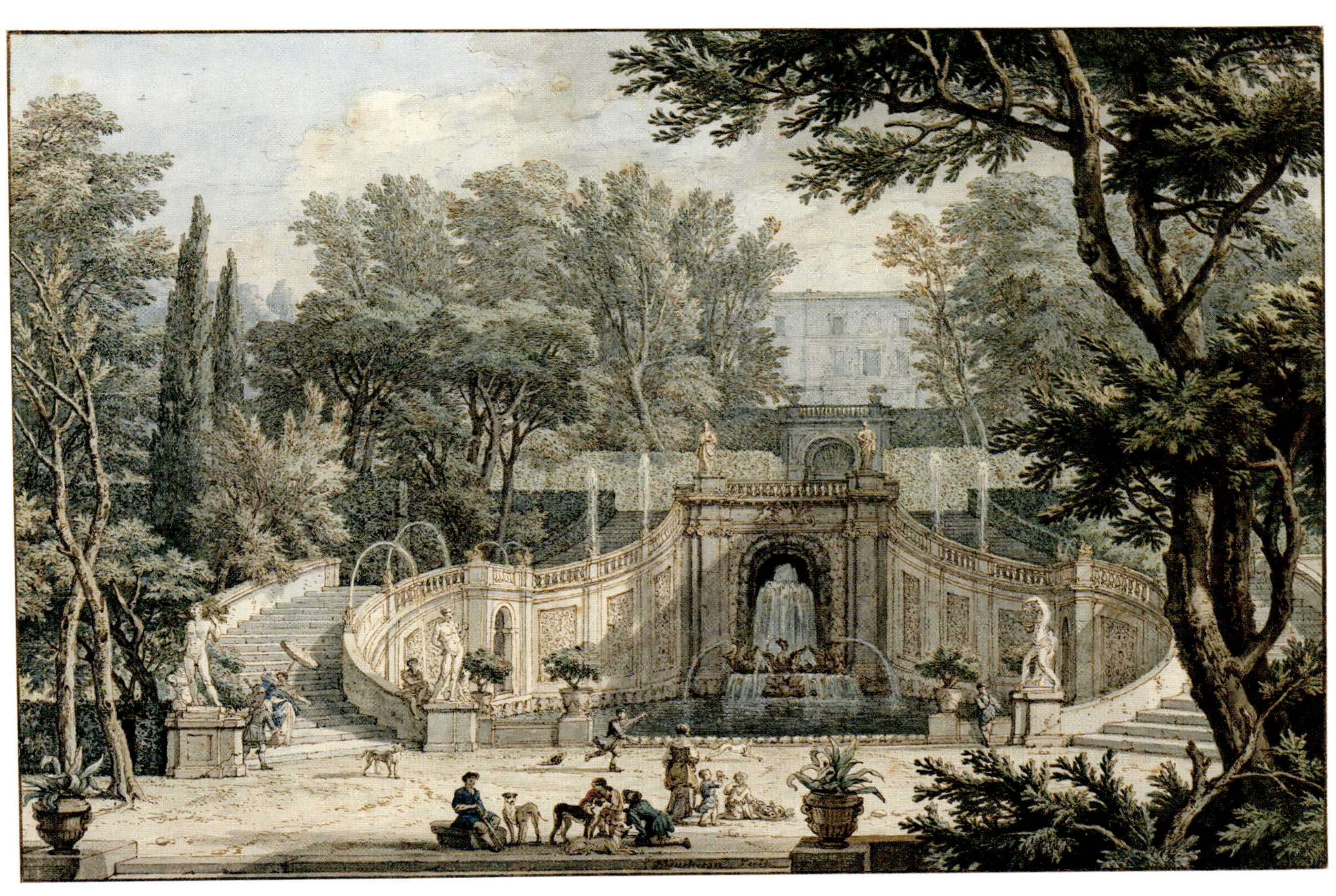

A draftsman, pastelist, and graphic artist who left a varied oeuvre. His first teacher was Frans Decker, and when he died in 1751, Cornelis van Noorde continued his studies with Taco Hayo Jelgersma (1702-1795), who had also been a pupil of Decker. In the meantime, Van Noorde produced ornaments, illustrations, decorated initials, and other items for the now world-famous printing works and type foundry that belonged to Johannes Enschedé, with whom he later became close friends. In 1761 Van Noorde became a member of the artists' Guild of St. Luke, and in 1772 he helped found the Haarlem Drawing Academy. His own death spared him from witnessing its closure in November 1795.
For the collectors in his home town, Van Noorde drew dozens of portraits of artists in the style of Taco Jelgersma. In addition, he was the acknowledged topographer of Haarlem and its surroundings, although he also recorded views in the north, east, and central regions of the country while on a journey in 1751. One of his sketchbooks from that tour is in the Haarlem Municipal Archives.
Van Noorde's watercolor copies of seventeenth-century paintings are particularly notable and have been regarded as his finest work. He was also an excellent graphic artist, producing etchings, woodcuts, and a few mezzotints. Among his most attractive are those prints executed in the crayon manner, in which he succeeded in capturing the effect of a drawing.

46 Frozen Canal with Skaters

Pen in gray and brush in watercolor; gray border (doubled at bottom, with a broad, brown wash frame around it)
173 x 241 mm
Signed at lower left, in pen: *C:V:Noorde.inv:1769.*
Inv. no. 1921:74

Although Van Noorde was primarily a topographical draftsman who repeatedly depicted the canals of his native Haarlem, in both summer and winter, this scene is an imaginary one. The *inv*[enit] after the signature indicates that the composition was not done from life (*ad vivum*), but emanated from his own invention. This is not to say, however, that this view does not resemble the city of Haarlem on the River Spaarne. The bridge with the low building on the left, for instance, is very reminiscent of the area near Eendjespoort (officially known as Leiden Gate) as it appeared in the eighteenth century.
This ice scene, with its ashen, snow-laden skies, has a light tonality, with few pronounced touches of color. The depiction of snow on the roofs, the foreground, and the tree was achieved simply by leaving the white paper blank.

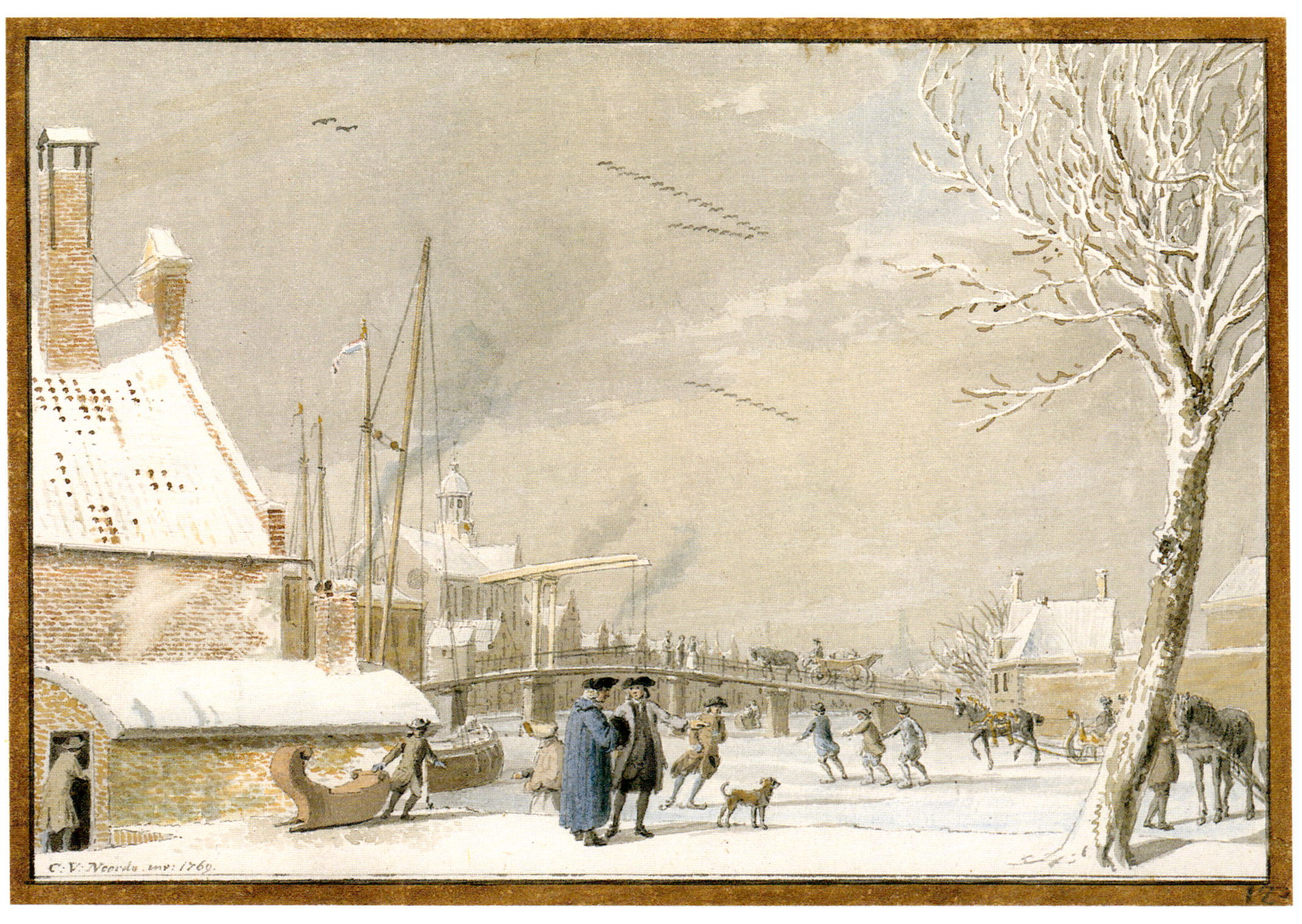
C: V: Noorde. inv: 1769.

Painter, draftsman, and etcher of landscapes and, to a lesser extent, of portraits. Hermanus Numan grew up in the northern city of Groningen, where his family ran a flourishing shop that produced lacquered and painted tinware. There he practiced decorative painting under the supervision of Johannes Franciscus Francé, until he was apprenticed in Haarlem to Jan Augustini (1725-1773), a specialist in wall-hangings who was also from Groningen. Numan was accompanied by Egbert van Drielst (see cat. nos. 17, 18), another native of the city. After four years Numan returned home and began working on commissions, mainly for portraits. To round off his studies, he went to Paris, in either 1768 or 1769, through financial support from the famous Petrus Camper, then a professor in Groningen. In the French capital he was taken under the wing of Hallé, and after several meetings with Jacques-Philippe Le Bas (1707-1783) he mastered the art of graphics.

In 1771, Numan returned to Groningen briefly before he settled in Amsterdam, where he enrolled in the Drawing Academy on October 2. During his Amsterdam period, Numan painted portraits, worked with Jurriaan Andriessen (see cat. nos. 1-5) on stage sets for the new Playhouse (the old one had burned down in 1772), and gave drawing lessons to distinguished amateurs. The topographical draftsman Jan Bulthuis (1750-1801), of Groningen, also regarded him as his teacher.

Numan was unquestionably one of the most accomplished watercolorists of his day. His palette is warm and mellow. He made his name as an etcher in 1797 with a series of twenty-four views of country seats, which he etched with fluent outlines that he then filled in with watercolor. The artist proved himself to be an innovator in topographical illustration by depicting modern country houses with gardens laid out in the English-landscape style.

47 View of Zandbergen House (Utrecht Province)

Pencil, pen in gray, brown, and black, and watercolor; black border
470 x 600 mm
On verso, inscribed at lower right, in a nineteenth-century hand: *H.Numan / Collectie* (Collection) *van der Dussen van Beeftingh / Verkooping* (Sale) *Rotterdam 29 / 30 Mei* (May) *1876 / n° 304 v.d. Catalogus* (in the catalogue)
Inv. no. 1951:173

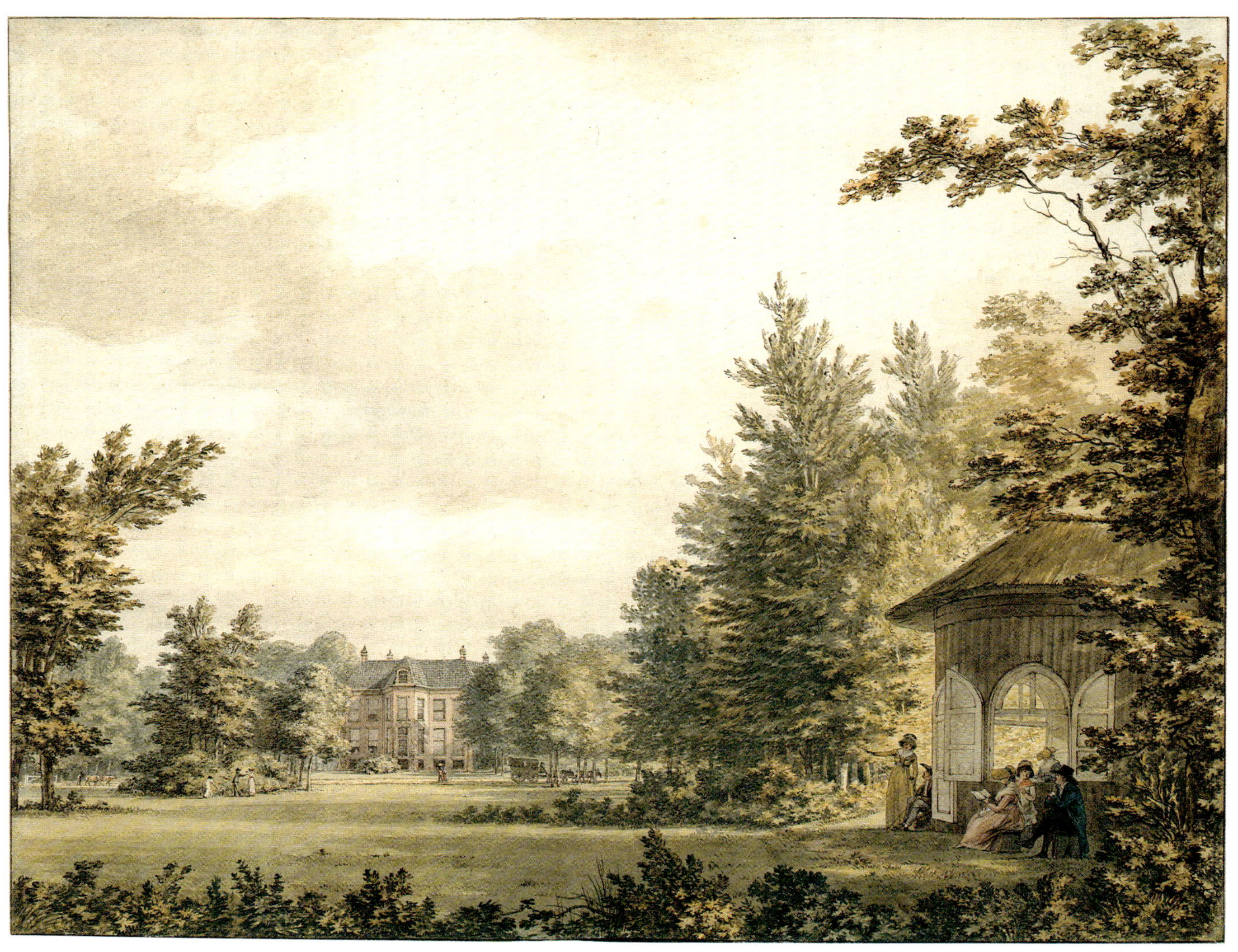

48 In Zandbergen Park

Pencil, pen in gray, brown, and black, and watercolor; black border
473 x 600 mm
On verso, inscribed at lower right, in a nineteenth-century hand: *H.Numan / Collectie* (Collection) *van der Dussen van Beeftingh / Verkooping* (Sale) *Rotterdam 29 / 30 Mei* (May) *1876 / n° 304 v.d. Catalogus* (in the catalogue)
Inv. no. 1951:174

Dating around 1800, these two interpretations of an idyllic form of country life may have been commissioned by the new owner of Zandbergen House, the Amsterdam merchant Willem Ebeling (1762-1802), who had bought the property from Laurens Johannes Nepveu on February 1, 1799. Ebeling's only son died there precisely fifty years later. The house had been built in 1654 by Jasper Schade van Westrum, who was immortalized in a famous portrait by Frans Hals that is now one of the treasures of the National Museum in Prague.

The first watercolor (cat. no. 47) shows the front of the house seen from the far garden, which was separated from the main residence by a sandy track, on which a covered carriage travels and a countryman drives his cattle. This is now a busy main road, the Amersfoortse Straatweg, that links Amersfoort with Utrecht and De Bilt. The road is still overlooked by Zandbergen House, located near the village of Huis ter Heide. The appearance of the house has changed very little, and it now belongs to the Seventh Day Adventists.

The pendant image (cat. no. 48) shows a leafy avenue in the park. The foliage of the trees, however, is a little amorphous and undifferentiated. Coincidentally, a poem from this very period speaks of Zandbergen's fir woods and endless avenues of beeches.

On the left a draftsman, perhaps Numan himself, is at work. Around 1800 he spent a great deal of time on country estates in the provinces of Holland and Utrecht. In 1792 he made two watercolors of Sparrendaal, not far from Zandbergen. (Those works are now in Leiden Print Room.) Between 1793 and 1797 he drew a series of views of country mansions, which he published in 1797 under the title *Vier-en-twintig printtekeningen* (Twenty-Four Print Drawings). It is possible that Numan also gave drawing lessons at some of these houses. This is suggested by a drawing, now is a private collection, of a young girl and an old woman sitting in a room by a window, which is inscribed *A.Ebeling naar* (after) *H.Numan 1806*. The draftsman was probably Antonie Ebeling, the son of Zandbergen's owner.

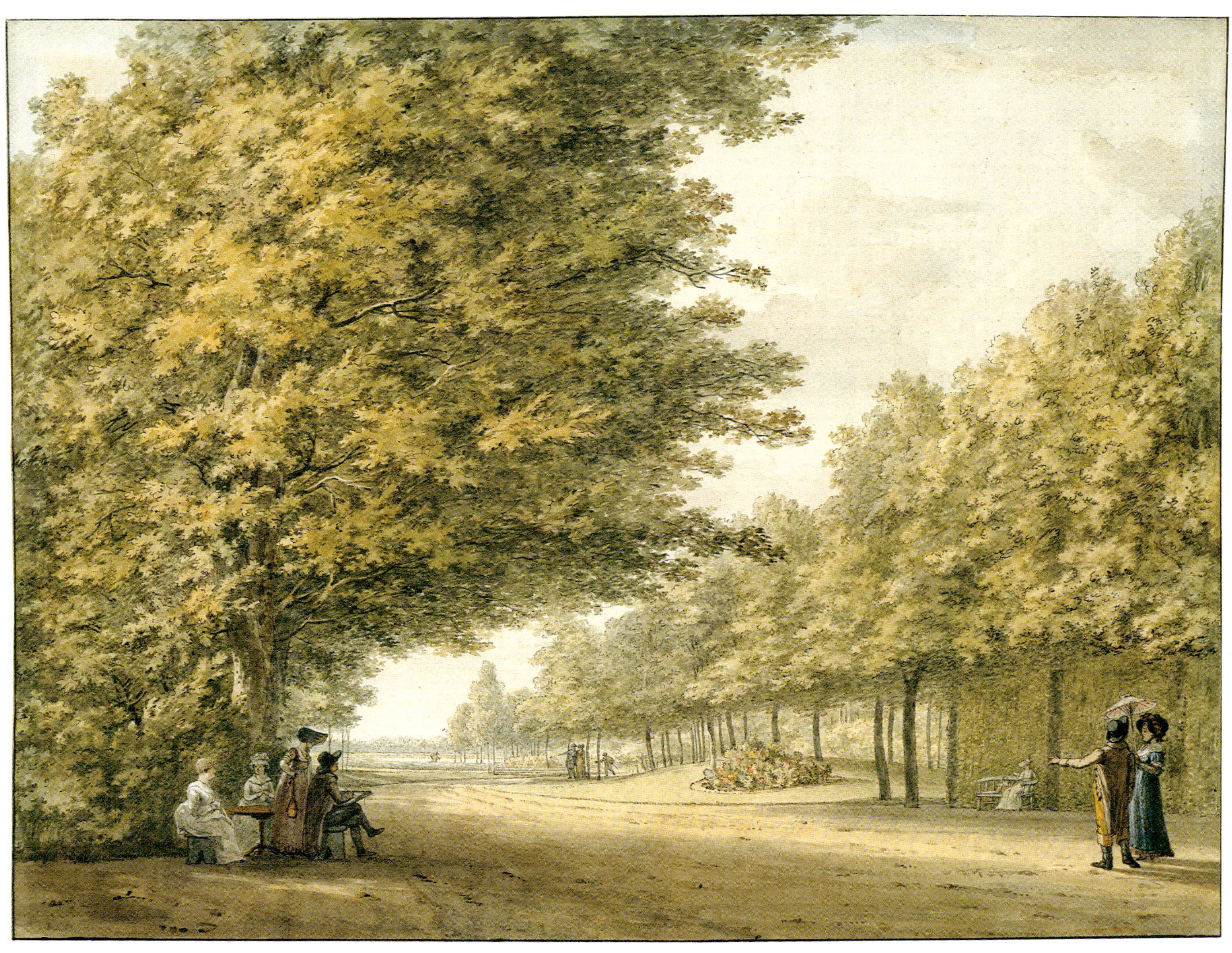

Elias van Nijmegen (Nijmegen 1667-1755 Rotterdam)

Painter of interior decorations and history pictures. Born in the city from which his family took its name, Elias van Nijmegen was one of the sons of a house and marbling painter. He was first taught by his father, who died at an early age, and then by his brothers, Gideon and Tobias. After having worked in various parts of the Netherlands for a few years, during which time he grew out of his craft-like background and became a more creative artist, Elias settled in Rotterdam. There he received many commissions and established a large workshop for painted interior decorations, which employed not only his sons but also three assistants and numerous pupils. Examining this studio's estate lends insight into the day-to-day operation of this once-famous workshop, and in some cases it has made it possible to identify dispersed history paintings as being the work of Elias or his son Dionys.

Van Nijmegen produced his drawings as an integral part of his business, for they served as designs for the many ceilings, overdoors, overmantels, and wall panels that were supplied by his studio. They do not stand as independent drawings, like those made by his grandson Gerard (see cat. no. 50). Pressure of work sometimes made him hasty, which, in turn, bred a certain superficiality. The shop, which was taken over by Elias's son Dionys in 1750, readily absorbed outside influences – Elias from Daniël Marot, and Dionys from Jacob de Wit. Few complete room or salon decorations by Elias van Nijmegen have survived, but some 250 drawn and often watercolored designs by father and son do exist and were purchased by the Amsterdam Print Room in 1969.

49 Design for a Painted Ceiling

Pencil, pen in brown, and watercolor; double brown border
340 x 440 mm
Signed at lower right, in pen: *E.V:Nijmegen*
Inv. no. 1968:152

This design for an illusionistic ceiling painting derives heavily from the example of Daniël Marot. The complex structure of a mock opening in the ceiling, which is surmounted by an open dome that is itself held up by narrow spandrels, is found in a series of prints by Marot that was published in Paris and also received a printing license in Holland in 1687. Van Nijmegen modified Marot's model by inserting a semicircular segment in the short sides of the massive frame that supports the extremely foreshortened balustrade, and by adding four different corner designs. Two of the medallions contain personifications of Fame and Abundance, each with an appropriate attribut of trumpet or cornucopia. The figures in the other two medallions are too sketchy to identify. In the large, central oval, Aurora (the dawn) brings light to banish the darkness. Depictions of Geography and Astronomy flank the central image. Space has been reserved for a rectangular chimney on the right short side. It has sometimes been possible to determine the buildings for which decorative designs in the Amsterdam Print Room were made, but unfortunately, that is not the case with this watercolor of a ceiling decoration.

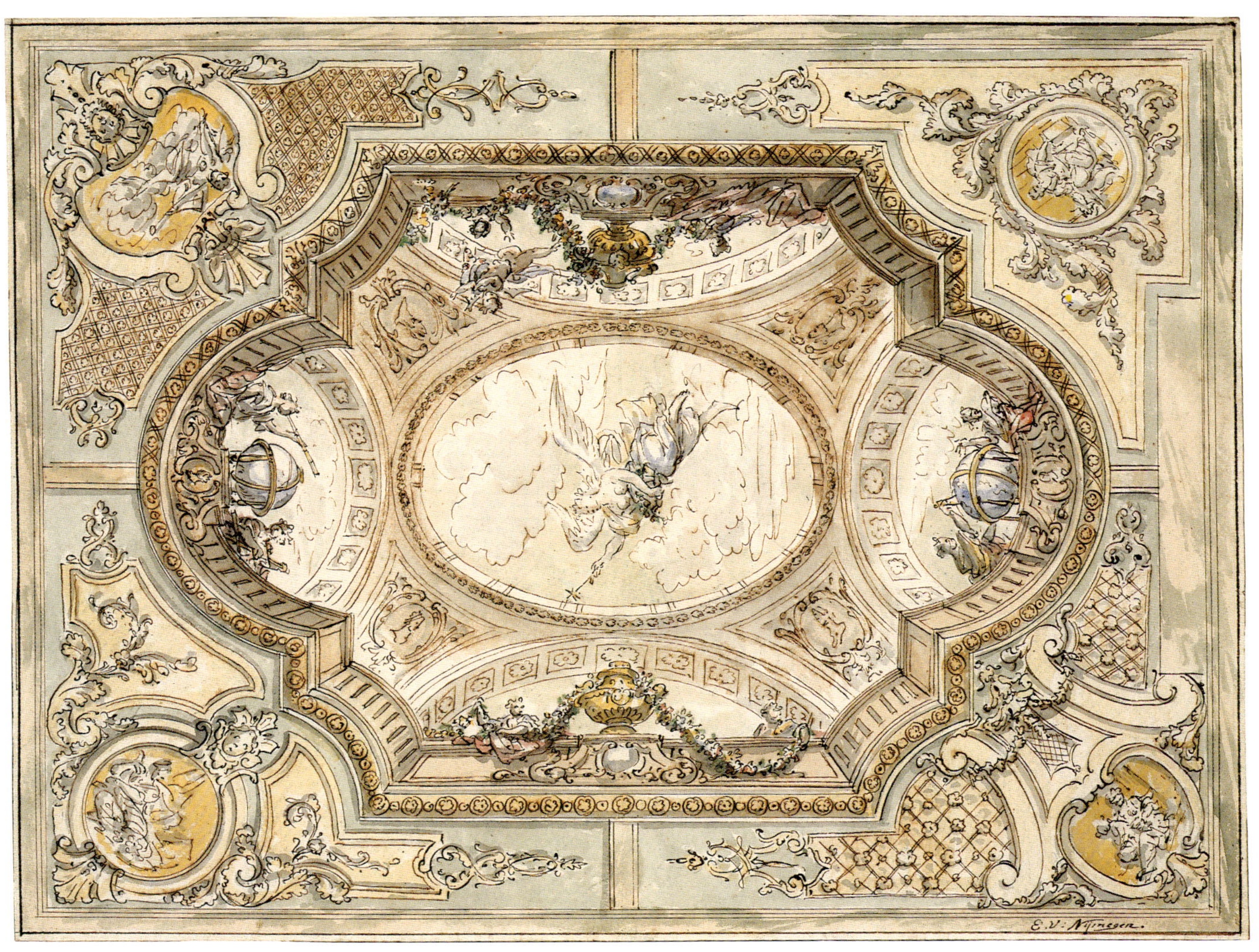
E.V: Nymegen.

Gerard van Nijmegen (Rotterdam 1735-1808 Rotterdam)

Painter, draftsman, and etcher of hill and mountain landscapes. Gerard van Nijmegen trained as an artist in the flourishing wall-decoration shop of his grandfather, Elias van Nijmegen (see cat. no. 49), in Rotterdam. By then, however, demand for this industry was on the decline, and around 1770 Gerard turned to portraiture and to cabinet paintings, mainly of woodland and mountain views. His admiration of the seventeenth-century landscapists Nicolaas Berchem and Adam Pynacker is reflected in his work, not so much in his choice of subject matter but more in the draftsmanship, lighting, and other stylistic features of his drawings.

In 1782, and again in 1788, Gerard traveled through Germany, where he recorded subjects that he later incorporated into a suite of etchings (1790-94) and eventually used in paintings and drawings. His love of mountains, winding paths, groves of trees, and waterfalls proclaims him a pre-Romanticism artist. Through good fortune, Van Nijmegen was able to live the life of a gentleman of leisure. He held posts on the committees of various institutions, and in 1795 served briefly as a member of the pro-French Council of Rotterdam. He also wrote poetry and collected art. In 1779-80 he conducted a correspondence with the Dutch novelist Elisabeth ("Betje") Wolff-Bekker.

50 Shepherd with His Flock in a Wood

Black chalk, pen in brown, watercolor, and gouache; black border
502 x 658 mm
On verso, signed at lower left, in pencil: *Gerard van Nijmegen na 't Leven* (from life) / *fec 1794 en 1795*
Inv. no. 1980:9

This is by far the most imposing of the eight drawings by Gerard van Nijmegen that are in the Amsterdam Print Room. At a spot flooded with sunlight on the edge of a wood, a shepherd keeps watch over a small flock of sheep. The scene's mood is redolent of the peace and quiet of an old wood. In addition, the vignette of the three men conversing while their dogs sniff the air strikes a rather trivial, anecdotal chord. The artist's inscription on the reverse, in a large, ornate hand, suggests that the drawing was made outdoors, directly from nature. That, however, is unlikely, given the large size of the sheet and the absence of folds. Van Nijmegen's words most likely mean that he made only the initial sketch "from life." Van Eynden and Van der Willigen make an interesting observation in this regard: "It is regrettable that this landscape painter, so worthy of merit, did not draw and paint more from nature. . . . He often relied on his vivid imagination and good memory, with which he supplemented in his pictures the rough sketches that he now and then drew from nature on white or gray paper." The harsh blue cast of this work is due to the discoloration of the original green.

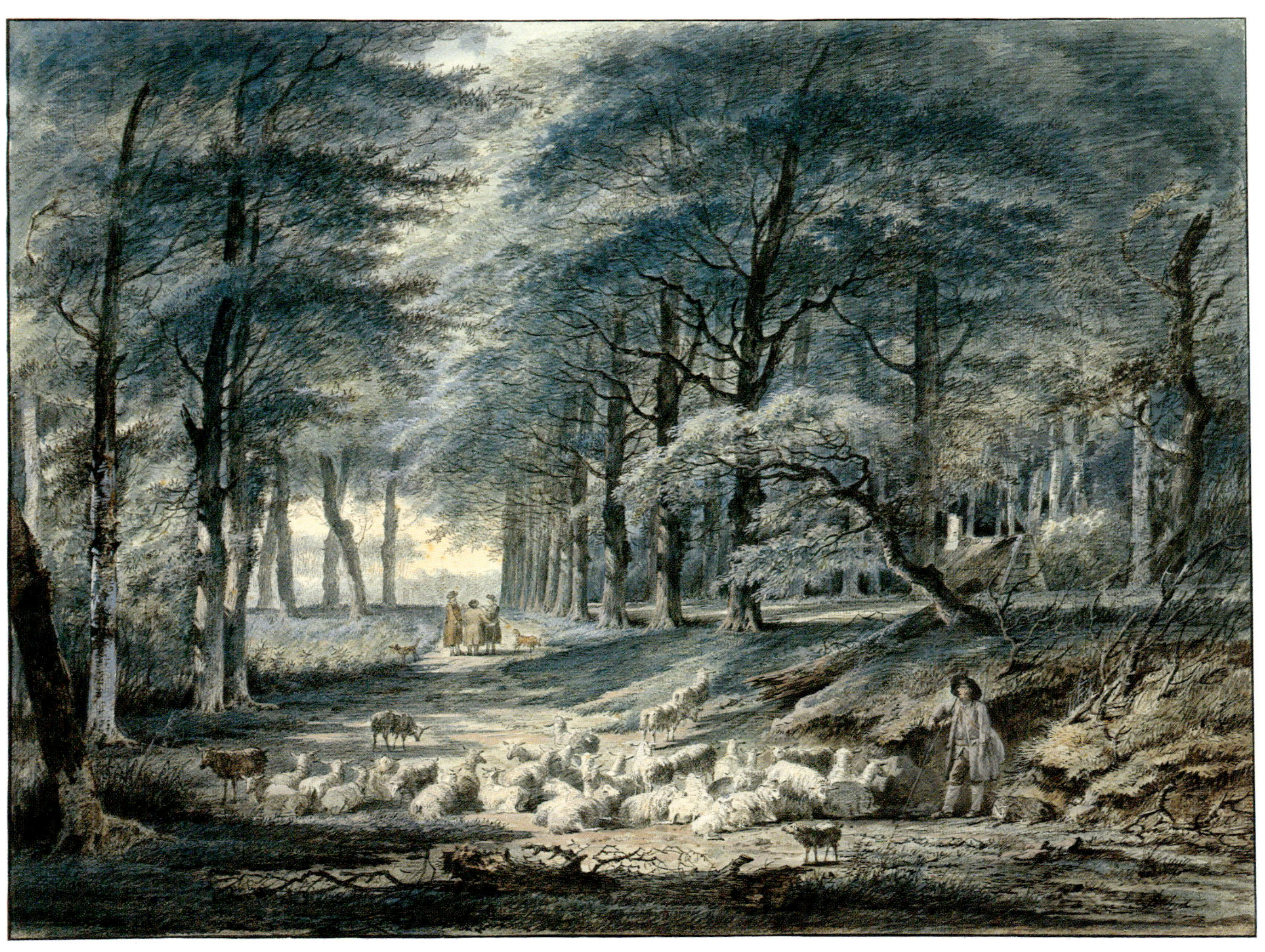

Johannes Huibert Prins (The Hague 1757-1806?)

Painter-draftsman of minutely detailed street scenes and interiors. Although Johannes Huibert Prins took to art at an early age, his father, who returned to Holland a rich man after a career in the colonies, insisted that he attend a university. Prins earned degrees at the University of Leiden in 1781 as Magister artium liberalium and Doctor philosophiae, but he then devoted himself solely to painting and drawing. He spent two years in Brabant and France, where he made numerous studies, but he found his greatest inspiration in Dutch art of the seventeenth century, particularly in the architectural paintings of Jan van der Heyden and his follower, Gerrit Berckheyde. It was from these two that he took his detailed depiction of masonry, as well as the habit of combining architectural elements from different sources to create imaginary buildings. This method was continued in the next generation by the Utrecht artist Jan Hendrik Verheyen (1778-1846). The nature of the relationship, if any, between these two artists is unknown.

Due to his restless nature, Prins moved from town to town, residing first in The Hague, then settling in Utrecht and later Leiden. In 1784, his talent for oratory led to his appointment to the committee of the Pictura artists' society in The Hague, but after a few years he quarreled with his colleagues and left for Leiden, taking the petty cash with him. Drink ruined his life, and he was forced to abandon first painting and then drawing. He apparently died by drowning in 1806.

51 Fair on a Market Square

Pencil, pen in gray and brown, and watercolor; fragmentary brown border
537 x 680 mm
Signed on a timber at left, in pen: *J.H. Prins inv.f.1793*
Inv. no. 1968:92

The setting for this scene was formerly identified, incorrectly, as Amstelveld in Amsterdam. It is, in fact, an imaginary location of the kind that Prins created in several other works, most of them dating from the 1780s and 1790s. One striking detail is that all the houses originate from a much earlier architectural period. None of them stems from the artist's own day, apart, of course, from the temporary marquees and stalls that have been erected on the square, such as the one with the signboard "De Afrikaansche leeuw" (The African Lion). The sign on the corner house on the right, which sells coffee, tea, and chocolate, gives its name as "In de Teeboom" (In the Tea Bush). Prins copied this seventeenth-century building, with some minor modifications, from a study in his sketchbook (p. 52, also in the Amsterdam Print Room). Other architectural details, such as the gable with the mock columns above the fair tent and the sculpted entrance to the house beyond the pillars on the left, came from the same sketchbook (pp. 76 and 84). Prins inscribed one of those sketches "Op de Houtmarkt" (On the Wood Market). From this it can be deduced that he composed such street scenes from drawings of real buildings, which he had gathered into a compendium that he could consult whenever he needed. The same applies to the figures. The man with the basket on his arm in the foreground, seen talking to a man in a gray coat with knotted tails, and the tall figure leaning against a pillar on the left are based on drawings by Prins that were included in a collection of figure models engraved by Matthias de Sallieth and published by Immerzeel in Amsterdam in 1818. (The figure of the loitering youth was reversed left for right.) Scenes of busy fairs and annual markets were evidently still popular in the eighteenth century and beyond. Dirk Langendijk (see cat. nos. 38, 39) and his son also specialized in the genre, and similar examples appear in the oeuvres of many other artists. Although clients liked images teeming with life, and an abundance of detail was certainly welcomed, no other artist surpassed Prins. He

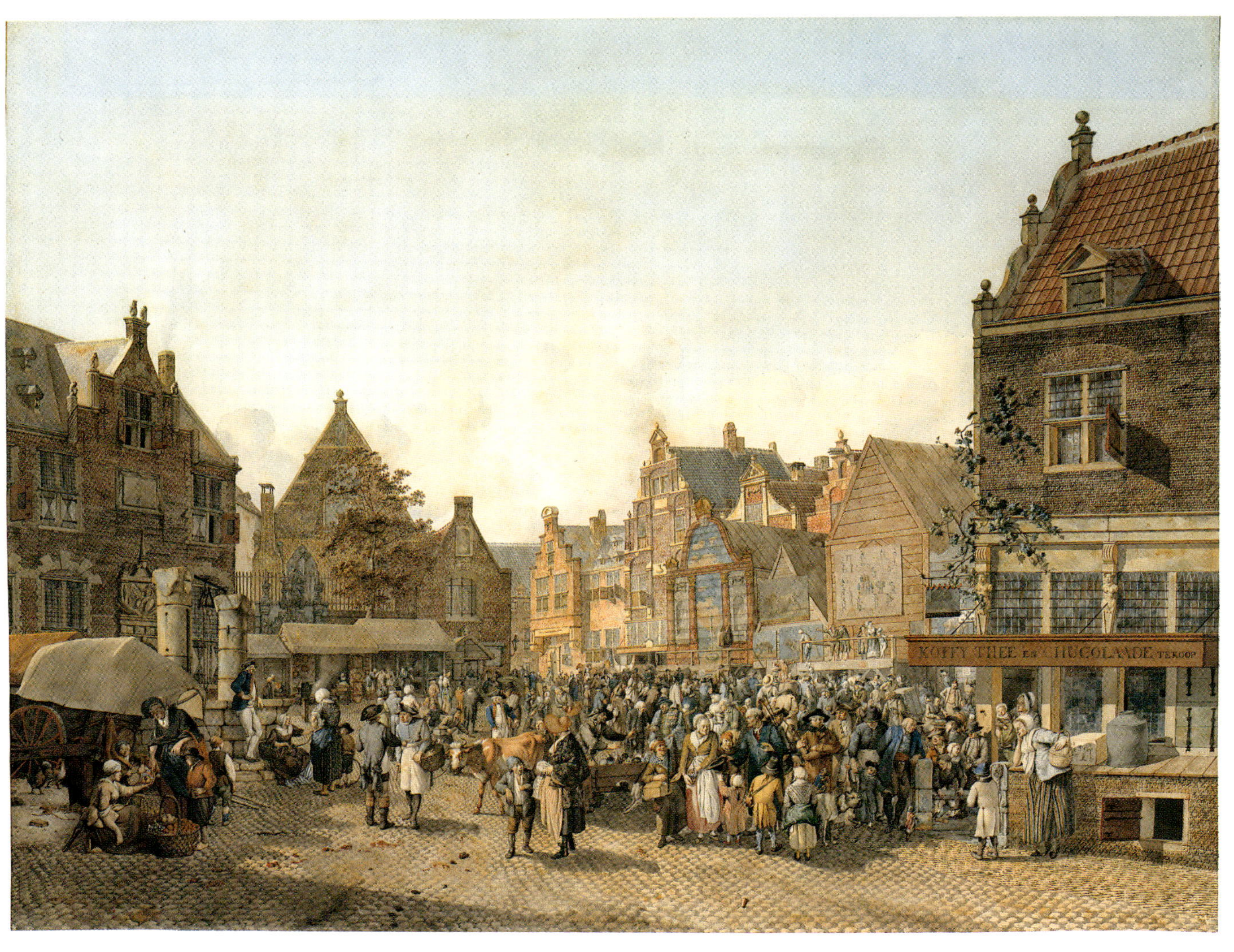
KOFFY THEE EN CHOCOLAADE TE KOOP

was well paid for such works, yet his meticulousness, was not always to the taste of connoisseurs. According to Adriaan van der Willigen in his *Geschiedenis der vaderlandsche schilderkunst* (History of Dutch Painting) of 1817, "In the depiction of masonry Prins was not seldom overly concerned with detail; the white pointing between the bricks is neatly reserved in many of his drawings, which although artful is unnatural when depicted on a reduced scale, and thus cannot be accounted as being germane to a masterly treatment."
Information on fairs in eighteenth-century Holland – how they were organized and what could be seen and bought at them – comes not only from painters and draftsmen but also from foreign visitors. The German traveler Sophie von La Roche, for instance, attended a fair in Rotterdam in 1787, shortly before this drawing was made, and saw dancing dogs and monkeys, acrobats on horseback (Langendijk often depicted the riding schools), dance halls, and stalls filled with food.
One year after Prins depicted this scene, the English romantic novelist Ann Radcliffe visited the Leiden fair. She was struck by the large numbers of countryfolk, many of whom wore traditional costumes, and in particular by the stalls offering luxury items, such as silver, clocks, and ormolu. The acrobats and the wild animals, which are commonly featured in Prins's works, are also mentioned in John Owen's account of a fair held in The Hague in 1791.

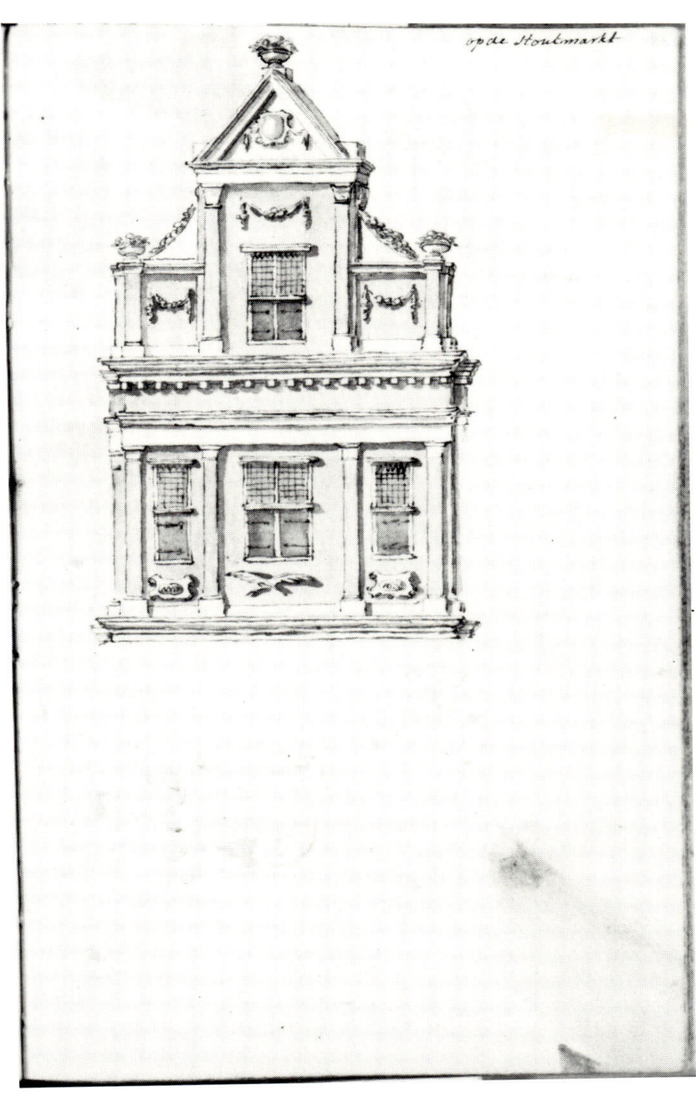

Johannes Huibert Prins, sheet from a sketchbook. Amsterdam, Rijksprentenkabinet.

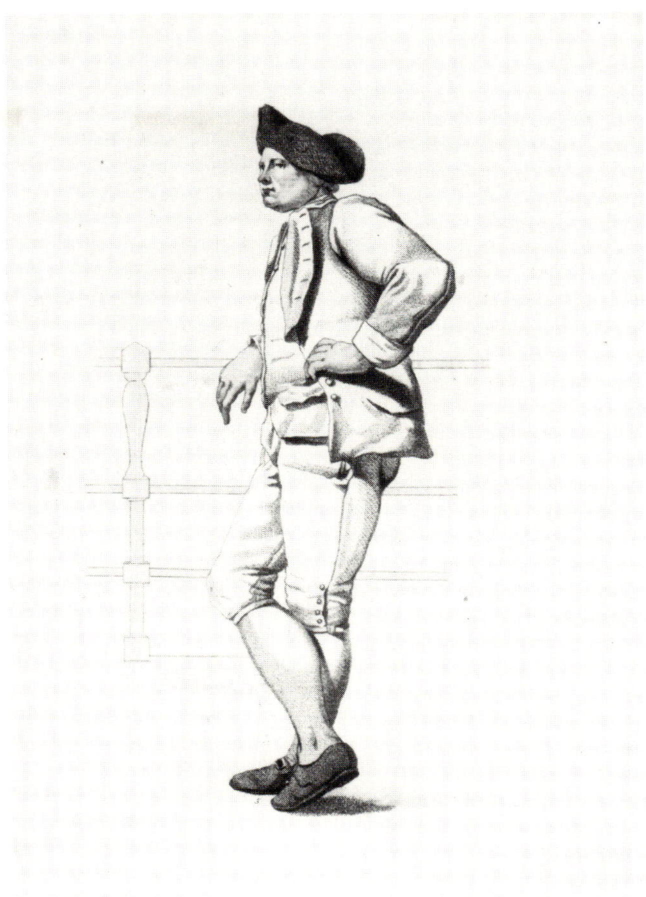

Etched by Matthias de Sallieth, after a drawing by Johannes Huibert Prins. In a book of model studies, dated 1818.

Cornelis Pronk (Amsterdam 1691-1759 Amsterdam)

Noted draftsman of topographical views and the nestor of an entire school of practitioners of this genre in the first half of the eighteenth century. Cornelis Pronk initially trained as a portraitist at the excellent studio run by Arnold Boonen, to which Cornelis Troost (cat. nos. 65-68), Philips van Dijk (1680-1753), and Johan Maurits Quinkhard were also apprenticed. In 1723, however, Pronk began specializing in the depiction of towns and villages, churches and castles. This led him to travel throughout the country, often accompanied by friends or pupils. He filled his sketchbooks (four of which are now in the Amsterdam Print Room) with studies from life, which he later used when he composed larger, more elaborate drawings and watercolors. These sketches also served as the basic material for the prints that Hendrick Spilman engraved for a ten-volume illustrated work, entitled Het verheerlijkt Nederland (The Netherlands Glorified; *see p. 28**), that was produced by the Amsterdam publisher Isaac Trion. Occasionally Pronk designed commemorative medals, and from 1734 to 1737, he made four series of models for the decoration of porcelain, so-called chine de commande, which were a great success. The direct pupils of this noted draftsman were Abraham de Haen (1707-1748), Jacobus Verstegen or Versteegen (1735-1795), and Hendrik de Winter (1717-after 1782).*

52 City Gate in Haarlem

Pen in gray and watercolor; gray border
137 x 207 mm (with inscription)
Inscribed: *Spaarwouwer Poort; te Haarlem*
(Spaarnwouder Gate, Haarlem)
Signed at lower right, in pen: *C:pronk del:ad viv.*
Inv. no. 1953:255

The only one of the many gates in the former walls around Haarlem that still survives today is the fourteenth-century Amsterdam, or Spaarnwouder, Gate. Here, it is shown at a time when traffic was not routed around it, as it is today. Through this narrow opening passed carts laden with goods, platoons of soldiers, elegant carriages, and herds of livestock. In Pronk's watercolor, a genteel couple is about to cross the bridge behind a man who pushes a large wheelbarrow bearing their baggage, much as is still done today in Venice. The man and woman are probably on their way to the horse-drawn ferry moored close by in the Amsterdamse Vaart. One or more of the boats departed each hour, and the clock on the gate tower was installed specially to ensure that they left on time. The scene has Pronk's characteristically sunny appearance, which he achieved by using light lines and a transparent wash in blond shades.

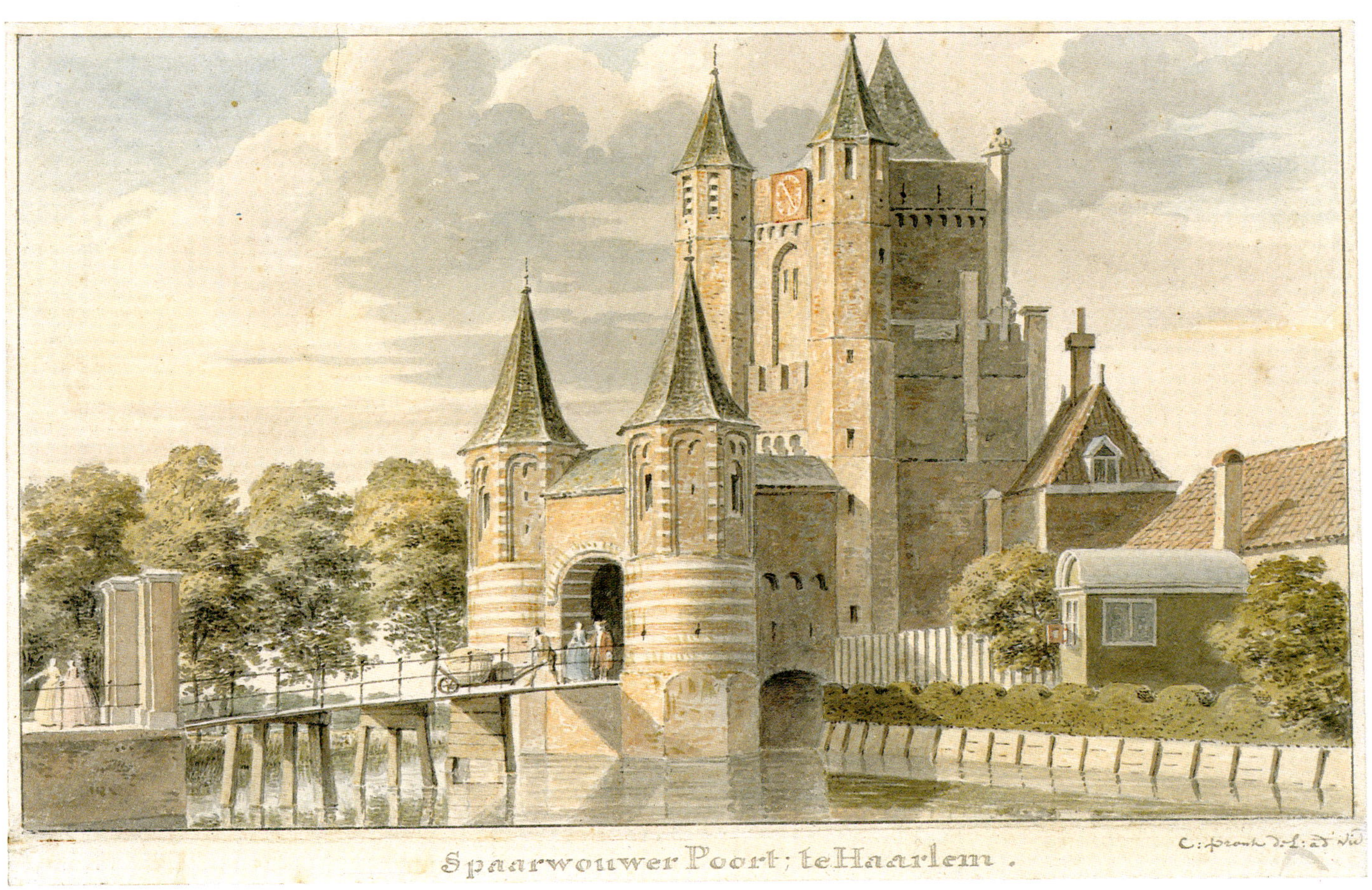
Spaarwouwer Poort; te Haarlem.

53 **Recreational Scene on a Frozen Waterway**
Pencil, pen and brush in gray, and watercolor; dark gray border
172 x 221 mm
Signed at lower right, in pen: *C:Pronk.Fecit.1748*
Inv. no. 1953:257

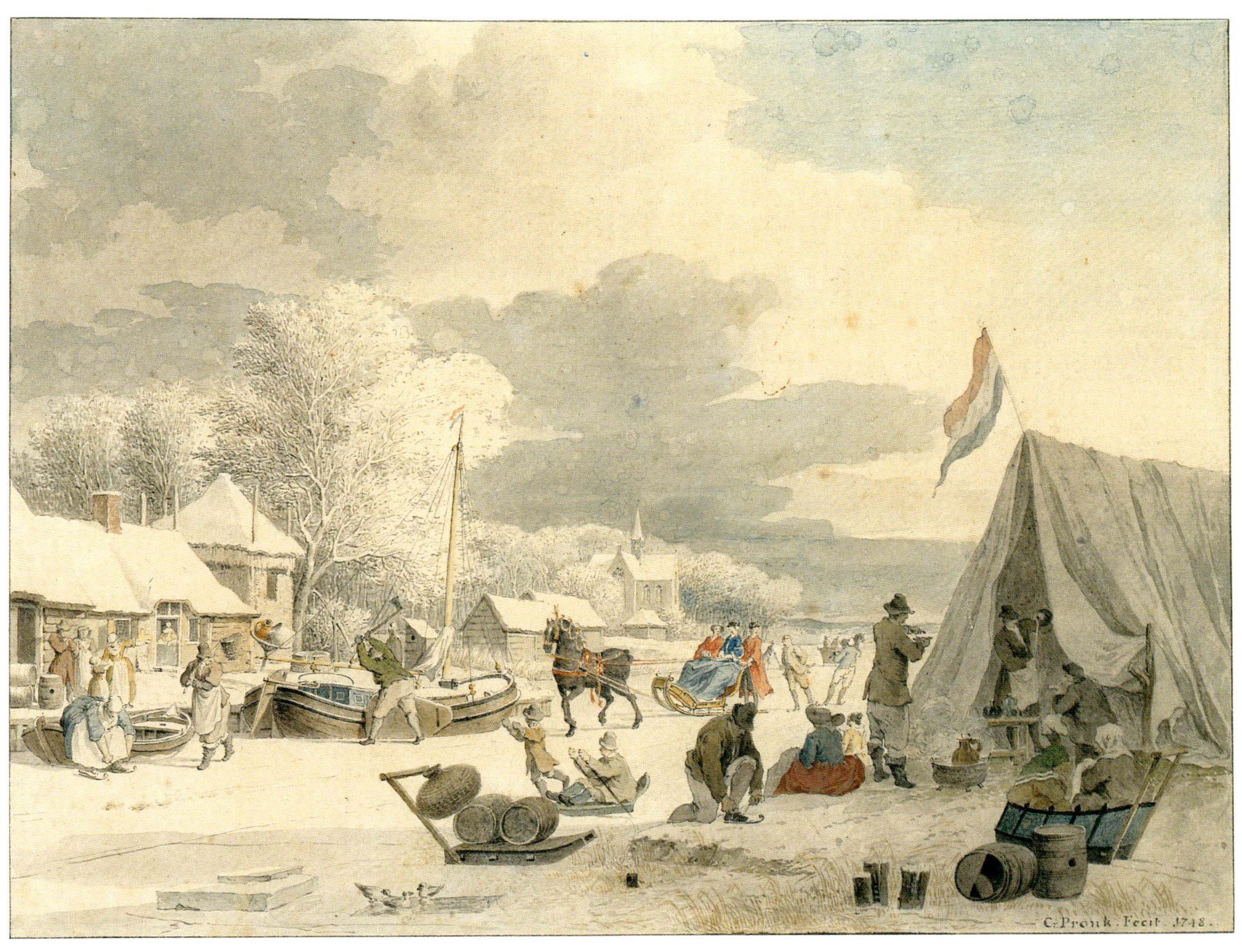
C. Pronk. Fecit. 1748.

54 **A Summer's Day in the Country, with Pleasure Boats and other Forms of Amusement near a Waterside Mansion**

Pencil, pen and brush in gray, and watercolor; dark gray border
170 x 223 mm
Signed at lower right, in pen: *C:Pronk.Fecit 1748*
Inv. no. 1953:258

These two drawings (cat. nos. 53, 54), which belong together, depict outdoor amusements in winter and summer. They are among the rare non-topographical scenes in the oeuvre of Cornelis Pronk, who specialized in recording actual buildings. Human figure, which are often present in his views of towns, villages, and castles in witty yet usually subordinate roles, have here been elevated almost to the main subject. All classes of society are represented in these two pictures of people amusing themselves in their spare time.

Since these two finely detailed drawings were probably framed and exposed to light for long periods of time, their color balances have shifted slightly. Soft, intermediate hues have faded a little, while the primary colors of red and blue have remained far less affected. Since the two drawings are not direct pendants in a compositional sense, they might have been part of a set that included scenes of spring and autumn.

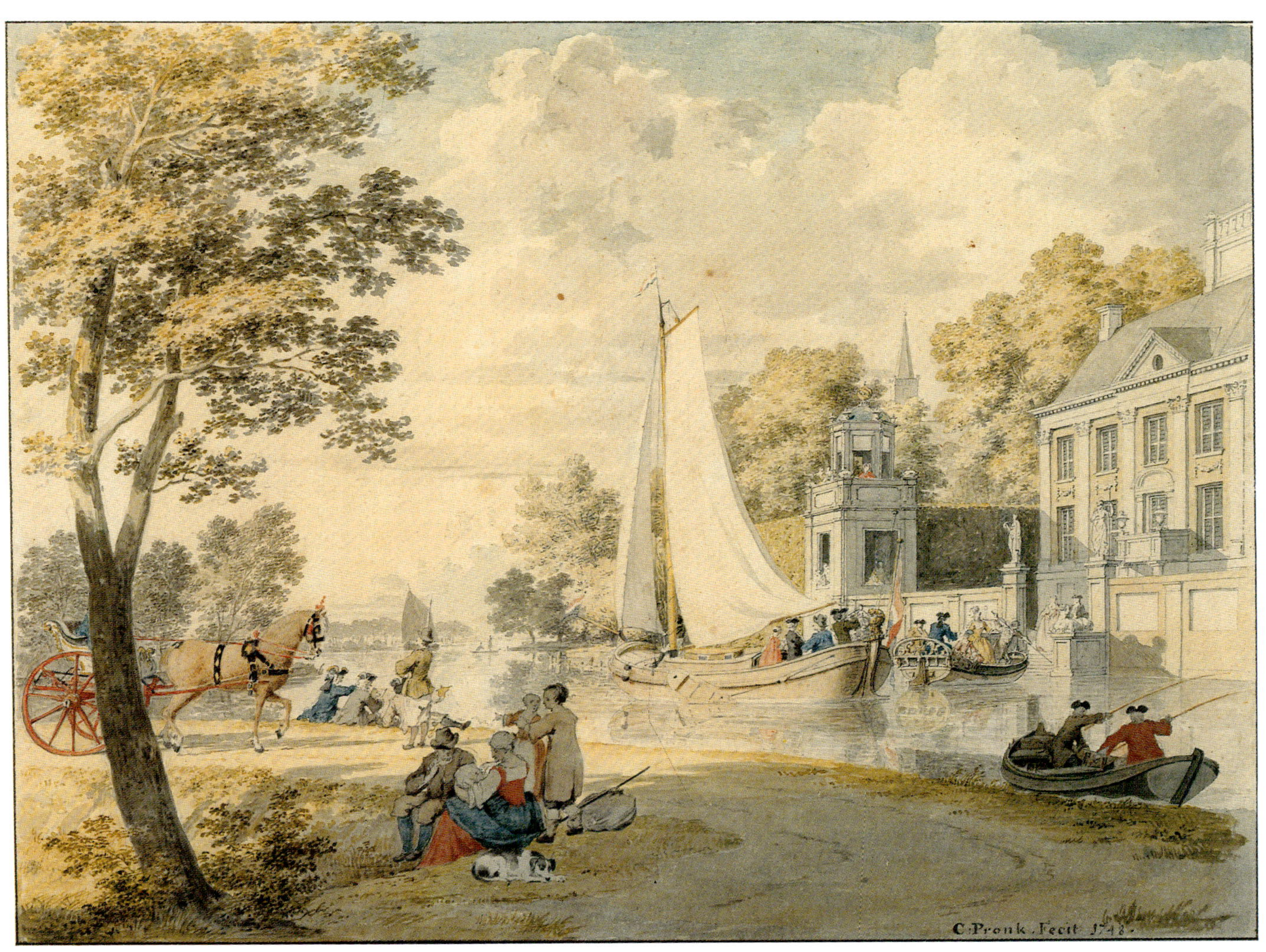
C:Pronk .Fecit 1748.

Aart Schouman (Dordrecht 1710-1792 The Hague)

A prolific and versatile artist who produced paintings, drawings, graphics, and stipple engravings on glass. In his day Aart Schouman was unrivaled as a watercolorist. Around the age of fifteen, he began an eight-year apprenticeship with Adriaan van der Burg (1693-1733) in his native Dordrecht. After his master's death, Schouman became an independent artist, earning his living chiefly as a painter of portraits and wall-hangings, although he also accepted more modest commissions. This is known from two notebooks in which he recorded orders for transparent, painted screens (chassinets), clock faces, window screens, and magic-lantern slides, as well as designs for church silver. Like many of his colleagues, Schouman also worked as an art dealer. Beginning in 1735 he received commissions from the province of Zeeland, and in particular from the town of Middelburg, where his brother Cornelis was active as a painter. From around 1748 he lived alternately in Dordrecht and The Hague. It was in The Hague, where the stadtholder had his court, that Schouman came into his own as an artist. His style of portraiture achieved charm and elegance, largely due to the influence of Philips van Dijk (1680–1753), who also drew his clientele from The Hague and Zeeland. (Schouman may have tried to succeed as court painter to the Landgrave of Kassel after Van Dijk's death.) In addition to that trip to Germany, Schouman went abroad twice, both times to England, in 1765-66 and 1775.

The artist's renderings of animals and birds, some in oils but most in watercolor, are probably his most important contribution to eighteenth-century Dutch art. In them he combined an exceptionally radiant palette with a rapid, transparent handling of the brush and an assured mise en page.

55 A Turkey and other Birds among Classical Ruins in a Park

Pencil and watercolor; black border with gilt edges
240 x 174 mm
Inv. Felix Meritis no. 137

The figures in this idealized landscape consist largely of birds that commonly would have been found in a Dutch park: a white Muscovy duck (*Cairina moschata L.*), a black crested hen in an aggressive pose as she protects her brood of multicolored chicks, a brown turkey cock perched on a fragment of sculpture, and a pink-and-white dove gliding in the sky above.

Through compositions of such as this, Schouman embellished on a tradition that had been developed in the seventeenth century by Melchior d'Hondecoeter and others. From the brush of the eighteenth-century artist, however, that tradition took on the distinctive look of interior decoration and acquired a new function as a room or salon painting. This particular example may well have been such a design. It hardly seems coincidental that all the birds are types reared by man, with not a wild specimen among them. Likewise, the setting is not unrestrained nature but a park that had been formed by human hands.

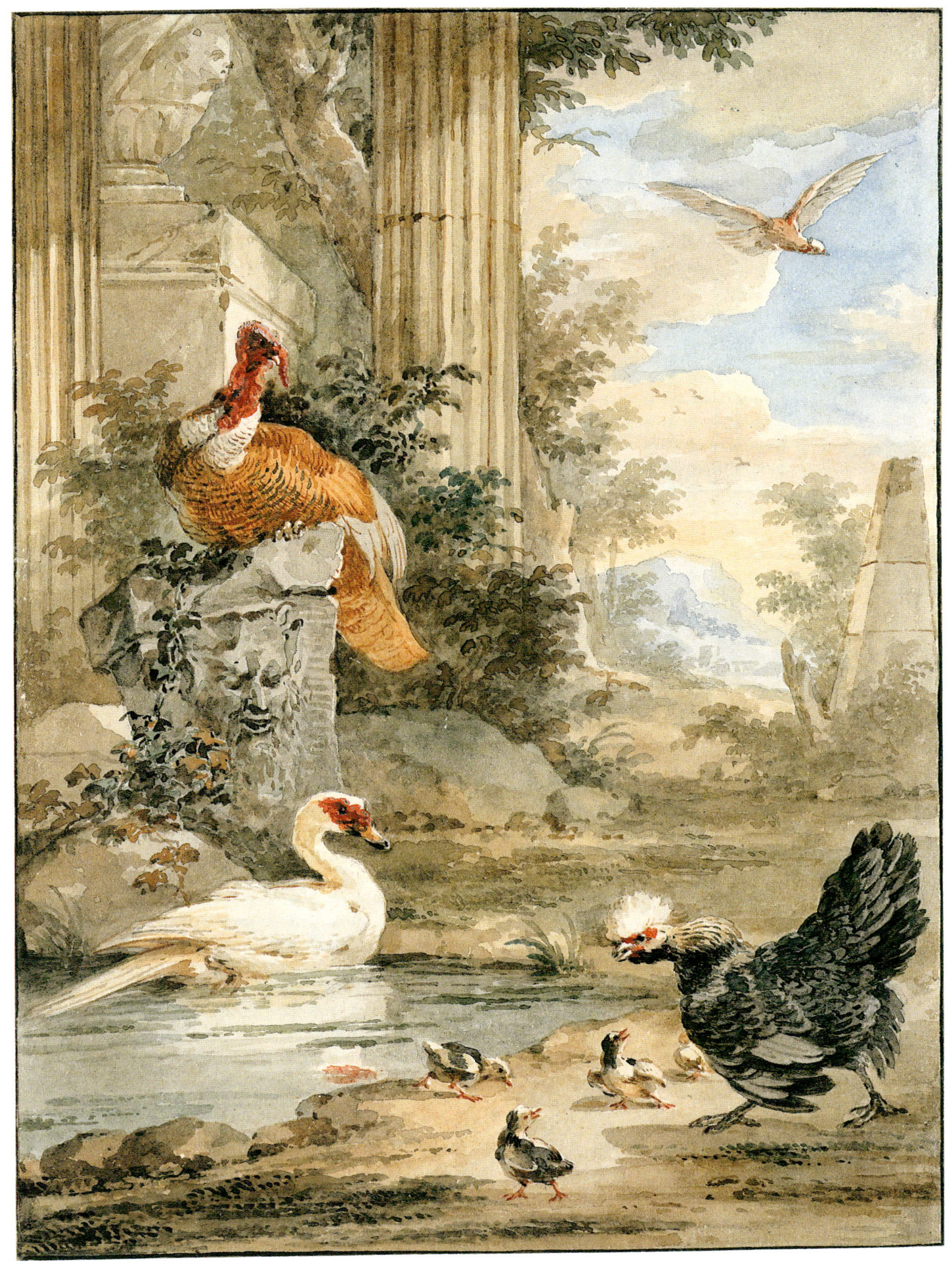

56 Exotic Birds: Cock-of-the-Rock and Leclancheri Painted Bunting

Pencil and watercolor; narrow brown border
366 x 258 mm
On verso, in Schouman's hand, in pen over pencil: *de Hoep Hen, Levens groote A.S. fecit int Cabint* [sic] *van Z.H.176..* (The hoopoe, lifesize, executed in His Highness's cabinet, 176.) [trimmed through the date, but probably 1762; see sale cat. A. Schouman, 1792, no. 316]
Inv. no. 1898 A 3707

The large orange bird that dominates the center of this drawing is a cock-of-the-rock (*Rupicola rupicola L.*), which Schouman called a hoopoe, that was taken from the stadtholder's natural history collection in The Hague. The smaller bird is a Leclancheri painted bunting (*Passerina leclancherii [Lafr.]*). The cock-of-the-rock was described by Arnout Vosmaer, director of the prince's cabinet, in his series of publications on his master's menagerie and bird collection, the first part of which appeared in 1766 (see also Tethart Haag, cat. no. 23). The issue that included mention of this bird was published in 1769. For the engraved illustration accompanying his description Vosmaer used another of Schouman's drawings, this one of the bird seen not from the left but from rear right (now in the library of the Artis Zoo in Amsterdam, reversed relative to the print). The model for both drawings was a stuffed specimen, based upon Vosmaer's statement that he was unable to see whether it was a male or a female, because he did not have a live bird, merely a stuffed specimen that had become very desiccated. He was evidently unaware that it is only the cocks that are orange; the hens are a dun color. The cock-of-the-rock is native to the mountainous regions of Guyana and northeast Brazil.

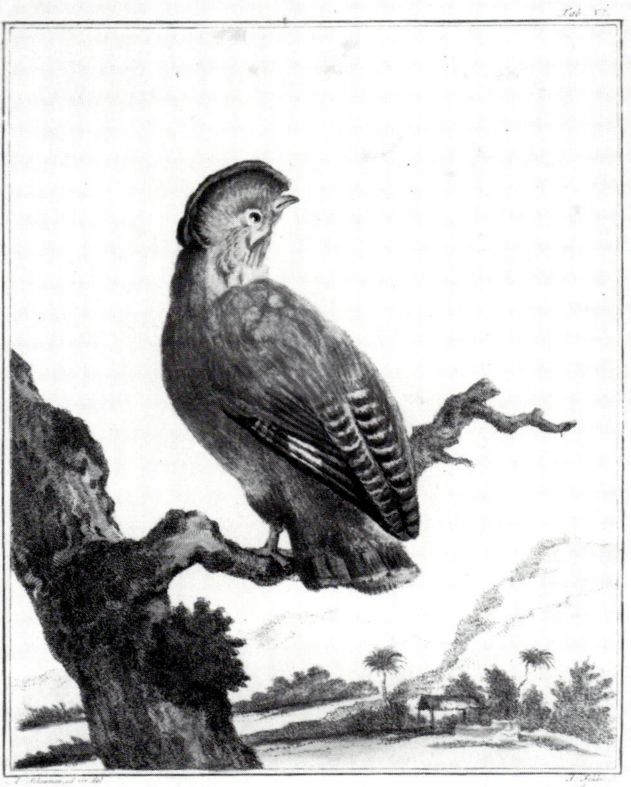

S. Fokke, after a watercolor by Aart Schouman. Etching in Regnum animale, 1769.

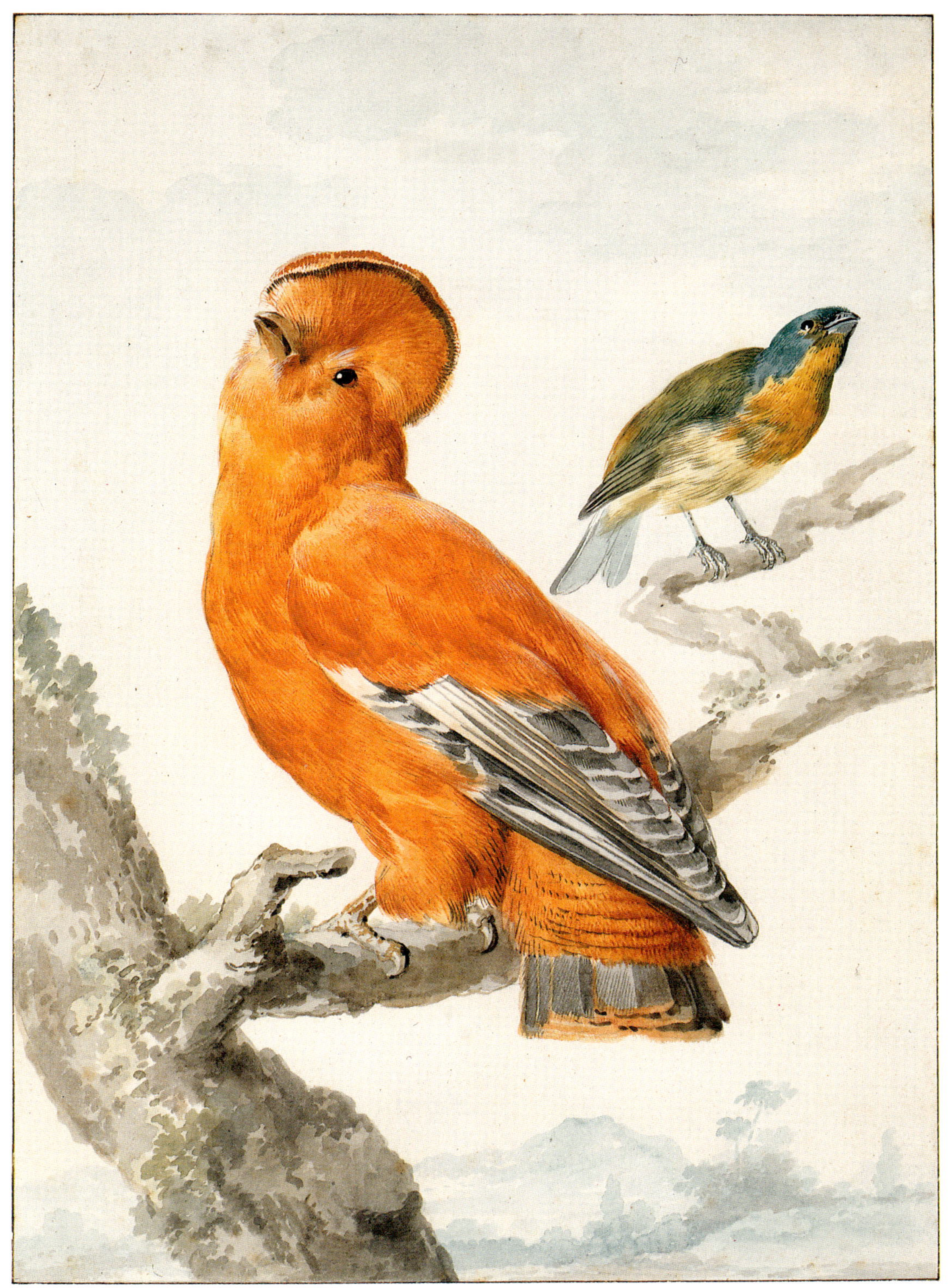

57 **Toucan**

Watercolor; narrow brown border
482 x 319 mm
Signed at lower left, with brush:
A:Schouman.1748.
On verso, in Schouman's hand: *Cawacawa of Braziliaanse Exter* (Cavacava or Brazilian magpie)
Inv. Felix Meritis no. 138

Quite clearly this bird, the red-billed toucan (*Ramphastos erythrorynchus Gm.*), was also drawn from a stuffed specimen, although this time Schouman did not say where the original was to be found. There were numerous collections of stuffed birds in the Netherlands at the time, so he would have had no shortage of models. It may have come from one of the collections in The Hague, to which Schouman had moved in or shortly before 1748, the year given in the inscription, although the artist never settled there permanently.

Beneath the bird, which perches on a tree branch, is the coastline of an exotic country, included as an allusion to the regions in Guyana and northern Brazil where the toucan lives in the wild. Schouman correctly observed that the toucan holds onto a branch with two toes, not three, like other species.

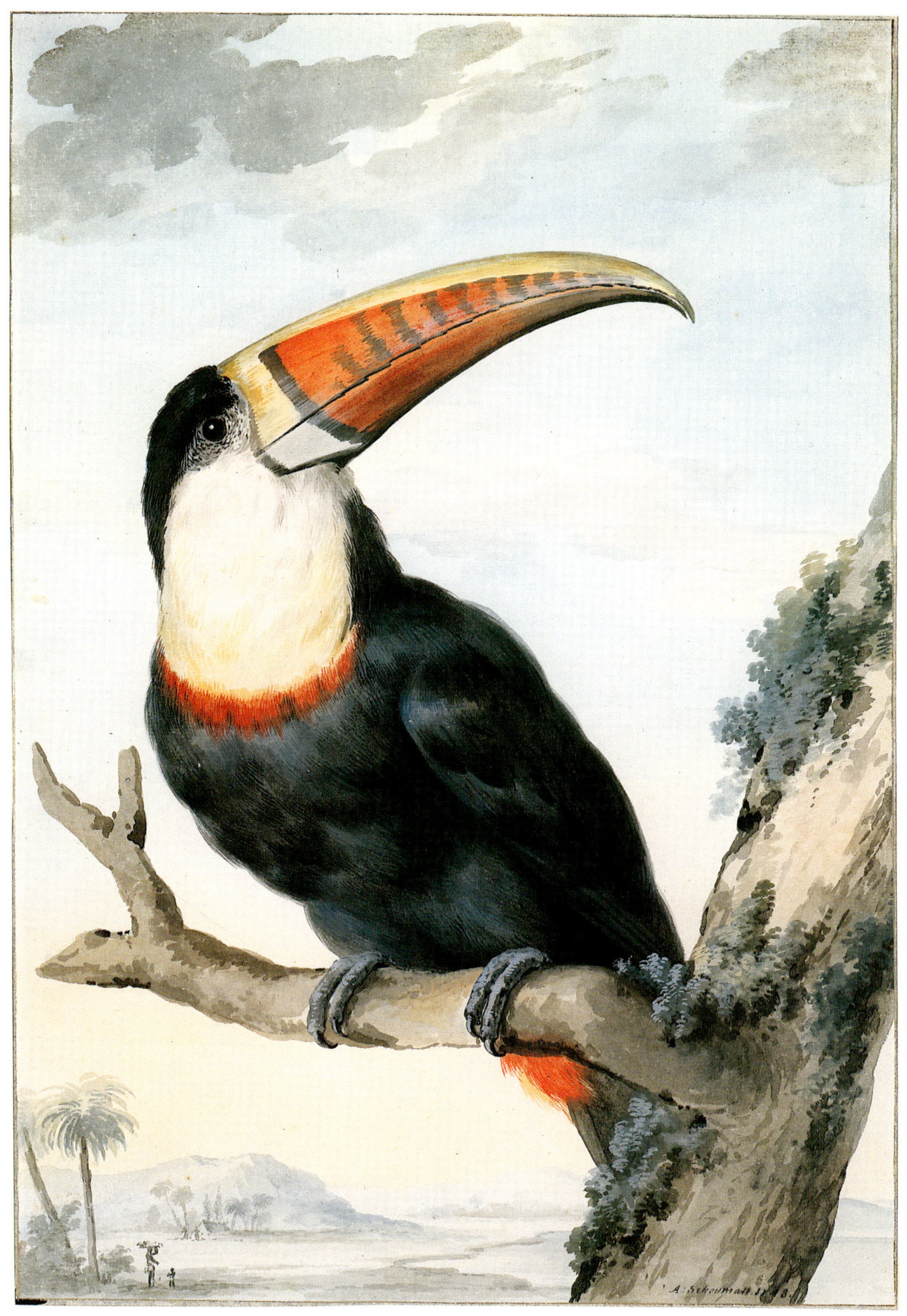
A: Schouman

58 Two Finches

Watercolor; brown border
339 x 244 mm
Signed at lower right, with brush:
A.Schouman.1752:
On verso, in Schouman's hand, in pen: *Een appel vink* [*of dik bec*] *en cheep Levens groot A.S.1752*
(A hawfinch [or grosbeak (inserted later)] and a brambling, lifesize)
In pen, old numbers: *An° 7/F.n°* –
Inv. no. 1898 A 3708

Unlike the exotic birds in the two previous watercolors (cat. nos. 56, 57), it is possible that these native finches – a hawfinch (*Coccothraustes coccothraustes L.*) and a brambling (*Fringilla montifringilla L.*) – were drawn from live specimens, although they may have been kept in an aviary or cage. The ungainly poses, however, are more suggestive of stuffed specimens. The distinctively watery Dutch landscape places the birds in their natural habitat.

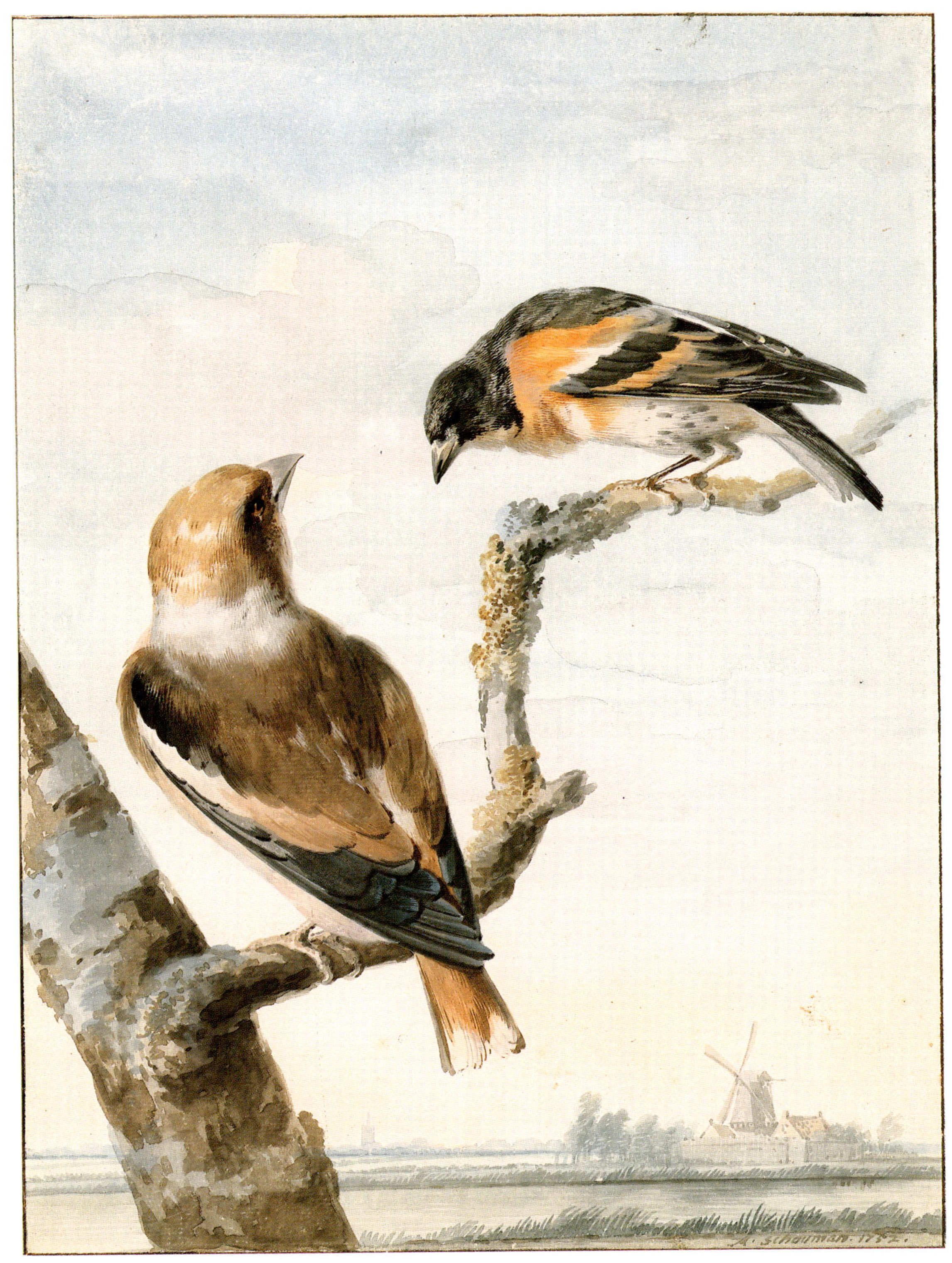
A. Schouman. 1752.

59 Pieter van Bleiswijk (1724-1790), Grand Pensionary

Watercolor over brown proof impression of mezzotint; brown border
183 x 123 mm (including bottom strip with inscription)
Signed at lower left, in pen: *A* [partly cropped] *Schouman fecit ad v.1787.*
Inv. no. 1901 A 4547

This portrait differs slightly from the other watercolors seen here in that the paint has been applied over a very light counterproof of a mezzotint, which accounts for the grid-like lines visible through the loose and painterly brushwork. The final print itself, which is reversed relative to this watercolor, exists in two states or versions, one with and one without the red seal that is displayed so prominently here. That seal was an important attribute of this dignitary, Pieter van Bleiswijk, for it symbolized his office of Keeper of the Great Seal of the Provinces of Holland and West Friesland, a responsibility he held in addition to his principal post of Grand Pensionary. The ambitious and vain Van Bleiswijk probably insisted that Schouman include the seal in the portrait.

This work actually seems to have been made in 1786, not 1787, as indicated in the inscription. Even by then, however, shadows were looming over Van Bleiswijk's political career. He was no longer trusted at court because of his maneuvering and manipulation, and in November 1787, when his period of office expired, he was not reappointed. That meant that he had to relinquish his seal, in reality and in the print as well. This explains why the second state shows him with merely a few neutral pieces of paper and an inkhorn. The space for the inscription was left blank, and this author knows of no later state. Perhaps Schouman decided not to complete the print. The copper plate was found years later as part of Schouman's estate.

On the other hand, perhaps more than political considerations made the further dissemination of Van Bleiswijk's likeness somewhat inopportune. Schouman's portrait is hardly a flattering reflection of his sitter's personality. The ex-Pensionary would undoubtedly have been more pleased by the superb portrait in pastels that Jean Etienne Liotard had made of him in 1756, when the sitter was at the start of his career. That work, unfortunately, has been lost to the Netherlands. Together with the companion portrait of Van Bleiswijk's wife, it has been in the possession of the Musée d'Art et d'Histoire in Geneva since 1911.

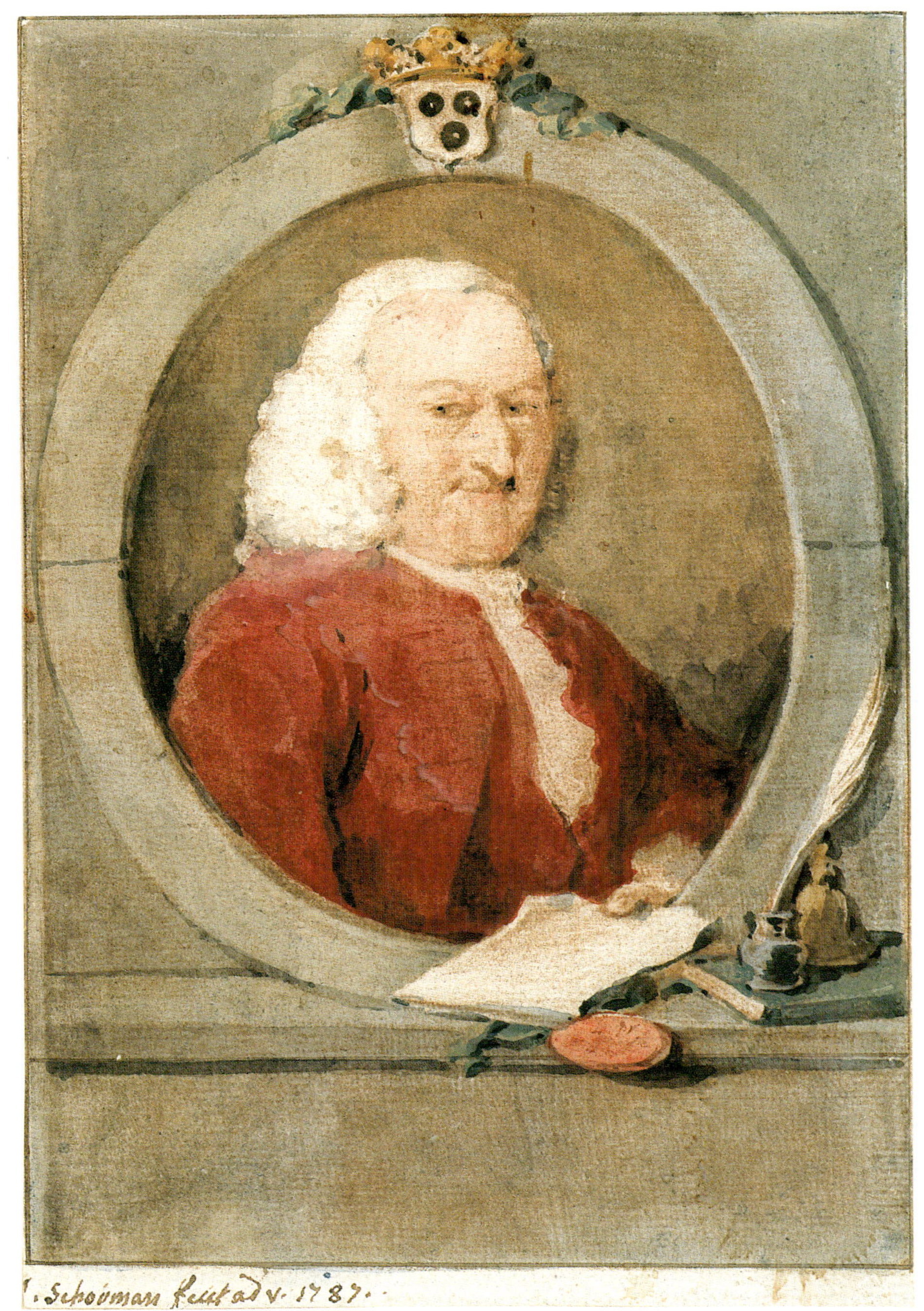

60 Portrait of a Gentleman in an Oval Frame

Watercolor; brown border
152 x 112 mm
Signed at lower right, with brush: *A.Schouman fec.ad.viv.1788* [?]
No inv. no.

The orange ribbon that this man displays so proudly on his breast identifies him as a supporter of Stadtholder Willem V of Orange, as was Schouman. The date in the inscription is a little difficult to decipher, but it is generally read as 1788, a year which the Orangist supporters had every reason to celebrate. In 1786, the stadtholder, his family, and court had been forced to flee The Hague for Nijmegen to escape a hostile, pro-French mob, but in September 1787, after the military intervention of his brother-in-law, the king of Prussia, Willem V was able to return. The following year saw his authority further strengthened by the Act of Guarantee, which enshrined the principle of the hereditary stadtholdership. It is little wonder that the prince's adherents took to wearing his colors. In Rotterdam, in 1789, the English traveler Samuel Ireland even saw horses decked out with orange ribbons.

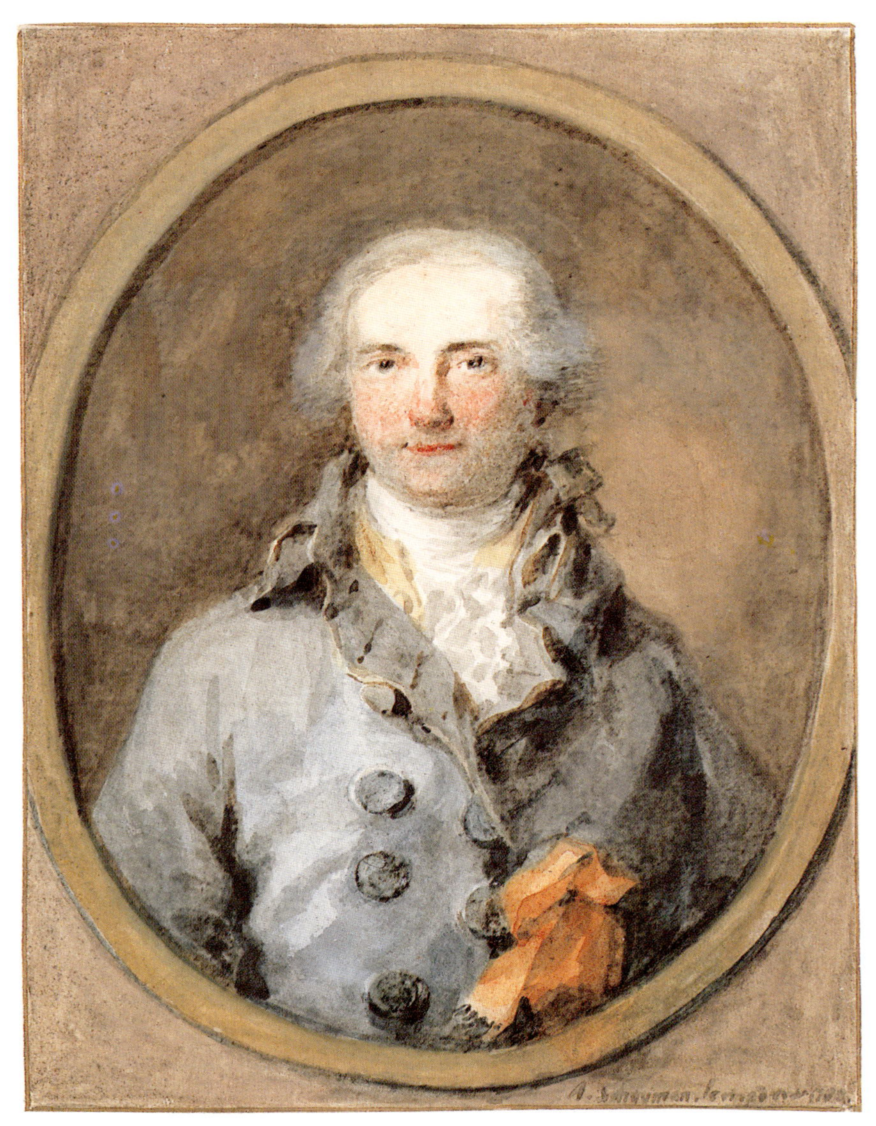

Hermanus Petrus Schouten (Amsterdam 1747-1822 Haarlem)

A topographical draftsman of German descent. Hermanus Petrus Schouten received his first training from his father and close collaborator Jan Schouten, who had been baptized Scholtz in Amsterdam in 1716. Next, Hermanus was a pupil of Paulus van Liender (see cat. no. 43) and of the collector and amateur draftsman Cornelis Ploos van Amstel, for whom he later drew a series of Amsterdam views. Schouten also worked for the art dealer and publisher Pieter Fouquet, for whose famous Atlas of Amsterdam he supplied dozens of drawings around 1770, most of which he also engraved.

In 1792, Schouten and his wife moved to Haarlem, yet he continued drawing views in Amsterdam. Similar to Prins (see cat. no. 51), Schouten's work proclaims his admiration for the detailed painting style of the seventeenth-century artists Jan van der Heyden and Gerrit Berckheyde. His palette, however, is far lighter and sunnier than theirs.

Schouten reached the peak of his career in the decade of 1780 to 1790, when his topographical views became increasingly detailed and precise. The Haarlem City Archives houses watercolors that he executed in the nineteenth century, which rival those by Prins in their detail. The forenames given to him in early lexica, Hubert Pieter, are based on erroneous information in Nagler's Neues allgemeines Künstler-Lexicon. Drawings signed simply H. Schouten are probably early works by the artist.

61 Luxemburgh House on the River Vecht

Pencil, pen in gray and brown, watercolor, and gouache; black border
441 x 431 mm
Signed at lower center, in pen: *H:P:Schouten*
Inv. no. 1921:197

This eighteenth-century building bathed in sunlight was Luxemburgh House, which once stood on the River Vecht, opposite the center of the village of Maarssen, near Utrecht. It probably received its name from the French Maréchal de Luxembourg, who occupied this part of the country in 1672. People soon associated the neighborhood with all the luxury that was being put on display there. Wealthy Jews of Portuguese descent had settled in Maarssen in the seventeenth century, and their numbers gradually grew. They built their own synagogue and lived in country houses, most of them on the Vecht. One of the most sumptuous of these residences was Luxemburgh, which belonged to the Pereyra family around 1775. A lavish party was held there when Stadtholder Willem V and his consort paid a visit on October 15, 1772. After a *déjeuner* at which the celebrated singer Magalli entertained – he was essentially the Luxemburgh house musician – the illustrious company strolled in the park, where they admired the waterfall, the aviary, and the more than forty garden statues and sundials.

Schouten's view of the house was made at a slightly later date, in the 1780s, when Luxemburgh belonged to Mozes da Costa Gomez de la Penha. The artist chose a position on the west bank of the river, behind the Swan Inn. He skillfully allowed the tree that shaded this corner of the scene to extend a branch to the left, causing its leaves to arch gracefully over the roof of Luxemburgh House. This rather artificial effect places the watercolor firmly within the conventions of eighteenth-century topography, although by this time a more modern manner had already become prominent.

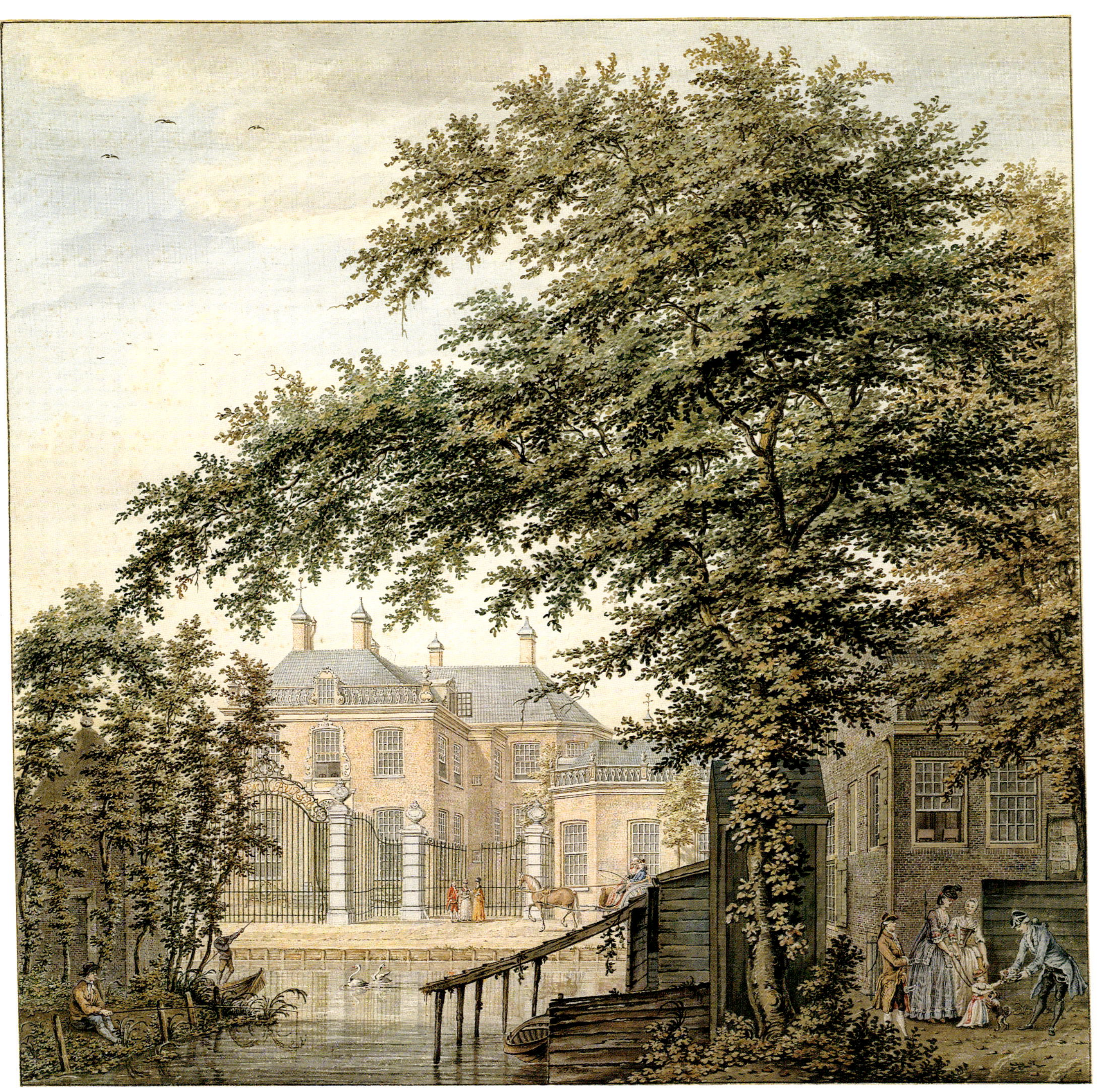

As painters and draftsmen, Abraham van Strij and his brother Jacob were the chief representatives of the Dordrecht school. Abraham studied first with his father, Leendert van Strij, a house painter and decorative artist, and then with Joris Ponse (1723-1783). As early as 1744, Abraham helped found the Pictura Drawing Society, and throughout his career he took an active part in the artistic and social life of Dordrecht. He and Jacob continued to run the workshop established by their father. The high caliber of works produced there is evident in a few intact sets of wall-hangings that date from the 1780s and 1790s, the workshop's heyday. Although Abraham van Strij originally painted still lifes – he later added portraiture and an occasional landscape to his oeuvre – his name is today mainly associated with genre scenes of interiors or courtyards. In this realm he was inspired by such seventeenth-century predecessors as Pieter de Hooch, Gabriel Metsu, and less frequently, Nicolaes Maes.

62 A Cobbler and His Family in an Interior

Black chalk, pen and brush in brown, watercolor, and gouache; black border
388 x 446 mm
Signed at lower left, in pen: *A.van Strij*
Inv. no. 1921:143

Light flooding in through a window or an open door was a favorite device of Abraham van Strij, and he handled the chiaroscuro effects that it generated with great refinement. In this case, however, the composition is not his own. It was borrowed from a painting by Aert de Gelder, a seventeenth-century pupil of Rembrandt whose work Van Strij could have seen either in the house of T.P.C. Haag, who acquired the picture in October 1792, or of Aart Schouman, its previous owner. Both, incidentally, had themselves made a watercolor copy of the picture. (Haag's is now in the Amsterdam Print Room; the other is lost.) Van Strij could also have taken one of those sheets as his model. Since dated scenes of interiors are only found in Van Strij's oeuvre after 1810, it seems likely that this undated sheet was made around then. The artist certainly did not adhere rigidly to his model but instead treated it as a point of departure for his own, individual interpretation. Indeed, De Gelder's *Holy Family in Joseph's Workshop* has been transformed into an anonymous cobbler's family. In the position where De Gelder situated the Virgin and Jesus, who reads a large book, Van Strij placed a young mother doing the laundry. The setting, too, has been changed: on the left a bedstead replaces the spiral staircase that leads to the floor above. The fact that Van Strij depicted a cobbler in this plain room coincides with the humble position then occupied by these craftsmen. They ranked lower than shoemakers and often lived in so-called pot houses, cellar-like structures that jutted out into the street. This home, however modest, is a cut above that, since it is on the ground floor, with a hatch on the right allowing access to a cellar. Van Strij's watercolor may have served as a preparatory sketch for a painting. This is suggested by the alternately broad and narrow brushstrokes, the pentimenti, and the large size of the sheet. The finished picture, if indeed one was ever executed, has not yet been located.

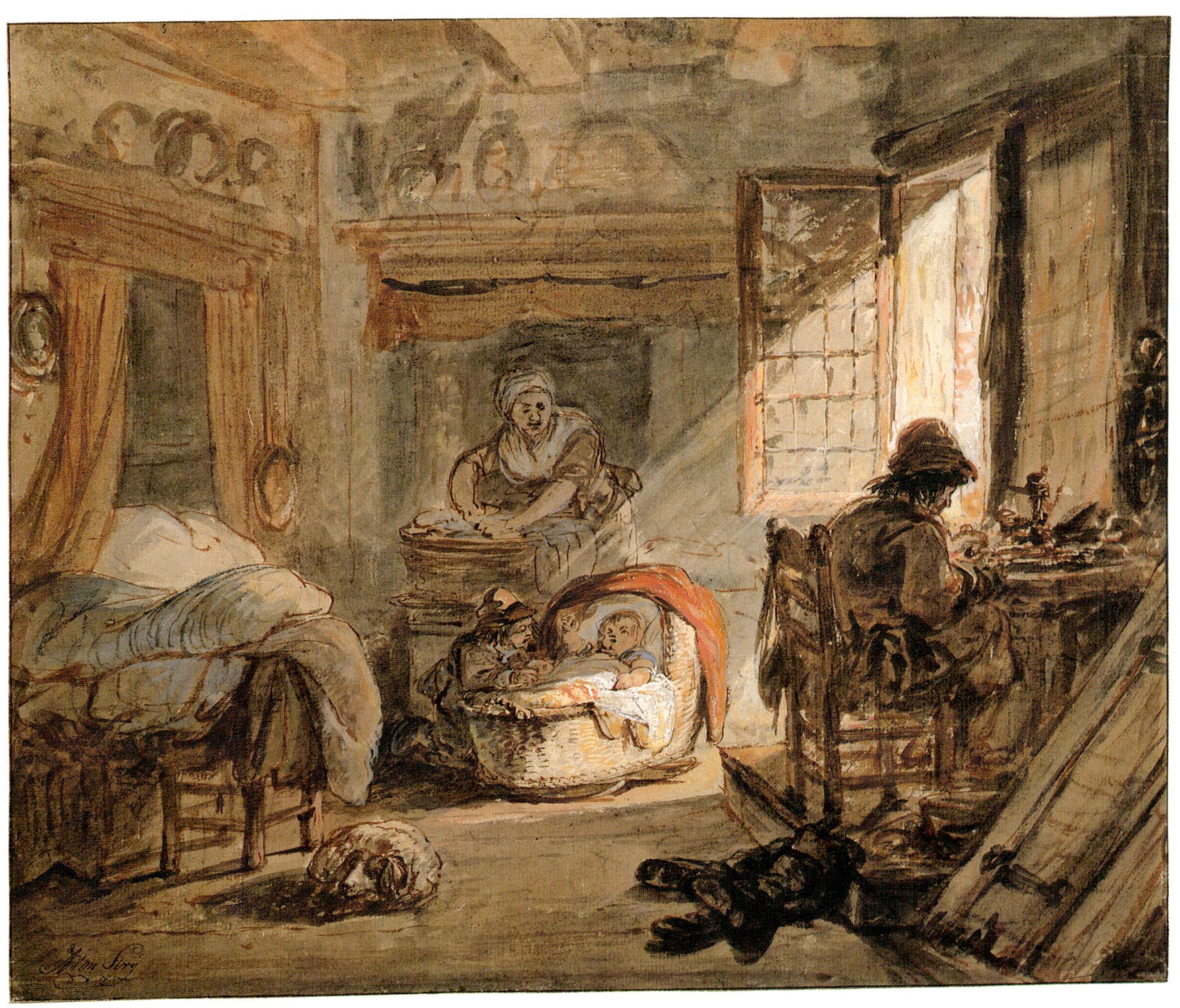

Jacob van Strij (Dordrecht 1756-1815 Dordrecht)

Painter and draftsman of cattle and landscapes. Together with his slightly older brother Abraham (cat. no. 62), Jacob van Strij learned the basic principles of painting in his father's studio. He lived for a while in Antwerp, where he worked under the supervision of Andries Cornelis Lens (1739-1822) and drew from the live model at the drawing academy. Like his brother, Jacob started out as a painter of wall-hangings, but with the encouragement of the collector and art dealer Jan Danser Nijman (died 1796), he turned increasingly to easel painting. His admiration for the seventeenth-century artist Aelbert Cuyp, also from Dordrecht, led him to copy and imitate Cuyp's landscapes populated with cattle. For a long time the skill that he developed in this area of specialty prevented Van Strij from being appreciated as a creative artist in his own right. He continually sought inspiration in nature, and even when crippled by gout, he would order a sleigh and have himself driven out onto the ice in the bitter cold in order to make sketches needed for a painting back in his studio. His work is rarely dated, which makes it extremely difficult to trace his stylistic development.

63 Watermill outside Dordrecht

Pencil, pen in brown, and watercolor; gray border (trimmed off on left)
286 x 418 mm
Signed at lower left, in pen: *J:van Strij.*
On verso, inscribed in pen (upside-down): *bij Smitshoek / buiten Dordregt* (near Smitshoek, outside Dordrecht)
Inv. no. 1887 A 1394

Aelbert Cuyp was the seventeenth-century Dutch master whom Van Strij most admired, but he was not the only source of inspiration. In this landscape, Van Strij was quite clearly recalling the drawings of Antonie van Borssum. Just how closely he approached his model in the choice of subject matter, the placement of elements on the horizon, and the pen-and-brush technique is illustrated by comparing it to two of Van Borssum's watercolor landscapes of meadows with mills (now in the Amsterdam Print Room; inv. nos. A 286 and A 287). Oddly enough, they came from the same collection as did this watercolor by Van Strij: the holdings assembled by Jacob de Vos (1803-1878).

Despite these similarities, it should be remembered that Van Strij's work is a radical adaptation of Van Borssum's drawing style, and not a slavish imitation of it. The inscription on the back confirms that Van Strij sought his inspiration at a spot not far from his home town of Dordrecht. The hamlet of Smitshoek (Smith's Corner, so named after the local smithy) was popular among artists for its picturesque buildings and rural surroundings.

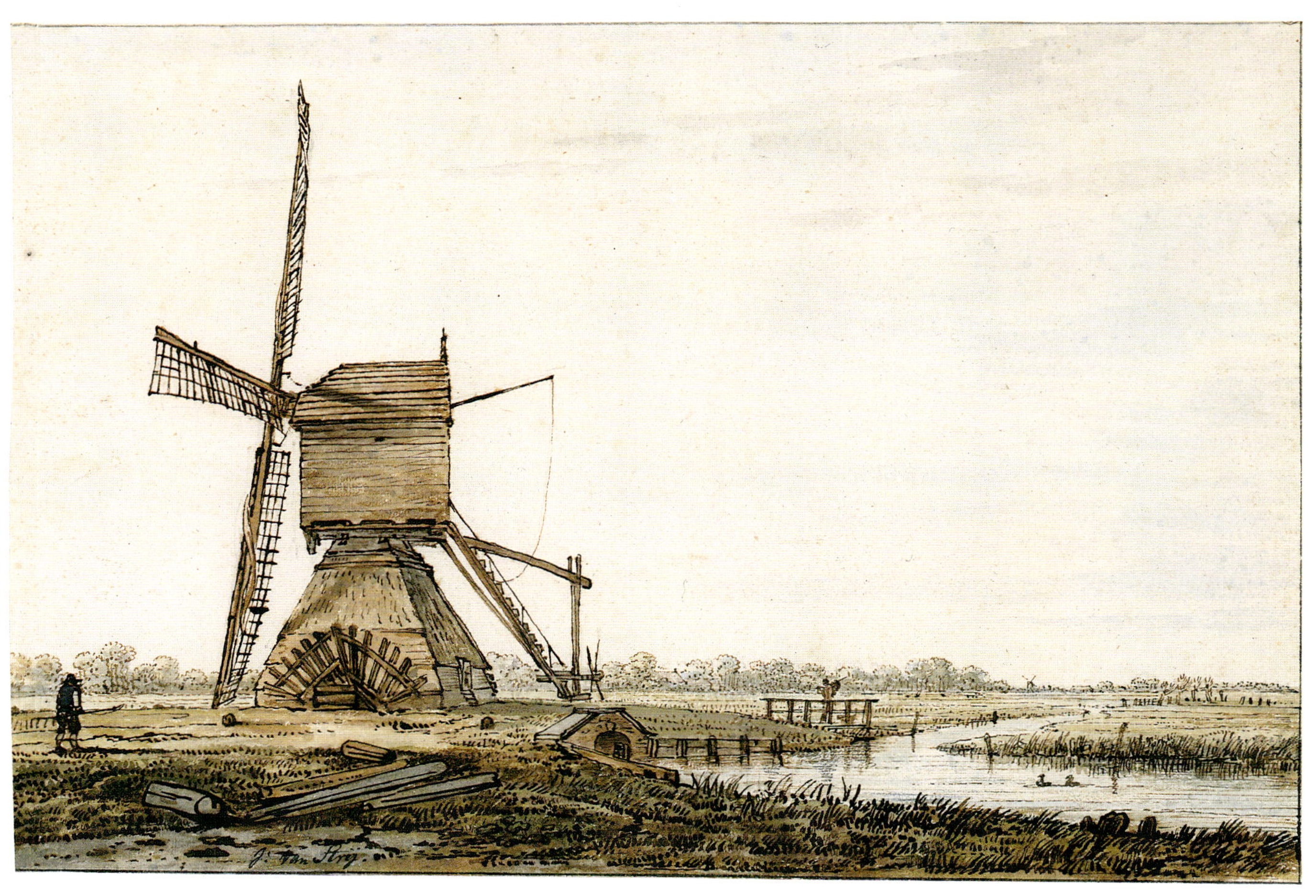

64 Old Farmhouse by a River

Pen in brown, and watercolor; brown border
207 x 306 mm
Signed at lower right, in pen: *J van Strij.*
Inv. no. 1902 A 4592

Subjects such as this were common in the region criss-crossed by rivers and waterways where Van Strij lived and worked. Depending on his mood, scenes could be recorded in a more topographical manner, as was done in the previous watercolor (cat. no. 63), or they could be incorporated into a freer composition, as he probably did here. In this scene of rustic tranquility, the dilapidated walls reveal a love of decay that Van Strij shared with many of his contemporaries. This scene probably dates from around 1800.

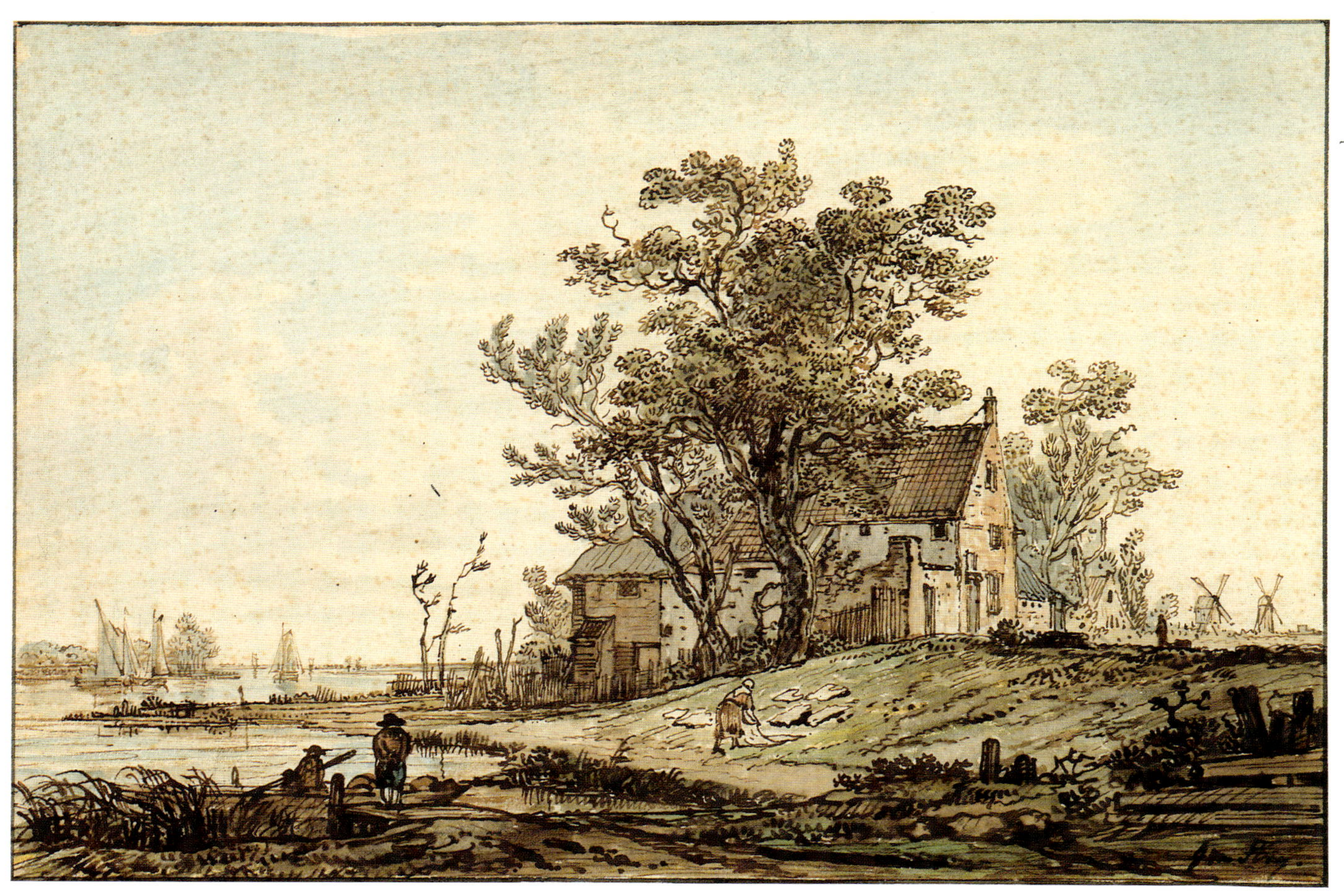

Cornelis Troost (Amsterdam 1696-1750 Amsterdam)

Versatile painter, pastelist, draftsman, and graphic artist who worked in a wide range of genres: portraiture, scenes from stage plays, depictions of life in the town and country, and military subjects. Born into an artistic family and brought into contact with actors from the Amsterdam Playhouse through his marriage, Cornelis Troost took some time to settle on a career. After several years of working as a comic actor, he began to emerge as a painter around 1724. He died only twenty-five years later, but in that short time he produced an extensive and varied oeuvre that elevated him to the vanguard of contemporary Dutch artists, and perhaps of artists throughout the entire century.

Troost never worked outside Amsterdam, but his inquiring mind was open to ideas from further afield. He incorporated elements from the work of modern and past masters into his own compositions with great facility. His main Dutch models were Jan Steen and Godfried Schalcken, and from the French school, Nicolaas Lancret, François Boucher, and Charles Coypel. Points of similarity are also shared with his English contemporary William Hogarth.

In his day, Troost's use of materials was considered strikingly original. He was fond of combining watercolor with gouache or chalk or both, and even in his pastels he did not eschew the use of the brush. Also remarkable in his oeuvre is a large number of sketches and preliminary studies, as well as many variants of specific subjects. Troost remains a highly individual, and unique, phenomenon in Dutch eighteenth-century art. He founded no school of which to speak, and he had only one real pupil: Jacobus Buys (see cat. no. 11).

65 Pefroen with the Sheep's Head (Scene from a Play)

Brush in gouache and watercolor; black border
273 x 269 mm
Signed at lower left, with brush: *C.Troost. 1740*
Inv. no. 1909:9

Troost was most renowned for his depictions of popular stage plays, which he often produced in many variants and in different techniques. This watercolor presents a scene from *Pefroen with the Sheep's Head*, an adaptation by IJsbrand Vincent of *Lubin ou le sot vengé*, a French work written by Raymond Poisson in 1661. Around 1741, a new edition of the play appeared. As in many farces of the period, the object of ridicule is the cuckolded husband, who is here named Pefroen. Troost shows him being scolded to tears and being sent back to the butcher to exchange a sheep's head. His wife Lijsje wags her finger and gives him instructions as she prepares to turn his absence to her benefit by retiring into the house with her lover Ritsaart, who already has his arm around her waist. To underscore the point, the signboard adds a heavy hint with the words *'t gekroonde hoofd* – the crowned head (with horns, of course). This version, largely in gouache, is a variant of a pastel that Troost had made a year earlier, which is now in the Mauritshuis in The Hague.

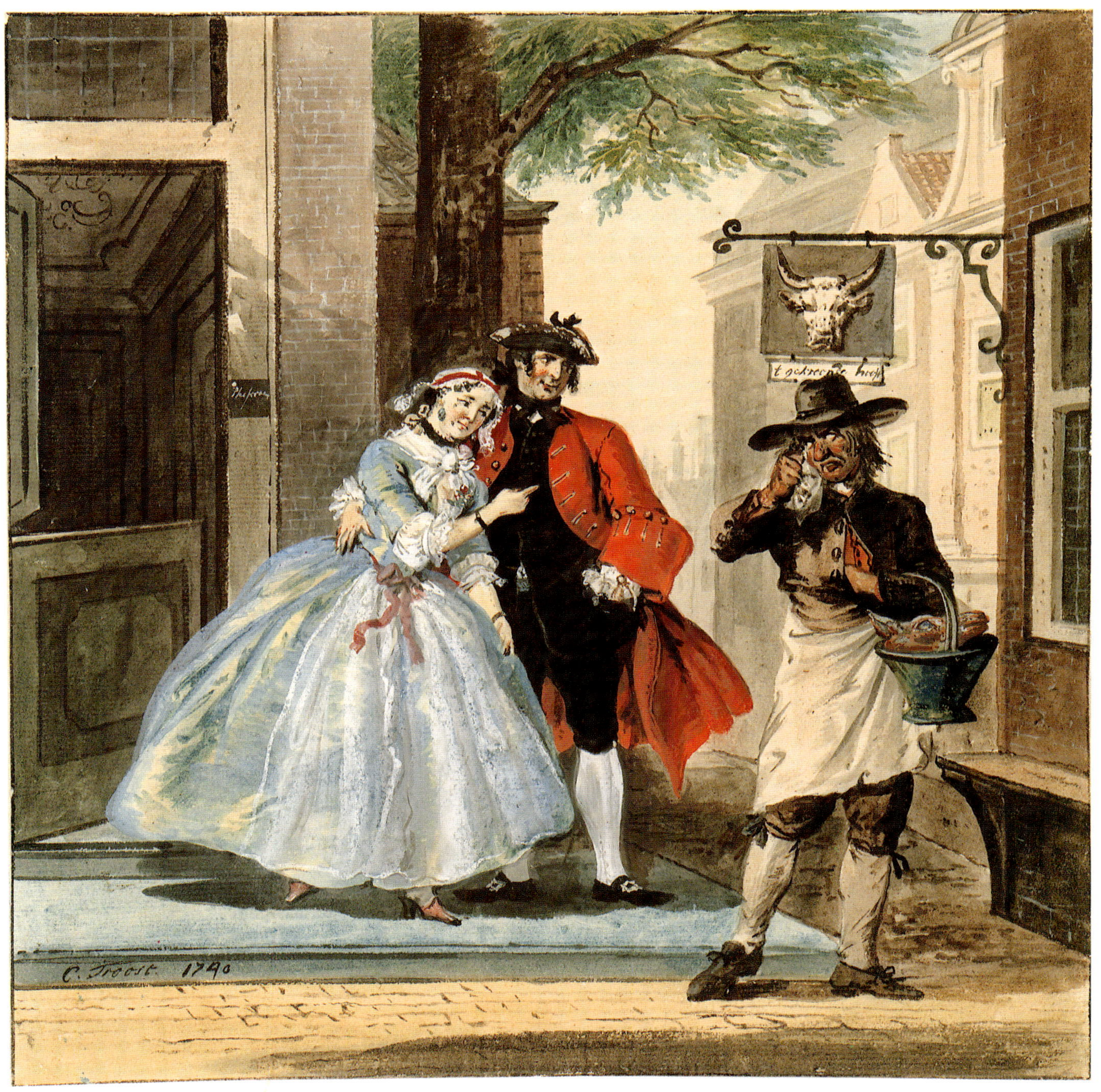
C. Troost 1740

66 **Family Listening to a Street Singer**

Black chalk, pen in brown, and watercolor on blue paper (now discolored); traces of black border; laid down
290 x 422 mm
Inv. no. 1981:82

The sketchiness of this drawing indicates that it is not a finished product but a preparatory design for a composition. In the final version, a pastel in the Troost collection in the Mauritshuis, the artist stayed fairly close to his initial conception. He did, however, reduce the number of figures from eight to six (dispensing with the milkmaid in the process), and he turned the street singer, seen half from the back, into an organ grinder who has turned his head to gaze roguishly at the viewer. Troost produced a separate preliminary study for this young man in chalk and pastel (now in the Print Room at Leiden). The color scheme of the watercolor exhibited here was severely modified in that pastel. As was so often the case, Troost may have been inspired by the work of his seventeenth-century predecessor Jan Steen, who also depicted an organ grinder giving a recital for a family on the doorstep of their house.

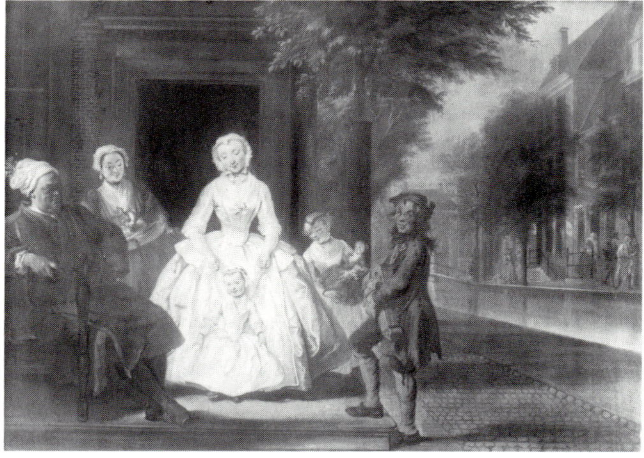

Cornelis Troost, The Organ Grinder. The Hague, Mauritshuis.

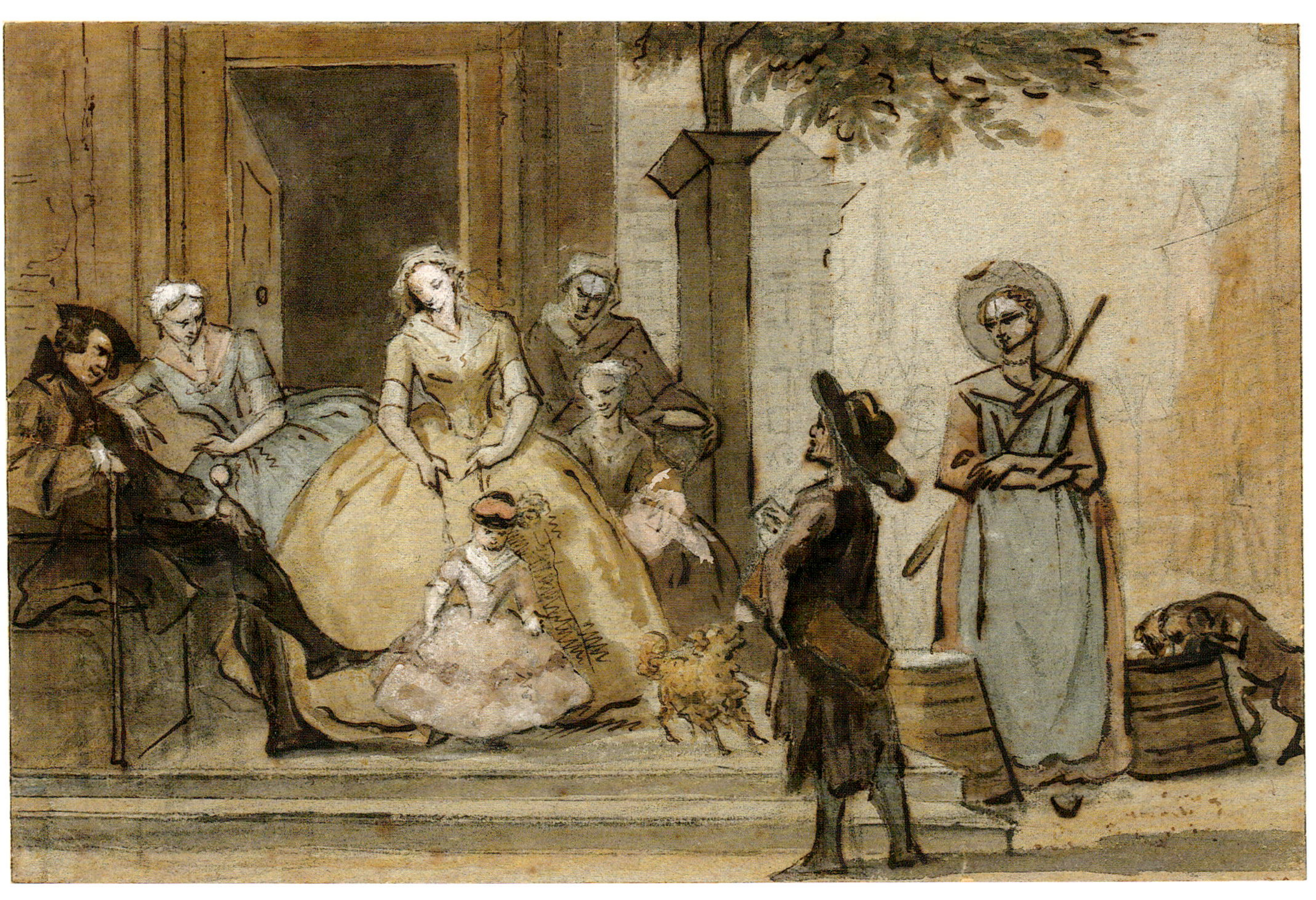

67 The Delivery Room

Pen in brown and gray, brush and gouache; brown and black border
260 x 420 mm
Signed at lower left, with brush: *C.Troost 1748*
Inv. no. 1953:227

Troost, himself blessed with children, depicted the subject of childbirth on several occasions. There are at least eight known painted or drawn variants of the theme, the first dating from 1737 and the last from 1749, the year before his death. The artist placed the event alternately in a prosperous or a modest home, by daylight or candle-light, in winter or summer. The constant in each work is the central group of a nurse feeding the baby, with the cradle on her left, and on her right a diaper basket covered with a fine rug. Little changed in this basic composition during those twelve years.

Here, a proud father gazes down approvingly at both the infant and the nurse. In the large four-poster bed, which has been moved to the salon for the occasion, the mother, looking a little pale and wan, awaits the instructions that are being written down by the aged doctor. At the window, a restorative draft is being prepared for her. The ornate vase standing in the hearth indicates that it is summer; in a variant in the Albertina in Vienna, a dog warms itself by the fire. The sumptuous decoration of the room may stem from Troost's early career as a painter of stage sets. He has made little attempt to depict a realistic interior, and consequently he has allowed his imagination free rein in the room's ornamentation. In a broader sense, he was continuing a seventeenth-century tradition that had flourished, above all, in Leiden through the work of Gerard Dou, Jan Steen, Quirijn van Brekelenkam, and Troost's slightly older contemporary Willem van Mieris.

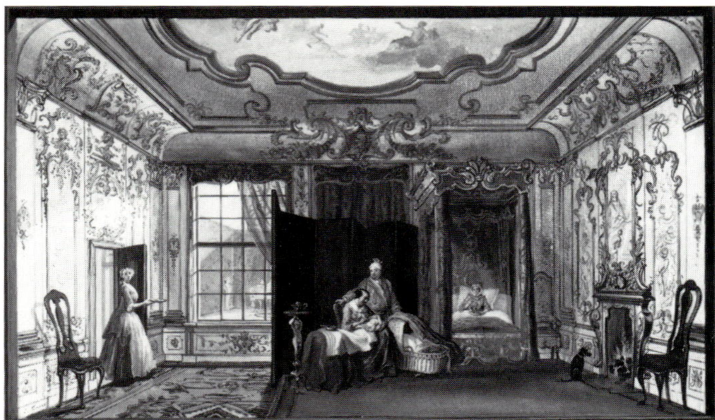

Cornelis Troost, Delivery Room. Vienna, Albertina.

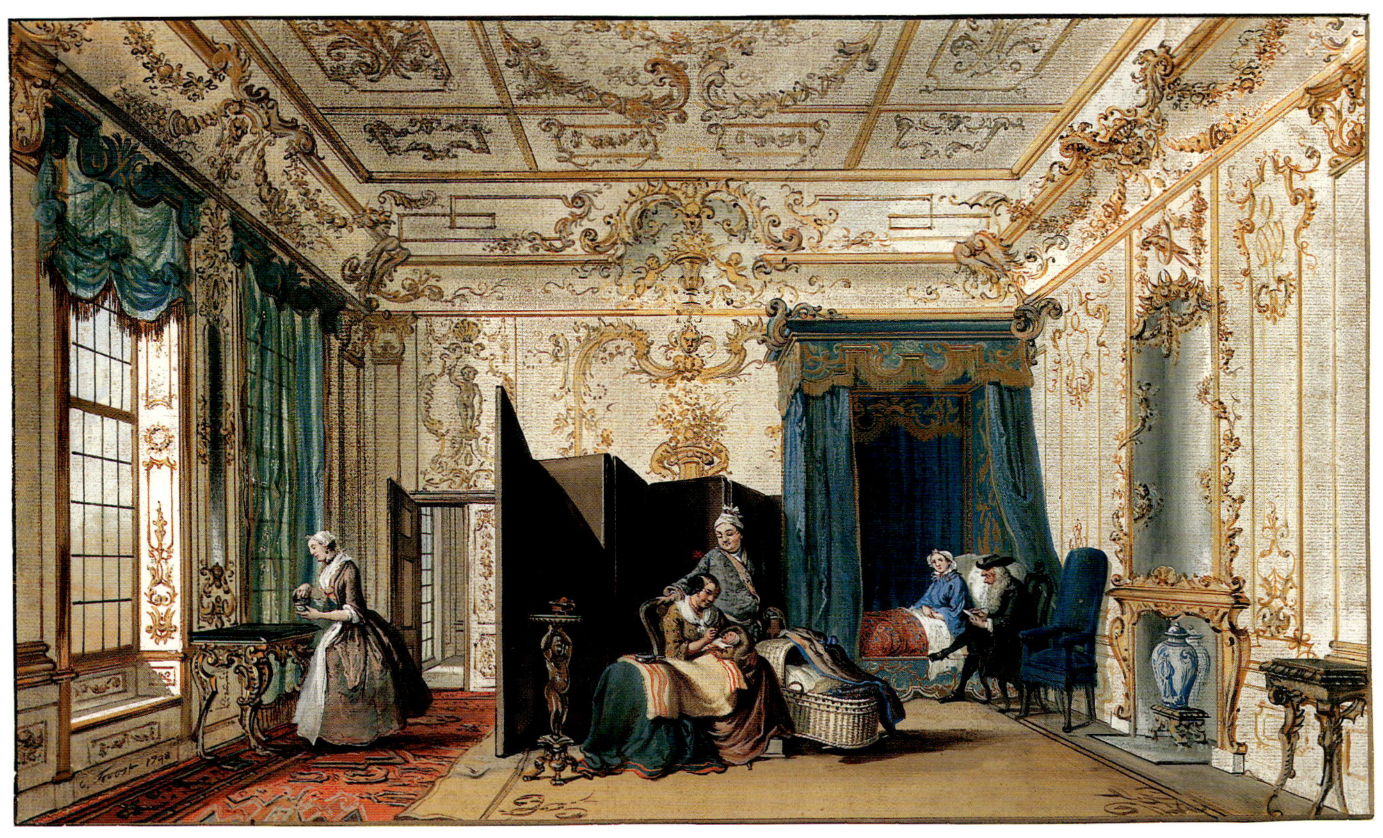

68 **Military Guardroom**

Brush in gouache; narrow gold border
312 x 485 mm
Signed at lower left, with brush: *C.Troost.1748*
Inv. no. 1953:226

In the seventeenth century, military guardrooms were depicted in the Netherlands by such artists as Willem Duyster, Pieter Codde, and Hendrik Pot. Troost, however, cast the subject in an entirely new mold. Instead of being untidy and shrouded in semidarkness, the guardrooms he depicted are spick-and-span and brightly lit, and just a little theatrical in construction. All date from the 1740s, which might be related to the rearming of European nations in response to the tensions aroused by determining the successor to Emperor Charles VI, who died in 1740. These animosities culminated in the War of the Austrian Succession (1741-48). The Dutch Republic enlarged its army, partly through the addition of foreign hussar corps. The swarthy man who wears a saber and a fur cap topped with a feather, and stands by the open fire, rather aloof from the rest, is undoubtedly a hussar officer.

In 1747, Troost produced a scene of a large guardroom (bought by the Mauritshuis in 1980). It contains numerous details that identify it as a propaganda piece for the stadtholder's pro-English party. In this gouache, the crowned arms of the Prince of Orange (Willem IV) hang beside those of the United Provinces to proclaim their shared loyalties.

This gouache became famous shortly after Troost's death through a full-size print engraved after it in 1754 by Jan Punt and Pieter Tanjé. It bears the title *Corps de Garde of Dutch Officers.*

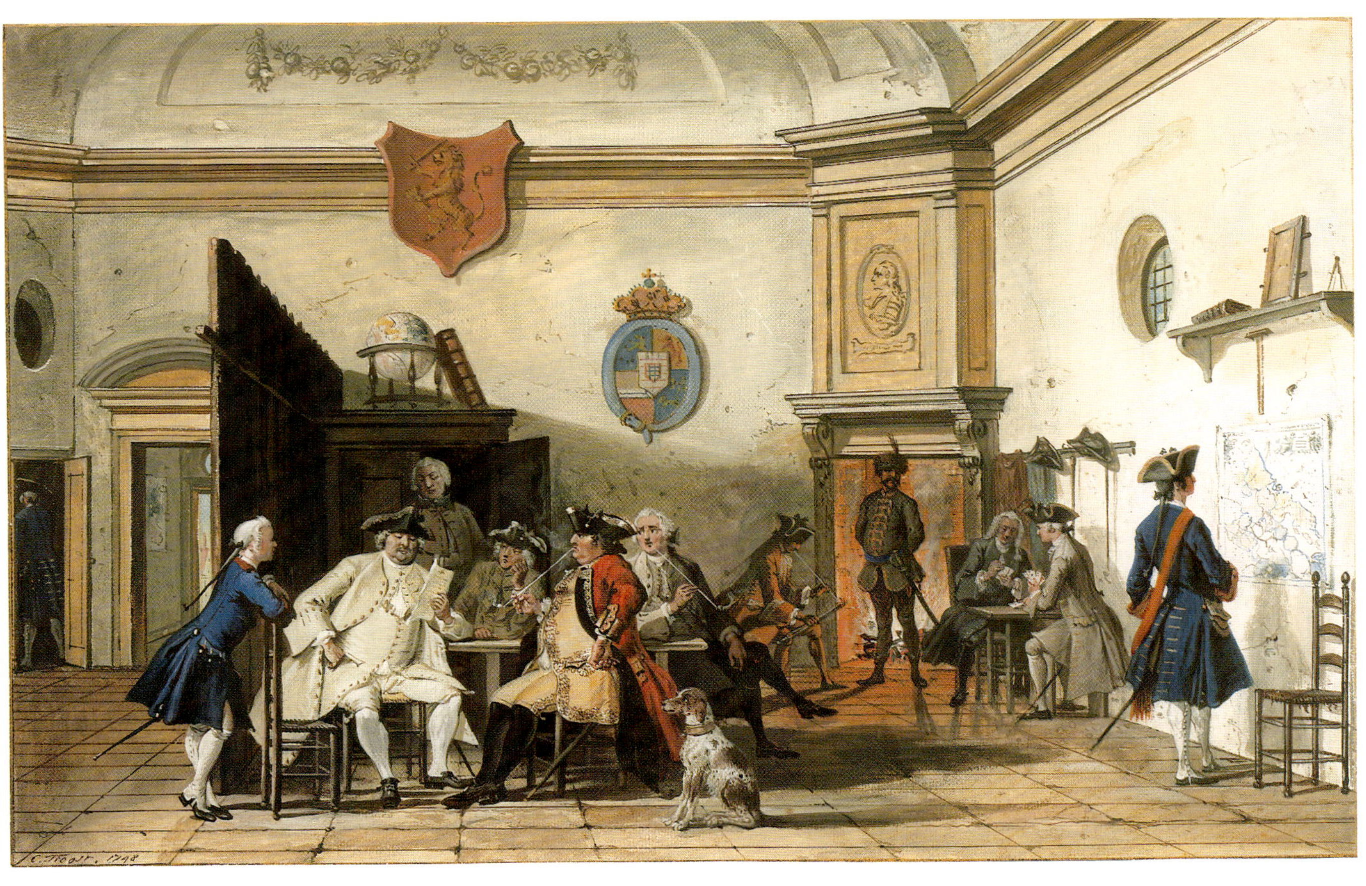

A well-known and very productive draftsman and engraver. For about ten years, Reinier Vinkeles was the pupil and assistant of the draftsman, engraver, and actor Jan Punt (1711-1779). In 1762, Vinkeles became a member of the local drawing academy, and he was appointed one of its directors as early as 1765. That same year he and Jurriaan Andriessen (see cat. nos. 1-5), and Andriessen's colleague Izaak Schmidt (1740-1818), took a sketching trip to Brabant, in the south of the country. Five years later Vinkeles traveled to Paris to study with the famous engraver Jacques Philippe Le Bas (1707-1783), with whom he also lodged. Among the Dutch artists whom he met there were Hermanus Numan (see cat. nos. 47, 48) and Izaak de Wit (1744-1809).

Upon his return to Amsterdam in 1771, Vinkeles was inundated with orders for stage and book illustrations, history prints, topographical views, engraved portraits, copies after paintings, and much more. According to Van Eynden and Van der Willigen, "More than 2,500 prints were engraved either by him or under his supervision, 1,500 of them to his own designs." Although this massive output did occasionally lead to drabness, he still managed to retain a sparkling spontaneity in works that date from his best period, the years around 1780. Some of them contain echoes of his time in Paris. His brother Hermanus worked in his studio, as did his sons Abraham, Johannes, and Reinier, Jr. His pupils were Jacob Ernst Marcus (1774-1826) and Abraham Hulk (1751-1817?).

69 Amsterdam, Dam Square with the Town Hall and Weigh House

Pen in gray, and watercolor; double gray border
230 x 345 mm
Signed on a bale in right foreground: *RVF.* [R and V interlaced]
Inv. no. 1968:97

The Dam, which is still the main square in the Dutch capital, is dominated by the severe lines of the seventeenth-century classicist Town Hall (now the Royal Palace), of which this is the main front. To the right is a glimpse of the New Church, and on the extreme right the Weigh House, which was demolished in 1808 on the orders of Louis Napoleon, who had been made king of Holland by his brother, the French emperor, and who had chosen the Town Hall as his residence. This eighteenth-century watercolor is, in essence, an updated version of the many seventeenth-century views of the Town Hall and Dam Square that were painted by the brothers Gerrit and Job Berckheyde. Vinkeles himself made several versions of this townscape, both colored and plain, all of which seem to date from the years 1764, 1766, or 1767. They are so similar to this, slightly smaller sheet that it must be given a comparable date. It was around this time, 1766-67, that Vinkeles arranged for the city's Drawing Academy to move into a room in the Town Hall.

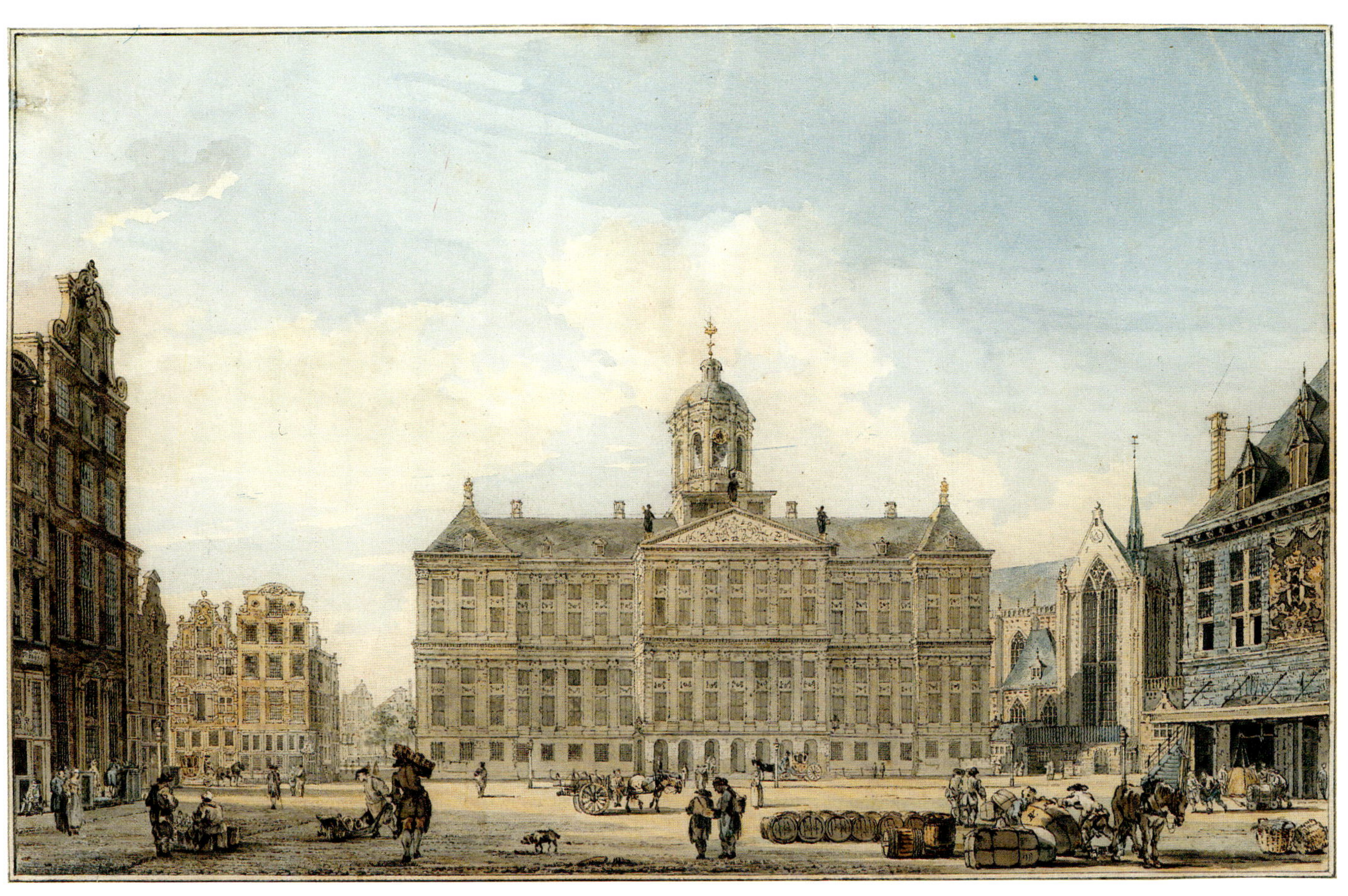

Jacob de Wit (Amsterdam 1696-1754 Amsterdam)

Celebrated history painter who specialized in room and salon decroations. At a very early age Jacob de Wit was apprenticed for several years to Albert van Spiers in Amsterdam, a now totally obscure painter of wall decorations. De Wit then trained with his godfather, Jacob (or Jacomo) de Wit, an art dealer in Antwerp, and shortly afterwards became the pupil of Jacob van Hal in the same city. He seems to have returned to Amsterdam in 1715, but his years in Antwerp were well spent. His direct and intensive confrontation with the art of Peter Paul Rubens and his pupils proved an important element in De Wit's artistic education.

De Wit's career in Amsterdam began in Amsterdam with a series of decorations for the Roman Catholic Moses and Aaron Church, which spawned commissions for other Catholic churches. His clientele rapidly expanded to include the ruling patrician families of Amsterdam, collectors elsewhere in the Republic, and patrons in Paris and London, and probably in Kassel and Lisbon as well.

The phenomenal speed at which he worked enabled him to meet an unceasing demand for chamber paintings and decorations for overmantels, overdoors, and ceilings. The artist's creative imagination led to lasting innovations in the embellishment of ceilings. His works in grisaille were particularly popular – virtuoso painted imitations of stucco in white and gray, known in Holland as "witjes" in a play on his name (Wit meaning white). This renowned artist received his most important commission from the burgomasters of Amsterdam for a painting measuring more than 5 by 12_ meters for the Council Chamber of the Town Hall, the subject being Moses Selecting the Seventy Elders.

Next to the portraitist Johan Maurits Quinkhard, De Wit was the highest paid painter in the city. In 1742 his annual income was assessed at 4,000 guilders, a sum matched only by a few apothecaries, surgeons, and preachers, but not by a single lawyer, goldsmith, or silversmith.

70 Hovering Cherubs with a Basket of Flowers

Pencil, pen in brown, and brush in brown, red, and gray; brown border
169 x 177 mm
Signed at lower left, in pen: *JdWit inv[t]&F.*
On verso, inscribed by De Wit: . . . *voor de wel Edl vrouw*
Mevrouw de Wed[e]. Jacob Cromhout vrouwe van Nie[uwerkerk] [cropped]
Inv. no. 1898 A 3751

De Wit habitually noted the client's name on the back of his designs, which makes them an invaluable source of documentary information. In this case, the full inscription would have read: *Geschilderd voor de wel Edele vrouwe Mevrouw de Weduwe Jacob Cromhout vrouwe van Nieuwerkerk* (Painted for the noble lady, the widow of Jacob Cromhout, Lady of Nieuwerkerk). There may also have been a date. Born in 1671, Jacob Cromhout van Nieuwerkerk died on November 21, 1722. His widow, herself a Cromhout, died on March 12, 1737, so De Wit's painting must have been executed some time between the years of 1722 and 1737.

There is little chance of discovering the house in which this small-scale decorative work (probably a ceiling piece) was installed. Jacob Cromhout, a wealthy Catholic, generously patronized his fellow Catholic De Wit at the start of his artistic career, and he commissioned decorations for several of his houses, both on Amsterdam's Herengracht and in his country seat in the Beemster polder, northeast of the city. That was in the period of 1717 to 1719. It seems that Cromhout's widow, who was still relatively young, wanted the artist to continue decorating one or more of her houses.

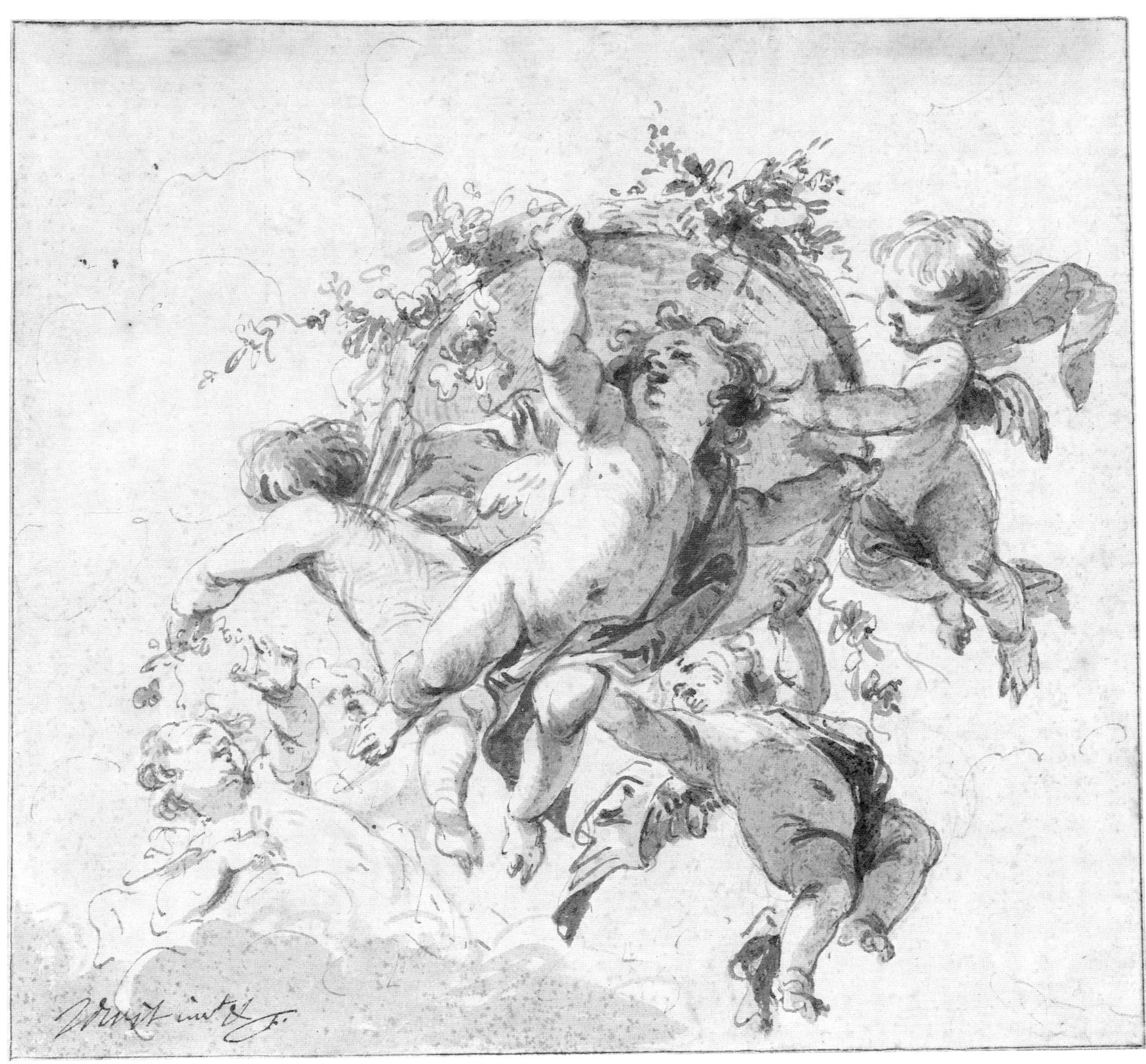

71 Design for a Ceiling Painting with Diana and Endymion (by J. de Wit) in an Architectural Frame (by Isaac de Moucheron)

De Wit's drawing:
Pencil, pen in brown, and watercolor; triple brown border (with quadrantal corners)
200 x 200 mm
Signed at lower left, in pen: *JdWit F inv^t^*.

Frame:
Pen in brown, brush in brown and gray
324 x 236 mm
On verso, below, (in De Moucheron's hand?), in pencil:
t zaeltjen van Moucheron / Hemzelf & J De Wit
(Moucheron's small chamber / himself and J. de Wit)
At lower left, in hand of A. VerHuell, in pen: *Der Vereeniging / Rembrandt aangeboden / 1884*
(Presented to the Rembrandt Society in 1884)
With stamp: A. Ver Huell
Penciled annotation by C. Hofstede de Groot:
Afkomstig van Ploos van Amstel (From Ploos van Amstel)
No inv. no.

The central scene shows Diana, the moon goddess, inflamed with love for Endymion and gazing down on him after he has been granted the gift of eternal sleep. The object of her love was actually a king's son who had decided to work as a shepherd in order to study the course and guises of the moon, which is why he is shown with an astrolabe and a sextant. De Wit's composition may have been inspired by a lengthy passage in Gerard de Lairesse's *Groot schilderboek* (Dutch edition, Amsterdam, 1707, pp. 128-30), which contains a detailed description of a painting of Diana and Endymion that was probably by the author himself.
This is actually a composite drawing in two parts. According to an inscription on one section, they jointly reproduce the ceiling decoration of a small room in the house of Isaac de Moucheron, the artist responsible for the ornamental frame. The two works have always been exhibited and reproduced as an ensemble, but in fact, the contours of De Wit's ceiling design simply do not fit into De Moucheron's frame. Moreover, the latter has paste marks that are now covered by De Wit's drawing.
In the Städelsches Kunstinstitut in Frankfurt-am-Main is a drawing with an annotation on the back in De Wit's hand, which reads: *Plaffon voor de Hr. Isac de Moucheron 1726 geschildert* (Ceiling painted for Isaac de Moucheron, 1726). And that sheet – of a sky scene with Flora above and putti holding flowers below – fits far better into De Moucheron's frame. It seems quite likely that this was De Wit's original design.
Since 1726, Isaac de Moucheron had been living on Prinsengracht, in a residence now numbered 794. The house's interior was evidently remodeled in the second half of the eighteenth century and again at the end of the nineteenth. The front room retains the wainscoting and a fireplace from De Moucheron's day, but the architecture depicted in this drawing can no longer be found there or in any other part of the house. De Wit's ceiling, which, according to his own annotation, was executed in 1726, must have been removed, for it has now completely disappeared. Sadly, then, this joint work is not the interesting document that records the friendly collaboration between De Wit and De Moucheron that it was thought to be. There is, however, an imposing monument to their association in the decoration in the front room of the Theater Museum in Amsterdam (Herengracht 168).

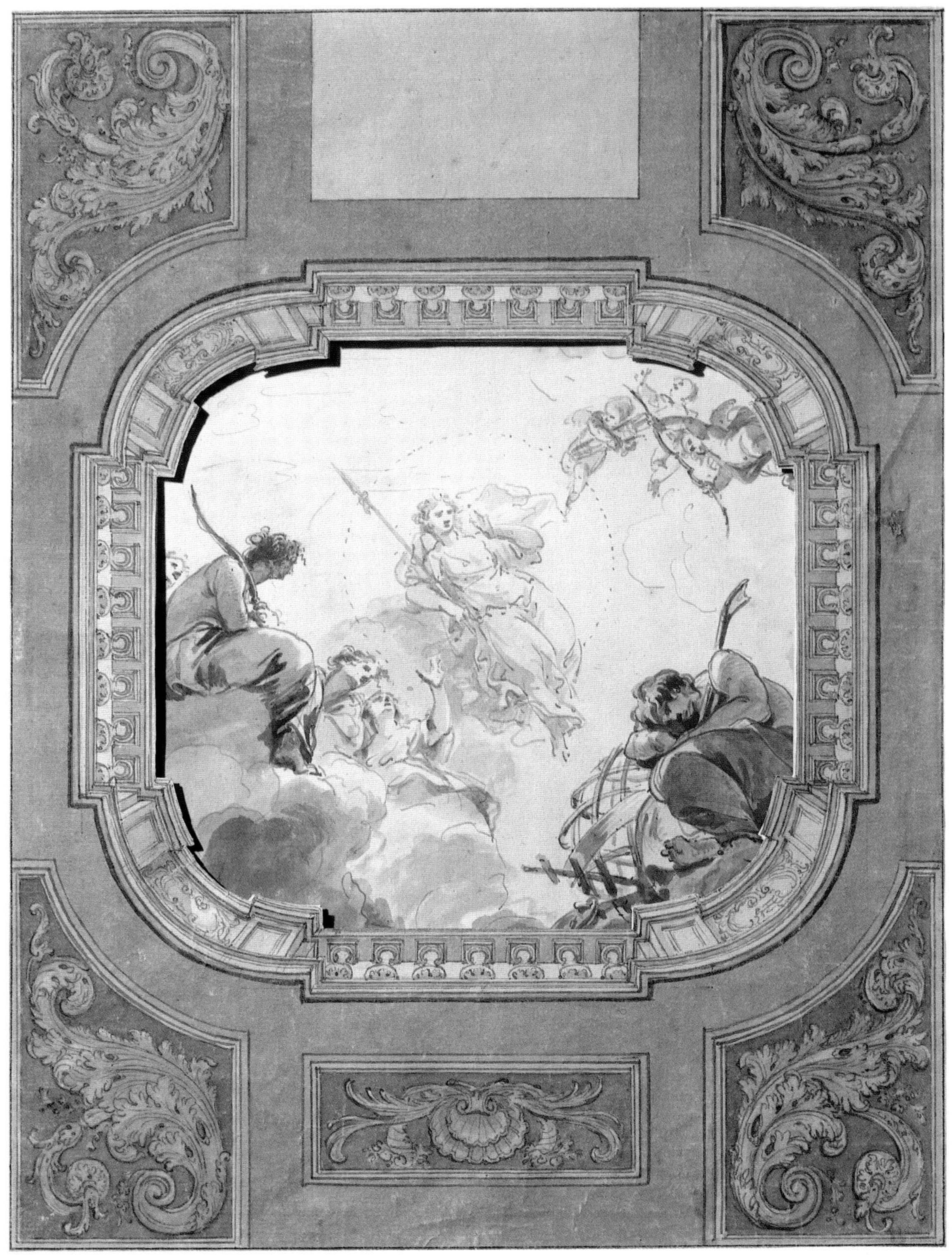

72 **Callisto, Cupid, and Jupiter with the Eagle**

Pencil, pen in gray-brown, watercolor in various colors, and gouache on brown prepared paper; gray border
260 x 156 mm
Signed at lower left, in pen: *JdWit F* [illegible] *1746inv^{t}*.
Inv. Felix Meritis no. 159

One of the companions of Diana, goddess of the hunt, was the beautiful and chaste Callisto. According to myth, when Jupiter set eyes on her, he instantly fell in love, and in order to satisfy his desire took on the guise of Diana herself (or her brother Apollo, as related in other sources). When Callisto was no longer able to conceal her pregnancy, Diana transformed her into a she-bear. She was slain by a hunter's spear, whereupon Jupiter took her into heaven as the constellation of the Great Bear. These are the broad outlines of the legend, of which there are numerous variants.

De Wit returned to this theme several times in his work. In 1727, almost twenty years prior to this drawing, he painted a work (now in the Rijksmuseum) in which Jupiter, disguised as Diana, embraces Callisto. That composition, almost the mirror image of this sheet, has a pendant image of Jupiter with a woman who is probably Mnemosyne, the ancient Greek goddess of memory. Both paintings are almost 2 meters high, and so were evidently executed as room decorations. It is possible that this particular drawing was a design for a similar canvas, and that it, too, was one of a pair.

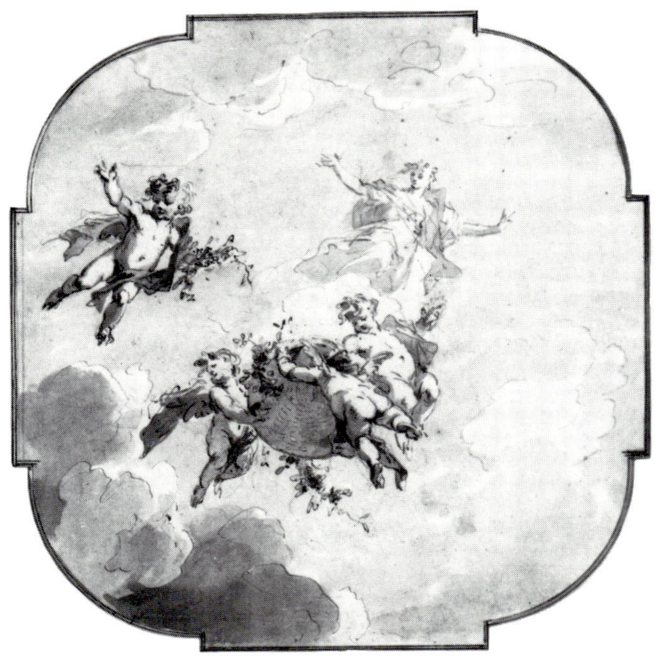

Jacob de Wit, design for a ceiling in the house of Isaac de Moucheron. Frankfurt-am-Main, Städelsches Kunstinstitut.

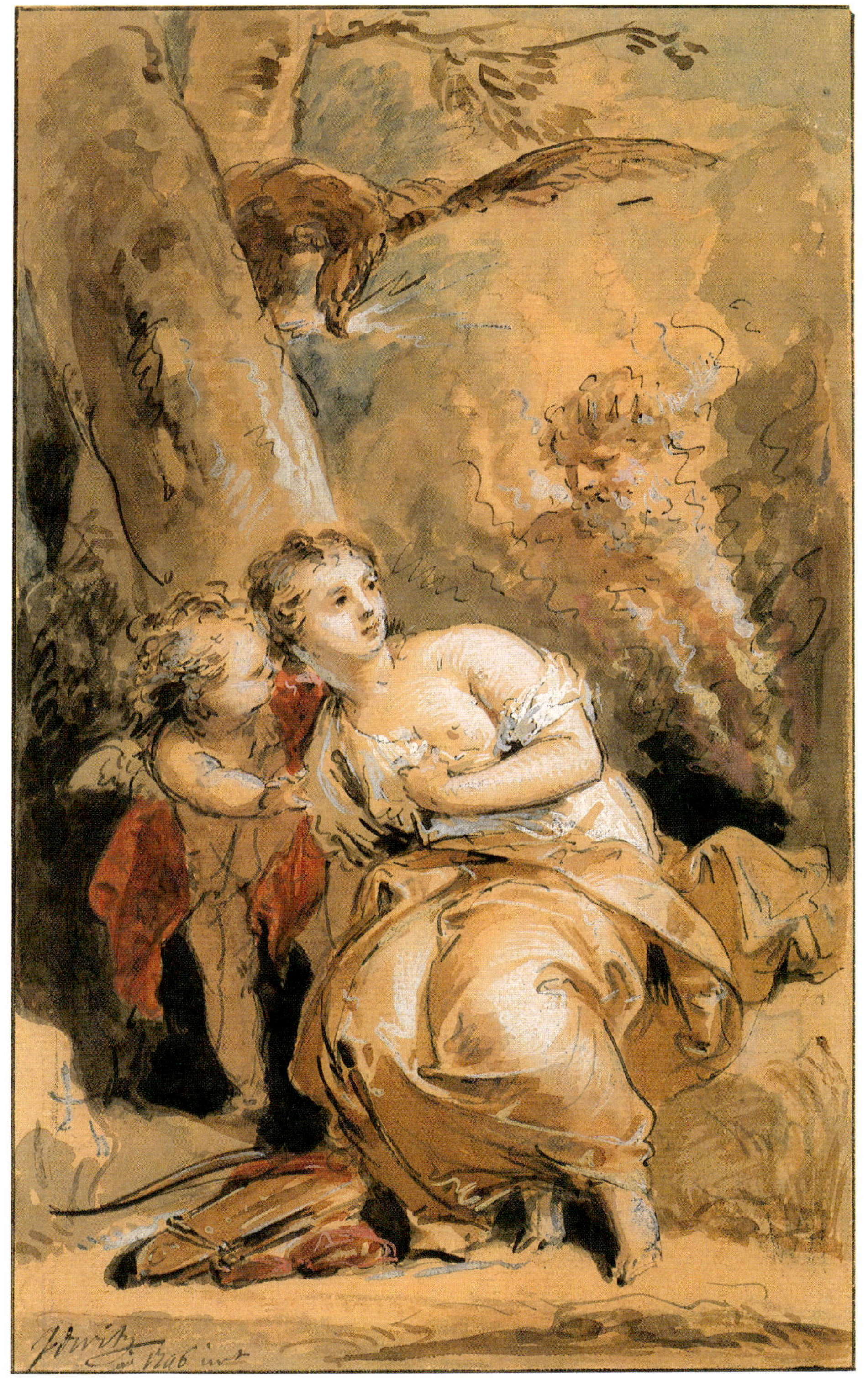

73 **Scene in the Garden of a Town House (from a Stage Play)**
Pen in brown, and watercolor; brown border
353 x 402 mm
Inv. no. 1906:22, as Anonymous, later attributed to Isaak Ouwater

The dress of the main character in this scene, a little girl seated by a rosebush, shows that this watercolor must date from the very end of the eighteenth century – probably, in fact, from the early years of the nineteenth century. That estimation rules out the drawing's traditional attribution to Isaak Ouwater, who died in 1793. Moreover, Ouwater was a true topographer who rarely depicted anything but towns, villages, and country houses, and this is a scene from a play. Although it is not explicitly depicted as such, the setting is clearly a stage, complete with a backdrop of a small garden with an exotic-looking tented bower (which could also be found in real life) and a painted floor canvas for the cobbles. The trees and architectural elements serve as stage wings and frame the entrance onto the stage. The girl plucks a rose and sits on a bench (that, in reality, would never have been placed so far off-center.) On the right two adults, who may be her parents, watch and listen with interest. It has not been possible to discover whether this is a scene taken from a published play or to identify the draftsman, although Pieter Barbiers would make a good candidate (see cat. nos. 6, 7). In addition to painting a large number of stage sets for the Amsterdam Playhouse, he had, from 1781, supplied a series of gouache decors for the miniature theater owned by Hieronymus, Baron van Slingelandt. This watercolor is very similar to some of those sets, which are now in the Theater Museum in Amsterdam, and especially to one entitled *Zomerbos* (Summer Wood). This watercolor may also have been a design for a set in one of the other miniature theaters to be found at fairs and in the houses of rich connoisseurs in Amsterdam and elsewhere.

74 **Watercolor box**
Anonymous owner, 1781
Wooden box with engraved labels on paper; box contains pigments, brush, and scraping knife
20 x 210 x 89 mm
Printroom, Rijksmuseum

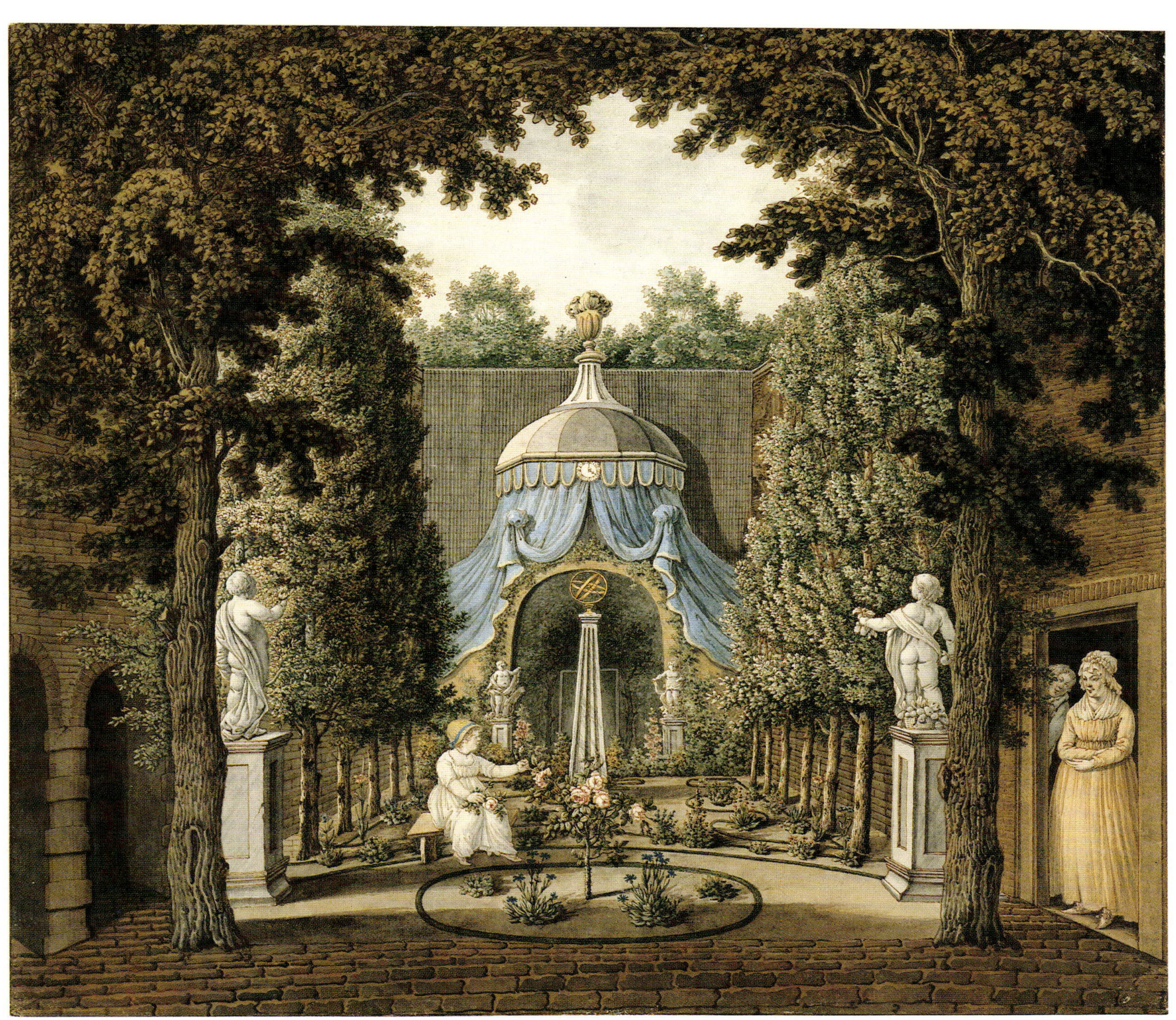

Bibliography and Notes (publications up to Spring 1990)

Introduction

On the practice of coloring seventeenth-century drawings see Ben Broos, "Improving and Finishing Old Master Drawings: an Art in Itself," *Hoogsteder-Naumann Mercury* 8 (1989), pp. 34-55.

Selected readings on eighteenth-century Dutch artists in France: L. Réau, *Historie de l'expansion de l'art français (moderne)*, 4 vols. (Paris, 1924-30), esp. vol. 2 (1928), p. 284; and J.G. Wille, *Mémoires et Journal*, ed. G. Duplessis, 2 vols. (Paris, 1857). Also see the artists' biographies by Weyerman, Van Gool, and Van Eynden and Van der Willigen, given in the section "Abbreviated Literature" (p. 173).

Sir Joshua Reynolds's manuscript notes for his travel journal are preserved at the Fondation Custodia in Paris. Various published editions exist. The one used here was edited by Edmond Malone, 3 vols. (London, 1809).

Other travel accounts cited: Thomas Bowdler, *Letters written in Holland in the Months of September and October 1787* (London, 1788); Katherine Fremantle, *Sir James Thornhill's Sketch-book Travel Journal of 1711* (Utrecht, 1975); Alexander Fergusson, *Letters and Journals of Mrs. Calderwood of Polton from England, Holland and the Low Countries in 1756* (Edinburgh, 1884); *The Memoirs of Charles-Lewiss, Baron de Pollnits, being the Observations he made in his Late Travels from Prussia through Germany, Italy, France, Flanders, Holland, England, etc. in Letters to his Friend*, 4 vols., 2d ed. (London, 1734-40); [C. A. Pilati de Tassulo], *Lettres sur la Hollande*, 2 vols. (The Hague, 1780); De la Barre de Beaumarchais, *Le Hollandois, ou Lettre sur la Hollande ancienne et moderne* (Frankfurt, 1738); Thomas Holcroft, *Travels from Hamburgh through Westphalia, Holland and the Netherlands to Paris*, 2 vols. (London, 1804); *Lettres de Madame du Boccage, contenant ses voyages en France, en Angleterre, en Hollande et en Italie, faits pendant les années 1750, 1757 et 1758* (Dresden, 1771); Thomas Pennant, *Tour on the Continent 1765*, ed. G.R. de Beer (London, 1948); A. Doedens, L. Mulder, and A.C. Bijsman, *Het dagboek van Sir Matthew Decker. Een Nederlandse Engelsman over Nederland in 1748 en de buitens in de 18de eeuw* (Baarn, 1987); C.H. von Heinecken, *Nachrichten von Künstlern und Kunst-Sachen*, vol. 2 (Leipzig, 1769); Wilhelm Tischbein, *Aus meinem Leben*, ed. Lothar Brieger (Berlin, 1922); Samuel Ireland, *A Picturesque Tour through Holland, Brabant and Part of Flanders, Made in the Autumn of 1789*, 2d ed. (London, 1796); and J. Grabner, *Ueber die vereinigten Niederlande. Briefe* (Gotha, 1792).
P.C. Hasselaer Collection: sale, Amsterdam, November 28, 1797.

Andriessen

Biography:
Van Eynden and Van der Willigen, vol. 3, pp. 12-15.
J. Knoef, "Jurriaan Andriessen," in *Tusschen Rococo en Romantiek* (The Hague, 1943), pp. 3-20. Knoef perpetuates the confusion, general at the time, with the "drawn diary" of Christiaan Andriessen. The situation was finally clarified by Miss I.H. van Eeghen in an article that appeared in *Maandblad Amstelodamum* in January 1964.
T.H. Lunsingh Scheurleer, "Een Amsterdamse zaal met wandschilderingen van Jurriaan Andriessen," *Bulletin van het Rijksmuseum Amsterdam* 1 (1953), pp. 19-24; and Scheurleer, "Naschrift," *Bulletin van het Rijksmuseum Amsterdam* 2 (1954), p. 47.

Cat. no. 2 (Mediterranean Coast with Pyramid)
Data on the La Borde, Sander, and Josèphe families were compiled at my request in the Amsterdam City Archives by T. Brockmeier, through the good services of B. Bakker. Supplementary information was obtained from the collection of newspaper announcements of births, marriages, and deaths at the Centraal Bureau voor Genealogie in The Hague, and from the Rijksarchief (Public Record Office) in Utrecht. See also M.N. van Loon and I.H. van Eeghen, *Het Huis met de paarse ruiten* (Alphen aan den Rijn, 1984), and *De Indische Navorscher* 3 (1937), p. 56.
The drawings by Van der Wal (or Wall) appeared at auction in Utrecht on April 10-11, 1935, no. 366, and April 18-24, 1939, no. 800.
For Andriessen's drawing of the large lake at Drakensteyn see sale, D.C. Meyer, Amsterdam, December 12-14, 1910, no. 1176. Another watercolor of Drakensteyn is in the Whitworth Art Gallery, Manchester (no. D/217/1926).
For views in De Vuursche by Jacob Cats and Egbert van Drielst see sale, Langerhuizen, Amsterdam, April 29, 1919, no. 133 (ill.), and sale, J. de Vos, Amsterdam, May 22-24, 1883, no. 649.

Cat. no. 4 (View of a Dike outside Amsterdam)
Zeeburg Inn on the Zeeburgerdijk, or Diemerdijk, is depicted in an anonymous engraving in the Amsterdam City Archives (inv. no. K112-13*a*).

Cat. no. 5 (Strollers on a Woodland Path near Heemstede)
Almost all the works that are discussed by G.H. Kurtz in "De tekenaar Jurriaan Andriessen in de omstreken van Haarlem," *Jaarboek Haerlem* (1943), pp. 57-61, are now attributed to Christiaan Andriessen.
On Manpad House see Kurtz, *Jaarboek Haerlem* (1954), pp. 44-61.

Barbiers

Biography:
Van Eynden and Van der Willigen, vol. 3, pp. 49-50; *Aanhangsel*, p. 193.
Barbiers died on his birthday, October 26. He was born in 1749, and not in 1748, as is so often stated.
One of the Thurkow panels was included in the exhibition catalogue *Dutch Masterpieces from the Eighteenth Century* (Minneapolis, etc., 1971), as cat. no. 3, pl. 88.

De Beijer

Biography:
Van Gool, vol. 2, pp. 199-200.
Van Eynden and Van der Willigen, vol. 2, pp. 37-39; *Aanhangsel*, p. 161.
H. Romers, *J. de Beyer. Oeuvre-catalogus* (The Hague, 1969); and Guido de Werd, *Jan de Beyer (1703-1780). Zeichnungen von Emmerich bis Roermond* exhib. cat., Cleves (Haus Koekkoek), 1980, with earlier literature. On p. 10 it is assumed that De Beijer was already studying with Pronk before 1731, but this is disputed by P.J. Klapwijk in *Leids Kunsthistorisch Jaarboek* 1985 (Delft, 1987), p. 185 and p. 199, n. 10.

Cat. no. 8 (Leiden Town Hall)
The drawing in Leiden is Bodel Nijenhuis Atlas, University Library, Leiden, inv. no. P308-IIN10.
The drawing in the Kunstsammlungen Weimar is inv. no. KK4785.
Beschrijving der Stad Leyden by Frans van Mieris: vol. 1 (Leiden, 1767); vol. 2, by Daniël van Alphen (Leiden, 1770); the print is in vol. 2, facing p. 365. For Van der Marck see vol. 2, pp. 424-25.
For the De Beijer portrait see sale cat. Van der Marck, Amsterdam, November 29, 1773, p. 220, no. 1796.

Cat. no. 9 (Merry Company in the Village of Houten)
For the Brussels drawing see Musées Royaux des Beaux-Arts, De Grez Collection, cat. 1913, no. 280, on the same sheet as *Huis te Vuilkoop*, which is dated 1749. A drawing in the Amsterdam Printroom (inv. no. A 4156) gives the same view but without the figures. It is dated 2 August 1749 and may be a copy (possibly by P. van Liender) after De Beijer's life sketch on which the Brussels drawing is based.
A third view of the village of Houten, but from the other side and dated 1737, is in the collection of the Rijksdienst voor de Monumentenzorg in Zeist (inv. no. Th-14-a).
A fourth, in the possession of the Fondation Custodia in Paris (inv. no. 9231), and likewise made in 1737, is a rather weak effort that also shows the village from the other side.

Cat. no. 10 (The Town Hall at Venlo)
Guido de Werd (Cleves, 1980) no. 155 (with earlier literature).

Buys

Biography:
Van Eynden and Van der Willigen, vol. 2, pp. 85-88.
Van Gool, vol. 2, pp. 272-73.
N.G. van Huffel, "Jacobus Buys," *Oude Kunst* 2 (1916-17), p. 272.
E.W. Moes, *Jacobus Buys, de Twaalf Maanden* (Amsterdam, 1908).
J.W. Niemeijer, "Een door Buys geschilderde familiegroep Ploos van Amstel teruggevonden," *Oud Holland* 81 (1966), pp. 34-43.
J.W. Niemeijer, "Jacobus Buys," in *Cornelis Troost 1696-1750* (Assen, 1973), ch. 10, pp. 119-23.
L. Buynsters-Smets, "Jacobus Buys als boekillustrator," *Documentatieblad Werkgroep 18de eeuw* 16 (1984), pp. 91-107.
R.J.A. te Rijdt, "Een door Jacobus Buys geschilderd portret van Floris Bontekoning en zijn familie," *Jaarboek Centraal Bureau voor Genealogie* 40 (1986), pp. 163-73.
For the purchase of his house see I.H. van Eeghen in *Maandblad Amstelodamum* 61 (1974), p. 26.

Cat. no. 11 (The Unexpected Twins)
For the actors see J.M. Coffeng, *Lexicon van Nederlandse Tonelisten* (Amsterdam, 1965).

The drawing of Spatsier, in brown ink and watercolor, is dated 1770 and is in the collection of H. van Leeuwen, Amerongen; see *De verzameling van H. van Leeuwen*, exhib. cat., Amsterdam (Rijksprentenkabinet), 1975, no. 25. The print is described in F. Muller, *Beredeneerde beschrijving van Nederlandsche Historieplaten*, vol. 4 (Amsterdam, 1882), no. 4092B. There is a specimen in the Amsterdam Printroom. A painting by Buys (location unknown) is mentioned by Van Eynden and Van der Willigen, vol. 2, p. 87.
For a painting with a scene from *Het Koffyhuis* see sale, Jac. Buys and others, Amsterdam, February 16, 1802, no. 4.

Cats

Biography:
Van Eynden and Van der Willigen, vol. 2, pp. 303-16.
C.P. van Eeghen, "Jacob Cats en de Husly's als decorateurs van het huis Heerengracht 310 [in Amsterdam]," *Jaarboek Amstelodamum* 38 (1941), pp. 133-55.
S.A.C. Dudok van Heel, "Jacob Cats e.a. als behangselschilders in de fabriek van Jan Hendrik Troost van Groenendoelen," *Maandblad Amstelodamum* 59 (1972), p. 151f.

Cat. no. 12 (Street Scene in Beverwijk)
The drawings by Tavenier are in the Haarlem City Archives and the Zaandijk Museum. The painting appeared at auction in Amsterdam (Mak van Waay) on September 29, 1970, no. 103 (reproduced in the catalogue).

Cat. no. 15 (Visit to a Nursery Garden)
There are two editions of the prints. In the first, the months are given their usual names; in the second they are referred to by their popular names: "Louwmaand," "Sprokkelmaand," "Lentemaand," "Grasmaand" and so on. The drawings by the engraver Visser Bender are in the Teyler Museum, Haarlem.
For the months as a theme see J.W. Niemeijer, *Cornelis Troost* (1973), pp. 422-23.
The first quotation is from [C.A. Pilati de Tassulo], *Lettres sur la Hollande*, vol. 2 (The Hague, 1780), p. 172.
The second is from *Journal of a Horticultural Tour through some Parts of Flanders, Holland, and the North of France in the Autumn of 1817* (Edinburgh, 1823), p. 211.

Jacob Helmolt was clearly interested in series of the months, for he also had one by Hendrik Meyer, executed in 1783. See Van Eynden and Van der Willigen, vol. 2, p. 262.
On the nurseries near Haarlem see J. Kuijlen, C.S. Oldenburger-Ebben, and D.O. Wijnands, *Paradisus Batavus* (Wageningen, 1983), pp. 54-59.

Van Drielst

Biography:
Van Eynden and Van der Willigen, vol. 3, pp. 34-39 (with his year of birth given incorrectly as 1746).
J.W. Niemeijer, *Egbert van Drielst 1745-1818, "de Drentse Hobbema,"* exhib. cat., Assen (Provinciaal Museum van Drenthe), 1968.

For Jan Vuring van Drielst see A.J. Elen, in *Delineavit et Sculpsit* 1 (1989), p. 22f. The drawing reproduced there with the name *JVDrielst* is entirely in the style of Egbert van Drielst, apart from the execution, which betrays a weak hand.

Cat. no. 18 (The Ruins of De Haer Castle)
Ruisdael's drawings have been catalogued, with critical apparatus, by J. Giltay in *Oud Holland* 94 (1980), pp. 141-208. His painting of Egmond Castle was on view in Holland in 1982 as part of the Ruisdael exhibition that was shown in the Mauritshuis in The Hague (cat. no. 19).

Dupré

Biography:
Van Eynden and Van der Willigen, vol. 2, pp. 393-97 (with the year of birth incorrectly given as 1752); *Aanhangsel*, p. 187.
See the letter from D. Versteegh to A. van der Willigen, dated December 17, 1818, in the Rijksprentenkabinet, Amsterdam.
For the painted tables and the like see sale, P. van der Schley and D. Dupré, Amsterdam, December 22, 1817, pp. 99 and 101.

Cat. nos. 19 and 20 (Views at the Villa d'Este and the Villa Conti)
Dupré's studio estate was auctioned, together with that of the art dealer P. van der Schley, in Amsterdam on December 22, 1817.

Cat. no. 21 (The Arch of Titus)
For Ducros's view of the Arch of Titus (in various versions) see P. Chessex, *Images of the Grand Tour. Louis Ducros 1748-1810*, exhib. cat., London (Kenwood, The Iveagh Bequest), Manchester (The Whitworth Art Gallery), and Lausanne (Musée Cantonale des Beaux-Arts), 1985–86, cat. nos. 1 and 73. That the vista through the gate to the Palazzo dei Conservatori is supposedly an "impossible view," and thus a deliberate distortion of reality (p. 46), is contradicted by the photograph in Ernest Nash, *Bild-lexikon zur Topographie des Antiken Rom*, vol. 1 (Tübingen, 1961), p. 133.
For the Arch of Titus itself see Marita Jonsson, *Monumentvårdens begynnelse* (Uppsala, 1976), pp. 108-28.

Grandjean

Biography:
Van Eynden and Van der Willigen, vol. 2, pp. 376-88.
J.W. Niemeijer, "Academies and other Figure Studies from Jean Grandjean's Roman Period," *Master Drawings* 12 (1974), pp. 351-58.
Reizen naar Rome, exhib. cat., Haarlem (Teyler Museum), 1984, p. 32f.

Cat. no. 22 (Arcadian Landscape)
The two Grandjeans shown at the Delft fair were acquired at a sale in Amsterdam, May 6-14, 1958 (cat. no. 131).

Haag

Biography:
Van Eynden and Van der Willigen, vol. 2, pp. 263-66.
In het zadel. Het Nederlands ruiterportret van 1550 tot 1900, exhib. cat., Leeuwarden (Fries Museum), 's Hertogenbosch (Noordbrabants Museum), and Assen (Provinciaal Museum van Drenthe), 1979–80, nos. 31-33 and 89-99.
As to whether he was actually appointed court painter see Wouter Slob, "De paardenschilder Haag (1737-1812) groeide op in Leeuwarden," *Leeuwarder Courant*, April 8, 1983.
C. Dumas, *Het verheerlijkt Den Haag*, The Hague 1984, p. 134.
For contacts with Schouman and Vosmaer see J.W. Niemeijer, "Het Kunstenaarsalbum van Arnout Vosmaer," in F.L. Bastet *et al.*, *De verzameling van Mr. Carel Vosmaer*, exhib. cat., The Hague and Amsterdam (Rijksprentenkabinet), 1989, pp. 149ff.
For his bird collection see H. Engel, "Alphabetical List of Dutch Zoölogical Cabinets and Menageries," *Bijdragen tot de Dierkunde* 27 (Amsterdam, 1939), p. 277f.
For his stay in Paris see J.G. Wille, *Mémoires*, ed. G. Duplessis, vol. 1 (Paris, 1857), p. 47.

Haag's father was Johan David Christiaan Haag. The elder Haag died at The Hague in 1760, not in 1758 or 1759, as stated in Van Eynden and Van der Willigen, vol. 2, p. 146, who give him the initials J.F.C. He was buried there on April 24, aged 58.

Cat. no. 23 (Stable Interior)
For the series of ten paintings of horses see J.C. Bierens de Haan, in *Meer om Cieraet als Gebruyck*, exhib. cat., Arnhem (Het Arnhems Museum) and Nijmegen (Commanderie van Sint Jan), 1990, no. 222.
For the quotation about horses see Charles Tennant, *Tour through Parts of the Netherlands, Holland [...] in the Year 1821-2*, vol. 1 (London, 1824), p. 139.

Hendriks

Biography:
Van Eynden and Van der Willigen, vol. 3, pp. 21-25; *Aanhangsel*, pp. 37-38.
I.Q. van Regteren Altena, J.H. van Borssum Buisman, and C.J. de Bruyn Kops, *Wijbrand Hendriks 1744-1831* exhib. cat., Haarlem (Teyler Museum), 1972 (with the earlier literature).
On his activities as a painter of wall-hangings in Amsterdam see S.A.C. Dudok van Heel, "Wijbrand Hendriks en de behangselmakers Remmers," *Maandblad Amstelodamum* 59 (1972), pp. 102-9.
C.J. de Bruyn Kops, "Wijbrand Hendriks en Felix Meritis," *Jaarboek Amstelodamum* 70 (1978), pp. 294-311.

For Hendriks's Gelderland period see "St. Lucas Gilde-Boek" [guild-book], Haarlem City Archives, fol. 189-4: *11 april 1786,*

Ontfangen van W. Hendriks de 4 Jaaren welke niet betaald waaren uyt de stadt zijnde (11 April 1786, received from W. Hendriks [the dues for] the four years that had not been paid, he being absent from town).

Cat. no. 26 (Landscape with Ruined Castle)
After its time in the Hoofman Collection, the painting in the Wallace Collection, of which there are several other versions, belonged to the Amsterdam art dealer J.B. van den Bergh from 1818 to 1833, which was in Nuyen's day.

For the iconography of Egmond Castle see J.G.N. Renaud, in *Maandblad voor Beeldende Kunsten* 17 (1940), pp. 338-45.

Henstenburg(h)

Biography:
Van Gool, vol. 1, pp. 248-56.

The sale, held at Mak van Waay in Amsterdam on September 26, 1972, included four drawings by Herman Henstenburgh, twenty-seven by his son Anton, or Antonie, as well as nine by Johannes Bronkhorst. All came from the Van Pallandt family collection.

Cat. no. 27 (Fruit with a Butterfly and a Snail)
W. Goeree, *Verligterie-kunde, of regt gebruik der Water-Verwen. Eertijds uytgegeven door . . . Mr. Geerard Ter Brugge, en nu . . . door W. Goeree* (3d ed., Amsterdam, 1697; reprint, Davaco, Soest, 1974), p. 84.

Horstink

Biography:
Van den Eynden and Van der Willigen, vol. 2, pp. 419-20.
M. Kersten, "Aanwinst: een familieportret uit 1796," *Teylers Museum Magazijn* 20 (Summer 1988), pp. 18-19.

J. van Huysum

Biography:
Van Gool, vol. 2, pp. 13-33.
F. Schlie, "Sieben Briefe und eine Quittung von Jan van Huysum," *Oud-Holland* 18 (1900), pp. 137-43.
M.H. Grant, *Jan van Huysum 1682-1749, including Catalogue Raisonné of the Artist's Fruit & Flower Paintings* (Leigh-on-Sea, 1954).
Christopher White, *The Flower Drawings of Jan van Huysum* (Leigh-on-Sea, 1964).

Cat. no. 29 (Sketch for a Still Life with Fruit and Flowers)
For the painting dated *1730* see sale, collection of Adèle, Lady Meyer, London (Christie's), May 30, 1930, no. 145, with ill. (preliminary drawing: British Museum 1895.9.15.1179, as indicated in White, *Flower Drawings*, 1964, no. 28). For the painting dated both *1732* and *1733* see collection of Sir Brian Mountain, Bart., Grant 1954, no. 162 (drawing Louvre 22.673, as indicated in White, *Flower Drawings*, 1964, no. 106). The drawing in the Dutuit Collection: see White *Flower Drawings*, 1964, no. 115.

M. van Huysum

Biography:
The best survey is still C. Hofstede de Groot's article in Thieme and Becker's *Künstlerlexikon*, vol. 18 (Leipzig, 1925), p. 209, even if he does, at the end, put words in Van Gool's mouth that are not to be found in the latter's *Nieuwe Schouburg*, vol. 2, p. 31. Van Huysum's dates are taken from the baptismal and burial registers in the Amsterdam City Archives.

For his pupils see "Ledenlijst honoraire leden der Amsterdamse Tekenacademie," Amsterdam City Archives (PA 265, no. 41A).

Cat. no. 31 (A Calabash, Two Peaches, and a Walnut)
For symbolism in eighteenth-century still lifes see M. van Boven and S. Segal, *Gerard & Cornelis van Spaendonck* (Maarssen, 1980).

Keyert

Biography:
A. Wassenbergh, "De decoratieschilders der 18de eeuw en het stadhuis te Leeuwarden," *Gedenkboek Leeuwarden 1435-1935* (Leeuwarden, 1935), pp. 153-58.

Kobell

Biography:
Van Eynden and Van der Willigen, vol. 2, pp. 373-76.
Wilhelm Tischbein, *Aus meinem Leben*, ed. L. Brieger (Berlin, [1922]), p. 84.
For contacts with Cornelis Ploos van Amstel see T. Laurentius, J.W. Niemeijer, and Jhr. G. Ploos van Amstel, *Cornelis Ploos van Amstel 1726-1798, kunstverzamelaar en prentuitgever* (Assen, 1980), ch. 5, "Artistieke contacten."
"Ledenlijst Tekenacademie Amsterdam," Amsterdam City Archives (PA 265, no. 43A).

Cat. no. 33 (Strollers and Skaters on a Frozen River with Ships)
Information on the cold spell of 1771 comes from the Koninklijk Nederlands Meteorologisch Instituut, De Bilt (November 21, 1989).

Krausz

Biography:
Van Eynden and Van der Willigen, vol. 3, pp. 98-99; *Aanhangsel*, pp. 65-66.
J. Knoef, "Simon Andreas Krausz," *Maandblad voor Beeldende Kunsten* 21 (1944), pp. 69-77.
L.J. Bol, *Tekeningen van Simon Andreas Krausz 1760-1825*, exhib. cat., Dordrecht (Dordrechts Museum), 1964.

The "lijst der beroemdste schilders" of 1806 was published by A. Bredius in *Oud-Holland* 19 (1901), pp. 242-44.

La Fargue

Biography:
Van Eynden and Van der Willigen, vol. 2, pp. 193-94; *Aanhangsel*, p. 178.
C. Dumas, *Het verheerlijkt Den Haag* (The Hague, 1984), p. 133 (with references to earlier literature).

Cat. no. 36 (Country Waterway near Voorburg)
The more detailed version of this drawing is in the Hague City Archives (inv. no. TO Voorburg-Broeksloot-kl 3); it measures 269 x 362 mm and is dated 1757.
For a view of the Broeksloot with Quarles House see Amsterdam, Rijksprentenkabinet, inv. no. 1921:282 (268 x 345 mm, dated 1757); other drawings are in the Hague City Archives.

Lamme

Biography:
Van Eynden and Van der Willigen, vol. 2, pp. 353-54.
Titia J. Geest, "Arie Lamme en zijn nageslacht, een Dordtse schildersfamilie," in *Vier historische opstellen* (Assen, 1959), pp. 13-33.

Cat. no. 37 (A Park with a Peacock and Poultry Startled by a Dog)
The barking spaniel is found, for instance, in Schouman's watercolor design for a wall panel in Oostkapelle House (destroyed in 1940), now in the Fondation Custodia, Paris (inv. no. 1407-101, ill. in *Tableau* 10 [1987], p. 77). The little dog is a stereotype motif in Dutch art. It occurs in a virtually identical jumping posture in a fruit piece by Henstenburgh in the Rijksprentenkabinet (inv. no. 1933:26) and, sometimes reversed left for right, in paintings by Adriaen de Gryeff, Jan van Haensbergen, Jan Weenix, and above all, Nicolaes Maes. Schouman's Dordrecht teacher, Adriaan van der Burg, depicted the animal in a portrait, dated 1729, of Maria Catharina Van Slingelandt-Van der Burch (Van Tets Collection).

Langendijk

Biography:
Van Eynden and Van der Willigen, vol. 2, pp. 154-365; *Aanhangsel*, pp. 184-85.
M.E. Deelen *et al.*, *Dirk Langendijk (1748-1805), tekenaar tussen kruitdamp en vaderlands gevoel* (Rotterdam, 1982), with earlier literature.

Cat. no. 38 (The Battle of the Pyramids)
The watercolor belonging to Her Royal Highness, Princess Juliana, is unsigned and measures 560 x 860 mm (Amsterdam, Royal Palace, inv. no. PA 115). The watercolors in Brussels, dated 1803, 1804, and 1805, are in the Musées Royaux des Beaux-Arts, De Grez Collection, cat. 1913, nos. 2191-95.

Cat. no. 39 (French Troops Capturing a City)
The related watercolor is in the Teyler Museum: see cat. H.W. Scholten, 1904, no. X36.
The uncolored drawing is in the Van Leeuwen Collection: see *De verzameling van H. van Leeuwen*, exhib. cat., Amsterdam (Rijksprentenkabinet), 1975, no. 76.
For the drawing of Bergen op Zoom see sale, Amsterdam (Sotheby-Mak van Waay), November 14, 1983, no. 98, with ill. (dated 1795). For the scene of fighting with St. Walburga's Church in Arnhem see Teyler Museum, cat. Scholten, 1904, X 40, no. 37.

Laquy

Biography:
Van Eynden and Van der Willigen, vol. 2, pp. 275-83.
G. de Werd, "Das Gnadenseilbild von W.J. Laquy aus dem Jahre 1786," *Kalender für das Klever Land* (1986), pp. 10-20.
G. de Werd, "Abschied an der Fähre von Spyck," *Kalender für das Klever Land* (1987), pp. 11-20.
For Laquy's teacher Beldieu (or Bildieu, as given by Laquy on his enrollment in the Amsterdam Drawing Academy), see Amsterdam City Archives (PA 265, no. 43A). That artist proved untraceable in the archives of both Bonn and Cologne.
On Braamcamp's patronage see C.J. Bille, *De Tempel der Kunst of het Kabinet van den Heer Braamcamp*, 2 vols. (Amsterdam, 1961).

Cat. no. 40 (Young Woman at Her Toilet)
For the erotic significance of the dog, candle, mules, etc., see E. de Jongh *et al.*, *Tot lering en vermaak*, exhib. cat., Amsterdam (Rijksmuseum), 1976, nos. 64 and 68.

Lauwers

Biography:
Van Eynden and Van der Willigen, vol. 2, pp. 405-7.
E. van Biema, in *Nieuw Nederlandsch Biografisch Woordenboek*, vol. 3 (Leiden, 1914), col. 743.
D. Coekelberghs, *Les peintres belges à Rome de 1700 à 1830* (Brussels and Rome, 1976), p. 400.

For the wall-hangings signed jointly by Lauwers and Barbiers see above, under the latter artist.

Cat. no. 41 (Drawing from the Live Model in an Old Building)
The portrait of Frans Post by Frans Hals was sold in 1773 in Amsterdam with the Van der Marck Collection and seems to have remained in the Netherlands, for there are copies from 1778 and 1790 by Jan Gerard Waldorp (ca. 1740-1808). See Seymour Slive, *Frans Hals* (London, 1970), no. 155, pl. 236. The two small pictures by Senave that are roughly the same size as Lauwers's watercolor – each panel measures 430 x 545 mm – are in the Musées Royaux des Beaux-Arts in Brussels (cat. of modern paintings, [1984], p. 552).
The model's stance could not be found among the 250 or so male academy studies from the Dutch eighteenth century in the Amsterdam Printroom.

Van Leen

Biography:
Van Eynden and Van der Willigen, vol. 3, pp. 56, 85, 481; *Aanhangsel*, p. 20.
Tussen zonnegoud en kaarslicht. Dordtse meesters 1780-1840, exhib. cat., Dordrecht, 1986, p. 38f.
Autograph manuscripts are in the Netherlands Institute for Art History (RKD) in The Hague (s.v. Willem van Leen and G.J. Verburgh).
Autograph manuscripts in the Rijksprentenkabinet, Amsterdam, include an account of a trip with friends from Rotterdam to Düsseldorf in 1804.
The very rare series of etchings has the title *Ge-etste bloemen door W. van Leen en gecouleurd door J.C. & J.A. Coebergh* (Delfshaven, 1801 [and 1804]).

Van Liender

Biography:
Van Eynden and Van der Willigen, vol. 2, pp. 220-22.
Jhr. G. Ploos van Amstel, *Portret van een koopman en uitvinder, Cornelis Ploos van Amstel* (Assen, 1980), pp. 31, 93, 127, 143.
Anet West-Braams, *Een schilderij centraal, "Gezicht op de Gaardbrug" [in Utrecht] van P.J. van Liender*, exhib. cat., Utrecht (Centraal Museum), 1980, with references to literature on the draftsmen members of the Van Liender family).
J., P. en P.J. van Liender en de stad Utrecht, exhib. cat., Utrecht (Gemeentearchief), n.d. [1978].

Cat. no. 43 (View in the Town of Montfoort)
For Van Liender as a precursor of Koekkoek see J. Knoef, "De landschapskunst van B.C. Koekkoek en haar oorsprong," *Maandblad voor Beeldende Kunsten* 20 (1943), pp. 1-7.

Meyer

Biography:
Van Eynden and Van der Willigen, vol. 2, pp. 262-63.
Hendrik Meyer was not born in 1737, as stated by P.A. Scheen and other authors. He was baptized in the Evangelical Lutheran Church in Amsterdam on September 30, 1744, as the son of H. Meyer and S. Hanning.
His house in Haarlem, which is said to have formerly been the home of the painters Cornelis Decker (before 1625-1678) and Philip Wouwermans (1619-1668), is featured in an aquatint in Samuel Ireland, *A Picturesque Tour*, vol. 1 (London, 1789), facing p. 116.
One of the wall-hangings in the Lakenhal Museum shows the Eendracht malt mill (formerly called "De Juffer"), which was only built in 1776. The date 1772 proposed for this painting (cat. Lakenhal 1983, no. 305f) is therefore untenable.

Cat. no. 44 (Harvest near a Village in a Hilly Landscape)
Village in Winter was auctioned successively in London, (Sotheby's) December 13, 1973, no. 179 (ill.); Laren (Christie's), March 23, 1976, no. 173 (ill.); and Amsterdam (Brandt), May 26, 1977, no. 164 (ill.).

De Moucheron

Biography:
Van Gool, vol. 1, pp. 362-67.
A. Staring, "Isaac de Moucheron als ontwerper van gevels en tuinen," *Oud-Holland* 65 (1950), pp. 85-103.
A. Zwollo, "Isaac de Moucheron," *Hollandse en Vlaamse vedutenschilders te Rome 1675-1725* (Assen, 1973), pp. 39-56.

For De Moucheron's family see *Nieuw Nederlandsch Biografisch Woordenboek*, vol. 7 (Leiden, 1927), i.v.
For De Moucheron as a colorist of old drawings see Ben Broos, "Improving and Finishing Old Master Drawings: an Art in Itself," *Hoogsteder-Naumann Mercury* 8 (1989), pp. 34-55.

Van Noorde

Biography:
Van Eynden and Van der Willigen, vol. 2, pp. 222-25.
Bert Sliggers, *Het schetsboek van Cornelis van Noorde 1731-1795. Het leven van een veelzijdig Haarlems kunstenaar* (Haarlem, 1982).

Numan

Biography:
Van Eynden and Van der Willigen, vol. 3, pp. 25-28; *Aanhangsel*, p. 5.
"Ledenlijst Tekenacademie Amsterdam," Amsterdam City Archives (PA 265, no. 43A), s.v. Numan and Bulthuis.
H.H. Heldring, "Een Groninger industrie in de 18de eeuw en de familie Numan," *Groningse Volksalmanak* (1962), pp. 33-41.

On the Augustinis (whose real name was Degelenkamp) see B.C. Sliggers, "Een inventarisatie van geschilderd behang te Haarlem, in het bijzonder dat van Jan Augustini (1729-73)," in *Liber Amicorum Jhr. Mr. C.C. van Valkenburg* (The Hague, 1985), pp. 323-41.
L. Buynsters-Smets, "Hollandse buitenplaatsen anno 1797. Een album van vier en twintig gekleurde 'Printtekeningen' door H. Numan," *Antiek* 14 (1979), p. 245.

Cat. nos. 47-48 (Zandbergen House and Park)
The information on the owners of Zandbergen is based on data from the Rijksarchief (Public Record Office) in Utrecht (communicated by letter, dated February 15, 1989). For the Ebeling family see *Nederland's Patriciaat* 33 (1947), p. 221, and *Nederland's Patriciaat* 65 (1980-81), p. 95; also see N. Plomp, "De Amsterdamse familie Ebeling," *Jaarboek Centraal Bureau voor Genealogie* 34 (1980), pp. 177-202. Incorrect information on Zandbergen's owners in 1800 is given in *Edele eenvoud. Neo-classicisme in Nederland 1765-1800*, exhib. cat., Haarlem (Frans Hals Museum and Teyler Museum), 1989, p. 246.
The ode to Zandbergen occurs in a volume of poetry by Pieter

Pypers of Amersfoort, *Eemlandsch Tempe, of Clio op Puntenburgh*, vol. 2 (Amsterdam, 1803), p. 151.

E. van Nijmegen

Biography:
Van Gool, vol. 1, pp. 256-64.
Van Eynden and Van der Willigen, vol. 2, pp. 3-5.
J.W. Niemeijer, "De ateliernalatenschap van het Rotterdamse schildersgeslacht Van Nijmegen," *Bulletin van het Rijksmuseum Amsterdam* 17 (1969), pp. 59-111.

G. van Nijmegen

Biography:
Van Eynden and Van der Willigen, vol. 2, pp. 247-53.
J.W. Niemeijer, "Gerard van Nijmegens 'Berglandschap met ossewagen' en het dagboek van zijn reis langs de Rijn," *Bulletin van het Rijksmuseum* 32 (1984), pp. 64-70 (with references to earlier literature).

Prins

Biography:
Van Eynden and Van der Willigen (vol. 2, pp. 426-39) base themselves on information from Adriaan Bemme, who knew Prins well (see letter from Van der Willigen in the Amsterdam Printroom).
Album Studiosorum Academiae Lugduno-Batavae (The Hague, 1875), pp. 1111, 1136.
For Prins's involvement with the Pictura artists' society in The Hague see Johan Gram, *De schildersconfrerie Pictura en hare Academie van Beeldende Kunsten te 's-Gravenhage 1682-1882* (Rotterdam, 1882), p. 89f; and A. Bredius, "Extract uit de notulen der Confrerie van Pictura...," *Oud-Holland* 19 (1901), pp. 235, 239, 240.

Nothing certain is known about the date or place of his death. C. Kramm, *Levens en werken...*, vol. 5 (Amsterdam, 1861), p. 1318, states that Prins drowned on his way to Vleuten, outside Utrecht. Van Eynden and Van der Willigen believe that the accident took place outside the White Gate in Leiden. Research in Leiden and Utrecht (Public Record Office as well as City Archives) failed to resolve the question.

Cat. no. 51 (Fair on a Market Square)
Eighteenth-century Dutch depictions of fairs are too numerous to list. Among the artists who treated the subject were P. Barbiers, H. van Brussel, J.A. Langendijk, C. Meijer, H. Pothoven, and R. Vinkeles. The Amsterdam fairs of a slightly later date are described, with additional data drawn from the eighteenth century, by Marja Keyser, *Komt dat zien! De Amsterdamse kermissen in de negentiende eeuw*, exhib. cat., Amsterdam and Rotterdam, 1976. See also *Uit in Amsterdam. Van Schouwburgen en kermissen tussen 1780 en 1813*, exhib. cat., Amsterdam (Nederlands Theater Instituut), 1985.
The collection of prints with figures is *Verzameling van verschillende gekleede mans- en vrouwenstanden. Naar het leven geteekend door de kunstteekenaars Perkois en Prins en in het koper gebragt door den kunstgraveur M. de Sallieth* (Rotterdam [J. Immerzeel, Jr.], 1818; reprint, Amsterdam [J. Immerzeel, Jr.], 1833).

Sophie Witwe von La Roche, *Tagebuch einer Reise durch Holland und England*, 2d ed. (Offenbach-am-Main, 1791), p. 154 (1st ed., 1788).
Ann Radcliff, *A Journey made in the Summer of 1794, through Holland and the Western Frontiers of Germany ...* (London, 1795), p. 50.
John Owen, *Travels into Different Parts of Europe in the Years 1791 and 1792*, vol. 1 (London, 1796), pp. 83-84.

Pronk

Biography:
J. van Gool, vol. 2, pp. 193-98.
Van Eynden and Van der Willigen, vol. 2, pp. 36-37.
C. Dumas, *Het verheerlijkt Den Haag* (The Hague, 1984), p. 139.
F. Gorissen, "Künstlerreise nach Kleve Anno 1821," *Heimatkalender für das Klever Land auf das Jahr 1962*, pp. 33-40, 153-54.
S.E. Pronk Czn, "Iconografie van Cornelis Pronk," *Pronkstukken* 12 (April, 1982), pp. 39-77.
For an unknown friendship between Pronk and Jacob de Wit see J. Knoef, "Een onbekende vriendschap?" *Kunsthistorische*

Mededeelingen 3 (1948), p. 13.
Also A.J. Gevers and A.J. Mensema, *Over de hobbelde bobbelde heyde. Andries Schoemaker, Cornelis Pronk en Abraham de Haen op reis door Overijssel, Drente en Friesland in 1732* (Alphen aan den Rijn, 1985).

On Pronk as a designer of porcelain decorations see C.J.A. Jörg, *Pronk porselein / Pronk porcelain*, exhib. cat., Groningen, 1980, in Dutch and English, with references to earlier literature.

Schouman

Biography:
L.J. Bol, "Aert Schouman, 'Overkunstig schilder in oly-en waterverv,'" *Tableau* 8-10 (1986-88); ten installments, with references to sources and earlier literature.

Schouman is supposed to have worked in The Hague for part of each year from 1748 onwards, but the Fondation Custodia in Paris owns a drawing that was made at Eikenhorst, a country estate just outside the city, and is dated October 18, 1747 (inv. no. 1407-167).

Cat. no. 56 (Cock-of-the-Rock and Leclancheri Painted Bunting)
For the drawing in Indian ink in the library of Artis Zoo, Amsterdam see Florence F.J.M. Pieters, "Notes on the Menagerie and Zoölogical Cabinet of Stadhouder Willem V of Holland, directed by Aernout Vosmaer," *Journal of the Society for the Bibliography of Natural History* 9 (London, 1980), pp. 539-63, esp. p. 548. This drawing, which is indented for transfer, is in turn based on a watercolor in the Teyler Museum, Haarlem (cat. H.J. Scholten, 1904, no. U 41). It has the same imposing look and dimensions as the sheet described here, but it shows a kingfisher as the second bird. According to Schouman's notes on the drawing's verso, written at the same height as the birds on the front, the cock-of-the-rock belonged to the *P*[rince] *v*[an] (of) *O*[range], and the kingfisher to *Mev. de Willem* (probably to be read as Mrs. Le Leu de Wilhem-Timmers, who died in The Hague in 1753, some years before the foundation of the stadtholder's natural history cabinet). Schouman, though, was also involved in the auction of Mrs. Le Leu de Wilhem-Pieck's collection of paintings in May 1770. The Haarlem drawing is not dated. Again accompanied by the painted bunting, the cock-of-the-rock appears in a large group of other birds in a watercolor by Schouman in the Fondation Custodia (F. Lugt Collection) in Paris (inv. no. 1407-107), and it is also found in the title print of *Regnum animale*.

Cat. no. 59 (Pieter van Bleiswijk)
For biographical information on Van Bleiswijk see J. Romein, in *Nieuw Nederlands Biografisch Woordenboek*, vol. 10 (1937), cols. 78-80.
Manuscript notes by J.P. van der Kellen, Rijksprentenkabinet, Amsterdam, s.v. Schouman.
For the copper plate see sale, A. Schouman, The Hague, December 10, 1792, p. 88, no. 82.

Cat. no. 60 (Portrait of a Gentleman in an Oval Frame)
Samuel Ireland, *A Picturesque Tour through Holland, Brabant and part of Flanders, Made in the Autumn of 1789*, vol. 1 (2d ed., London, 1796), p. 33.

Schouten

Biography:
Van Eynden and Van der Willigen, vol. 3, pp. 44-45; *Aanhangsel*, p. 12.
I.H. van Eeghen, "De kunstenaarsfamilie Schoute(n)," *Maandblad Amstelodamum* 47 (September 1960), pp. 129-36.
J.W. Niemeijer, "Zwei Münstersche Domansichten von H.P. Schouten," *Westfalen* 39 (1961), pp. 234-37.
A.W. Gerlagh, "De familie Schouten. Een 18de-eeuws tekenatelier in de praktijk," *Bulletin Koninklijke Nederlandse Oudheidkundige Bond* 88 (1989), pp. 20-29.

For Schouten's contacts with Ploos van Amstel see T. Laurentius, J.W. Niemeijer, and Jhr. G. Ploos van Amstel, *Cornelis Ploos van Amstel 1726–1798. Kunstverzamelaar en prentuitgever* (Assen, 1980), p. 188.

Cat. no. 61 (Luxemburgh House on the River Vecht)
Jac. Zwarts, "Uit het verleden der Portugeesche Joden in de Vechtstreek," *Jaarboekje [...] Niftarlake* (1920), pp. 15-35.
Also see Jac. Zwarts, "Luxemburgh (Overkerck)," *Jaarboekje [. . .] Niftarlake* (1943), pp. 22-72.

For Magalli see D.F. Scheurleer, *Het muziekleven in Nederland in de tweede helft der 18de eeuw in verband met Mozart's verblijf aldaar* (The Hague, 1909), pp. 321-22.

A. van Strij

Biography:
Van Eynden and Van der Willigen, vol. 3, pp. 59-62.
J. Erkelens, "De gebroeders Abraham en Jacob van Strij, een biografie van twee Dordtse schilders," *Oud Holland* 90 (1976), pp. 186-99.

Cat. no. 62 (A Cobbler and His Family in an Interior)
For Aert de Gelder's painting (which is no longer known in the original) see K. Lilienfeld, *Arent de Gelder. Sein Leben und seine Kunst. Quellenstudien zur Holländischen Kunstgeschichte, herausgegeben unter der Leitung von Dr. C. Hofstede de Groot*, vol. 4 (The Hague, 1914), p. 150, no. 59.
Another borrowing analogous to the one in this watercolor is found in a drawing of a drunken man in the Printroom of Leiden University, which was modeled on the figure of Belshazzar in De Gelder's painting in the Getty Museum of Art in Malibu. Thus, in both cases a biblical scene was the basis for a genre picture. See E. Koolhaas-Grosfeld, in *Op zoek naar de Gouden Eeuw*, exhib. cat., Zwolle, 1986, figs. 27 and 28; see also cat. no. 64.

On cobblers see [J. Ter Gouw?], "Ambachten, I. Schoenlappers," *De Oude Tijd* 6 (Haarlem, 1874), pp. 257-62. Another nice illustration is Adriaan van Ostade's etching, B.27.

J. van Strij

Biography:
Van Eynden and Van der Willigen, vol. 2, pp. 414-18.
J. Erkelens, "De gebroeders Abraham en Jacob van Strij, een biografie van twee Dordtse schilders," *Oud Holland* 90 (1976), pp. 186-99.

Cat. no. 63 (Watermill outside Dordrecht)
On Smitshoek see J. Alleblas *et al.*, *Was getekend Dordrecht 1780-1960* (Zwolle and Dordrecht, [1988]), p. 91.

The year in which the collector Jacob de Vos died is incorrectly reported as 1882 in Lugt's *Marques de collections*; he actually died in Amsterdam on July 8, 1878. There is a nineteenth-century copy of the drawing in the Royal Library, Windsor Castle (cat. Van Puyvelde, no. 99, as A. van Borssum).

Troost

Biography:
J. van Gool, vol. 2, pp. 241-59, with the date of birth incorrectly given as 1697.
Weyerman, vol. 4, pp. 107-10.

J.W. Niemeijer, *Cornelis Troost 1696-1750* (Assen, 1973), with earlier literature. For the identity of Troost's wife see Jhr. G. Ploos van Amstel, "Cornelis Troost en zijn vrouw Suzanna Maria van der Duyn," *Maandblad Amstelodamum* 66 (1979), pp. 64-65. For information on his surviving children see I.H. van Eeghen, review of J.W. Niemeijer, *Cornelis Troost* (Assen, 1973), in *Maandblad Amstelodamum* 60 (1973), pp. 117-20, esp. p. 120.

Cat. no. 66 (Family Listening to a Street Singer)
For the picture by Jan Steen see Hofstede de Groot, no. 438 (Rothschild Collection), Ascott House, Leighton Buzzard (now The National Trust). Nicolaes Maes depicted the same subject (Rijksdienst Beeldende Kunst, The Hague, illustrated in *De ontdekte Schijndeugd, of de wereld van Cornelis Troost*, exhib. cat., The Hague, n.d., p. 17).

Cat. no. 68 (Military Guardroom)
A variant of this painting, probably identical with no. 728 in this author's monograph on Troost, was auctioned by Phillips in London on May 13, 1986, as no. 6, and later in New York by Christie's on January 11, 1989, as no. 183 (color. ills. in both catalogues). The gouache is now in the collection of Mr. and Mrs. Roger Gordon, Boston.

Vinkeles

Biography:
Van Eynden and Van der Willigen, vol. 2, pp. 316-25.
Algemene Konst- en Letterbode, February 9, 1816, p. 83; February 10, 1816, p. 100; and June 19, 1816, p. 166.

Guido Jansen, "De brieven van Reinier Vinkeles aan Volkert van der Plaats," *Maandblad Amstelodamum* 77 (1985), pp. 107-21.
J. Knoef, "Het grafisch oeuvre van Reinier Vinkeles," *Elsevier's Geïllustreerd Maandschrift* 43 (1933), pp. 374-82.
E. de la Fontaine Verwey, *De illustratie van Nederlandsche letterkundige werken in de XVIIIde eeuw* (Amsterdam, 1934), pp. 98-119.

Cat. no. 69 (Amsterdam, Dam Square with the Town Hall and Weigh House)
Other versions include: a) Amsterdam City Archives, Atlas Splitgerber, no. S 649M, gray wash, 265 x 403 mm, signed and dated 1766; b) Amsterdam City Archives, Atlas Splitgerber, no. S 650M, gray wash, 260 x 401 mm, signed and dated 1767; c) sale, Atlas Wurfbain, Amsterdam, May 6-11, 1912, no. 38 (ill.), watercolor, 340 x 430 mm, signed and dated 1764; d) sale, C. Ploos van Amstel, Amsterdam, March 3, 1800, no. D.18, watercolor, engraved by Frans de Bakker and reproduced as such in Jan Wagenaar, *Amsterdam in zijne ... geschiedenissen*, vol. 2 (pt. 3, 1st bk.), which was published in 1765. The scene closely matches that of the uncolored drawing mentioned, no. S 65M in the Amsterdam City Archives, Atlas Splitgerber.

De Wit

Biography:
Van Gool, vol. 2, pp. 218-38.
Weyerman, vol. 4, pp. 104-06.
Mr. A. Staring, *Jacob de Wit 1695-1754* (Amsterdam, 1958).
Jacob de Wit, De Amsteltitiaan / Jacob de Wit, The Titian of the Amstel, exhib. cat., Amsterdam (Koninklijk Paleis), 1986, with bibliography.

For De Wit's income see W.F.H. Oldewelt, *Kohier van de Personeele Quotisatie te Amsterdam over het jaar 1742* (Amsterdam, 1945).

Cat. no. 70 (Hovering Cherubs with a Basket of Flowers)
For the Cromhout family, which became extinct in 1764, use was made of information in the Centraal Bureau voor Genealogie en Heraldiek in The Hague.
For Jacob Cromhout's houses on Herengracht see *Vier eeuwen Herengracht* (Amsterdam, 1976), nos. 366, 368, 372, and 376.
A similar design in oils, now in the Hermitage in St. Petersburg (illustrated in A. Staring, *Jacob de Wit*, fig. 79), is clearly intended for a small ceiling painting.

Cat. no. 71 (Design for a Ceiling Painting with Diana and Endymion)
No. 794 Prinsengracht belonged to De Moucheron; he bought it in 1726 for 9,000 guilders. According to the *Kohier der Personeele Quotisatie van 1742*, this was also the home of D. Kok, of private means. Further along the canal dwelled the well-known engraver Jacobus Houbraken (1698-1780).

Unknown artist

Cat. no. 73 (Scene in the Garden of a Town House)
A similar tent is depicted in a watercolor that Jordanus Hoorn made of his own house and garden in Amersfoort shortly after 1800. For an illustration see F. Livestro-Nieuwenhuis, *Jordanus Hoorn, een Amersfoortse kunstenaar in zijn tijd, 1753-1833* (Amersfoort, 1983), p. 78.
For miniature theaters see J.W. Niemeijer, *Cornelis Troost* (Assen, 1973), pp. 50-51, with previous literature. For additional information see Ben Albach, "Oorsprong en bestemming van het Van Slingelandt-toneel," *Jaarverslag Toneelmuseum* 1974, pp. 24-32; and Tuja van den Berg, "Het miniatuurtoneel van baron van Slingelandt," *Ons Amsterdam* (February 1982), pp. 33-37.

Abbreviated literature

Van Eynden and Van der Willigen
Roelof van Eynden and Adriaan van der Willigen. *Geschiedenis der vaderlandsche schilderkunst, sedert de helft der XVIII eeuw.* 3 vols. plus *Aanhangsel* (Supplement). Haarlem, 1816-40.

Van Gool
Johan van Gool. *De nieuwe schouburg der Nederlandsche kunstschilders en schilderessen.* 2 vols. The Hague, 1750-51.

Weyerman
Jacob Campo Weyerman. *De levens-beschryvingen der Nederlandsche konst-schilders en konst-schilderessen.* 4 vols. The Hague and Dordrecht, 1729-69.

Index

The authors of art-historical and historical publications are not listed, with the exception of writers of eighteenth- and nineteenth-century travel accounts and a few contemporary authors.